LET ME LIVE

Selected from

THE AMERICAN NEGRO: HIS HISTORY AND LITERATURE

William Loren Katz

GENERAL EDITOR

LET ME LIVE

Angelo Herndon

With a new preface by Howard N. Meyer

ARNO PRESS and THE NEW YORK TIMES
NEW YORK 1969

*

Library of Congress Catalog Card No. 69-18566

*

Manufactured in the United States of America

To my unhappy, oppressed people who no longer assent to the white exploiters' command "to walk humbly and to speak low"—to those heroic spirits who face persecution, imprisonment and even death, fighting to break the shackles of economic bondage and social injustice that bind all Negroes in America—to them this book is dedicated with undying solidarity.

IT IS NOT VERY LIKELY THAT ANGELO HERNDON EVER saw Art Young's old *Masses* cartoon, "He Stirreth Up the People," depicting Jesus as an outlawed agitator. It was published in 1913, the very year of Herndon's birth. If he had seen it, he might not have been able to express so unselfconsciously the idea that struck him as he and a group of fellow Communists, black and white, were paraded in chains through the streets of Birmingham in 1931: "Christ jeered by the hoodlums of Jerusalem as he dragged his cross to be crucified at Golgotha."

The parallel between his adolescent religious fervor, and the selfless drive to serve his fellow man that marked his later youth as an agitator, recurs throughout his autobiography. It was published when he was twenty-three years old, awaiting the Supreme Court's final verdict on a Georgia judge's twenty-year sentence.

When he was arrested in Atlanta in 1932, on the charge of inciting insurrection that led to his becoming the center of a *cause celebre,* a search of his room turned up among the "incriminating" documents, a pamphlet by a Bishop Brown entitled *Christianism and Communism.* Herndon's book opens with his childhood introduction to the One who "gave His life so that all of us might be saved," and closes with his reply to a friend who had urged him to jump bail because of the prospect of a Supreme Court ruling that would send him to certain death on the chain gang: "Death itself is not the greatest tragedy that can happen to a man, rather, the greatest tragedy is to live placidly and safely and to keep silent in the face of injustice and oppression."

Let Me Live describes the early life of a black child born in southern Ohio, who was obliged at the age of thirteen to go into the mines in Kentucky. He went on to Birmingham, where during the 1920's he continued to suffer under the double burden of race and poverty. Whether in mines or on construction gangs, the conditions under which he worked were so appalling that it is no exaggeration when he says, "We worked like galley slaves." This was not as difficult for him to endure as the anguish he felt each time he encountered the fear that blocked southern blacks from uniting.

In 1929 began the administration of a president who announced, as the nation's middle and upper classes were enchanted by a steadily rising stock market, "We in America today are nearer to the final triumph over poverty than ever before in the history of our land." Soon afterwards an economic crisis caused business failures, farm foreclosures, and widespread unemployment, the impact of which was felt most acutely by black Americans. Statistics alone cannot begin to make clear to those under fifty how awful were the conditions of that time.

This was when, as even the most hostile historians of the American Communist Party, Irving Howe and Lewis

Coser, have written, "All through these bitter years the Communists stood almost alone" in espousing the cause of the American Negro. Angelo Herndon saw this for himself, after being introduced to communism by a leaflet that began: "Workers of Birmingham, White and Negro: Would you Rather Fight—or Starve?" Thus began his association with the Party that led to his arrest and indictment, which in turn led to the production of his autobiography.

His story may lack, as literature, the poetry and passion of works such as Richard Wright's *Black Boy,* but it has virtues of its own. It restores to us a segment of neglected history and does so with sufficient merit to have prompted the literary critic, Harry Hansen, to call it, "a document of the highest importance to Americans." The style has simplicity and frank ingenuousness of the sort that characterizes a "primitive" painting, and displays the honesty of that genre as well.

Herndon's case is a significant, if minor, chapter in American Negro history, and in American radical history as well. Yet he is not mentioned in any of the numerous scholarly or popular histories of Americans of African ancestry that are now in print. The Herndon case is barely touched upon in works about the thirties. Nevertheless, there was in that period no other single cause for which the diverse and often hostile branches of the "old left" united as successfully, and as the facts of the case came to be widely known, that won as many liberals and conservatives to their side.

An early local leader of the Atlanta Herndon Defense Committee was a young Georgia Tech professor named

C. Vann Woodward. A later coordinator of nationwide "Free Herndon" activities was Mary Fox of the non-Communist League for Industrial Democracy. An NAACP brief signed by young Thurgood Marshall sought a rehearing after the Supreme Court's initial dismissal of the case. The pre-C.I.O. and most antiradical American Federation of Labor adopted at its 1936 convention a resolution offered by Brother A. Philip Randolph, calling for Herndon's freedom:

> WHEREAS, The conviction of Herndon is equivalent to the conviction of the labor movement, since any labor organizer, white or black, may be picked up and sentenced to the chain gang under this archaic and barbaric law.

There was more truth than rhetoric to Randolph's resolution. The Georgia law under which Herndon had been arrested for possessing Communist literature and recruiting Party members, forbade inducement "to join in any combined resistance to the lawful authority of the state," as constituting "an attempt to incite insurrection." The statute in question was a century old and was originally aimed at rebel slave Nat Turner and abolitionist William Lloyd Garrison: the crime defined was "exciting insurrection or resistance on the part of slaves, Negroes, or free persons of color." The postbellum reenactment dropped the reference to race, but preserved the death penalty.

It is not only because of the origin of the law used against him that Herndon's case belongs in race relations history. The motives and techniques of the prosecution were faithful to the racist character of the old statute. Herndon's arrest was prompted by his leadership of a then unheard of and frightening action, an integrated demonstration of black and white unemployed, to protest a cut in relief rations. For some time he had been known as a Communist, but had not been "punished" except for intermittent illegal raids, arrests, and beatings. The indictment under which he was tried included the words "to establish and to set up a group and combination of persons, colored and white." This was the heart of his real offense, though that was not an element of the crime defined in the twentieth-century version of the slave insurrection law.

Angelo Herndon's autobiography ends with the suspenseful question that was to be answered within six weeks after publication, "What will the Supreme Court's decision be?" The 1937 court, inherited intact from Hoover's presidency, could not have been insensible to the struggle launched by President Roosevelt to reconstruct its membership after it had repeatedly struck down key New Deal legislation. Perhaps in this case, as in others in the spring of 1937, the court seized the opportunity to embellish its image. In granting freedom to Herndon, by a narrow five–four majority, the court took a major step in the revival of the Fourteenth Amendment to the United States Constitution, a process that practically began with the slightly earlier Scottsboro cases.[1]

These decisions played a major role in the line of cases that brought about a restoration of the Fourteenth Amendment's originally intended function as guardian of human rights. As such they were an essential part of the prelude to the Warren Court's determination that "civil rights" and "civil liberties" are interdependent and inseparable. The very special meaning of the ruling in Herndon's case to our time is illustrated by the use made of it by Dr. Benjamin Spock's attorneys in the appeal against his conviction for conspiracy to obstruct the draft: "Speech may not be punished because of its dangerous tendency to induce violations of law."[2]

The lawyer who established this principle in his successful argument of the case in the Supreme Court was Whitney North Seymour, Sr., former Assistant Solicitor General under President Hoover, with whom were associated Professors Herbert Wechsler and Walter Gellhorn of Columbia Law School.[3] The attorney who secured such eminent counsel and was the real spark plug of Herndon's legal defense on appeal was Mrs. Carol Weiss King.[4]

Angelo Herndon did not return to Georgia after he was freed. As a marked man he would not have survived very long. His place was taken by young blacks whose interest had been aroused by the events that brought him to national notice.[5] The Southern Negro Youth Congress, through which many worked, was the direct predecessor of the youngsters who sparked the Civil Rights Revolution of our day.

For a few years Herndon remained a figure in the Harlem Communist Party and the Negro liberation movement as well. He was the moving force behind the reissue by Pathway Press of the complete Frederick Douglass autobiography. He and his associates in this venture sought to launch a "Negro Publication Society of America" in 1941, but it failed after its first reprint was issued. In an introduction to that work, Herndon decried "the unfortunate contrast of American history over against Negro history. . . . The time is long overdue when the story of America's unsung heroes must be told." When this premature venture collapsed, he left political life, went into business in Chicago, and later broke with the Communist Party.

Among the papers found on Angelo Herndon when he was arrested in 1932 was a pamphlet recurrently using the phrase "Self-Determination for the Black Belt," part of the Communist line on the Negro question in the early thirties. The demand for an autonomous black state, one that ran across and included the "belt" of states and counties in which Negroes were in a majority, was phrased in the language of Moscow ("No armed forces of American Imperialism should remain in the territory of the Black Belt."), but the idea is a thoroughly native product that has recurred throughout our race relations history. When the American Communists attempted to exploit the slogan, they were undoubtedly responding to the recent and temporarily stunning success of the flamboyant nationalist-separatist, Marcus Garvey. As Gilbert Osofsky has perceptively observed, "Garvey offered American Negroes temporary psychological escape from what many believed to be a hopelessly racist nation."

Nationalism and ultra-separatism are not necessarily durable or valid credos, but as always, when they recur in the Afro-American community, they must be recognized as a response to the racism of nonblack Americans. Fourteen years of nullification of the "law of the land" laid down in the school desegregation decisions, tokenism, and virulently increasing white racism, have combined to produce a response in the black community that again offers proof that those who do not learn from history are condemned to repeat it. The "Black Belt" booklet's "demand for complete separation," is reechoed to our discomfiture today without the moderating caution, "Negro communists must carry on among the Negro masses an energetic struggle against nationalist moods directed against all whites, workers as well as capitalists. . . ."[6]

There is much in the story of Angelo Herndon's transition from unquestioning faith in Christianity to unquestioning faith in communism that is relevant to our time. Each of his faiths failed him. They did not, at least as practiced, provide the answer to his quest for the brotherhood of man. We are said to be moving in the direction of two separate nations within a nation, and many well-meaning people say that "Integration has failed." Perhaps a judicious response would be to say of integration and the Fourteenth Amendment's still unfulfilled promise of justice and equality, what William Booth's biographer said of Christianity: "The Christian ideal has not been tried and found wanting; it has been found difficult and left untried."

Howard N. Meyer
ATTORNEY AND CIVIL RIGHTS HISTORIAN

NOTES

[1] Because the present volume was first published prior to the final court ruling that freed Herndon, it included as Appendices Six and Seven the court decisions initially rejecting his appeal. In the first Herndon case, the Supreme Court (295 U.S. 441) dismissed his appeal in 1935 on technical grounds eloquently denounced by Justice Cardozo (pp. 395–403 herein), with the concurrence of Justices Brandeis and Stone.

Herndon's lawyers won their way back to the Supreme Court on a writ of habeas corpus, and Chief Justice Hughes and Justice Roberts joined the earlier dissenters, the latter writing the prevailing opinion on the merits of the case (301 U.S. 242). The court ruled, in essence, that the mere "dangerous tendency" of Herndon's advocacy was insufficient to justify abridging freedom of speech and assembly. Wrote Justice Roberts:

> His membership in the Party wholly fails to establish an attempt to incite others to insurrection. . . . In these circumstances to make membership in the Party and solicitation of members for that Party a criminal offense . . . is an unwarranted invasion of free speech.

As Professor Zechariah Chafee pointed out, the Roberts opinion in the Herndon case rejected the Georgia Court's view that the defendant could be found guilty if he intended an insurrection "at any time within which he might reasonably expect his influence to continue"—a departure from the classic "clear and present danger" test that was, however, countenanced in the later Dennis case by the Vinson Court. Professor Chafee's appraisal of the overall case expresses a viewpoint arguably applicable to most, if not all, "sedition" prosecutions:

> My guess is that the men concerned in this prosecution were not worried in the slightest about any plotted insur-

rection or the possibility of a new Liberia between the Tennessee Valley Authority and the Gulf of Mexico. But they were really worried, I suspect, about something else that Herndon really wanted—his demand for equal rights for Negroes. If he got going with that, there was clear and present danger of racial friction and isolated acts of violence by individuals on both sides. They were afraid, not that the United States Constitution would be overthrown, but that it might be enforced.

[2] *Herndon* v *Lowry,* 301 U.S. Reports, p. 242.

[3] Benjamin J. Davis, a young Atlantan, was one of the trial attorneys. Drawn into the Communist Party by his experiences during the trial, Davis later migrated to New York City, where he became the first black, Communist, city councilman.

[4] Carol King was a personality who defies classification. A specialist in the law of immigration, dedicated to justice and equality, she won the friendship and esteem of many of the officials whose intended victims—including Harry Bridges—she saved from the jaws of exile. She was a great-souled woman who was a credit to the American bar. Her warm and gracious personality will not be soon forgotten by those who fell under its spell. To the young lawyers of the thirties whom she persuaded, enticed, and cajoled into contributing to her scholarly publication, *The Bulletin of the International Juridical Association,* the editorial board meetings over which she presided at her Chelsea brownstone home, her face framed with closely cropped curly hair and bright eyes peering through heavy glasses, will always be a pleasant memory.

[5] His brother Milton had gone to Spain to join the Abraham Lincoln Brigade of American volunteers fighting the Franco rebellion that had Hitler's and Mussolini's support. His presence there was noted with approval by one young journalist: "Milton Herndon is in Spain now—fighting for the loyalists," Leonard Lyons wrote warmly to Angelo in his column, "And so many other members of your race are in the same battalion, fighting against the Italian fascists, to avenge the defeat in Ethiopia." Milton Herndon died in Spain.

[6] See Appendix Six, p. 386.

ILLUSTRATIONS

ONE

I WAS BORN ON MAY 6, 1913, in the little steel and coal-mining town of Wyoming, Ohio. My earliest recollections are wrapped in mist. It was only at the age of six that I first became conscious of the world, and the experience which initiated me into it was—tragedy.

I was then ill in bed, and the tenderness and concern of my mother, brothers and sister moved me very deeply. My illness had made me keenly sensitive to all that went on about me. Never before had I loved the members of my family so passionately.

My mother Harriet (we children used to call her Hattie familiarly, for she was a friend as well as a mother to us) is a mulatto Negro. She has Indian and white blood in her veins. I always thought her beautiful, and even to this day she looks as young and charming as my sister. My illness had upset her very much, so that she neglected her housework. She constantly hovered over me and looked at me with anxious, brooding eyes. Child though I was, I sensed her distress and my heart went out to her in sympathy and gratitude.

The days that passed were endlessly long and dreary. When I was left alone I could not sleep. I constantly would cry for Mother and I could find no rest until she came to my bedside.

One night she came into my room crying softly. She took me up and clasped me in her arms, saying:

"What hurts Mother's child, tell me? Now you must hurry up and get well fast."

My mother had a marvelous voice. When she sang, the world was filled with light for me. I shall never forget the day when she came to my bedside and began to sing.

Thou who made the heavenly waters, stand by me!
Stand by me!
O, stand by me in the days of false pretension!
Stand by me!

On the wall opposite my bed hung a large picture of Jesus. He seemed to be looking down upon me with grave searching eyes. When my mother came to the end of her song, she pointed to the picture and said to me with deep feeling:

"He will stand by you."

I asked her: "Who is Jesus?"

She answered that Jesus is God's only begotten son and that He gave His life so that all of us might be saved. Those who do not believe in Him will go to hell and be burned with fire and brimstone. But those who believe in the Saviour will surely go to Heaven and have life everlasting.

I asked her: "Do you think Jesus can make me well?"

Piously my mother answered: "Jesus can do anything He wants to."

Every night she knelt by my bed, and as I looked into the searching eyes of Jesus on the wall, she prayed with deep emotion:

"O Lord, I bow not for form nor fashion but with sincerity and truthfulness to You who can destroy but will defend, to come to my aid at this hour of need! O, Lord, You know how powerless and helpless I am down here in man's sinful world. Please, Lord, spare my little son!"

My mother was very religious. God was always with her.

That was quite natural; her father and great-grandfather were preachers. She often used to say to me: "Some day, Gelo, you too are going to be a preacher." This made me feel very proud. I asked her how preachers were made, were they born preachers or were they sent by God? My mother, who had an Old Testament conception of righteousness, answered severely that "Jack-leg preachers" who claim they have been sent to teach and lead the people out of sin and to bring heaven here on earth only want to fill their pockets. But a real, true, God-sent preacher has the teachings of the Bible at heart. He is willing to sacrifice everything he has for Kingdom Come.

My illness had become the concern not only of my own family, but of all our friends and neighbors. One night, when my father had returned from work, I overheard a conversation between him and my mother about doctors' fees and medicine. They were at their wits' end. I heard my mother say:

"We have no money to buy medicine for Gelo. What shall we do?"

My father looked grave and worried. He answered:

"What is there to do? We will just have to wait until I make some money."

My mother was desperate and insistent; no matter what happened she must have money immediately.

That night she called on her dear friend Mrs. Josephine Tolbert, who lived just around the corner from us. They belonged to the same church and very often attended prayer meetings together in neighbors' homes. As usual, Mrs. Tolbert did not fail her. She lent her money for medicine.

2

It was about this time that I first became aware of my great-grandmother, Mariah Evelyn Herndon. Prior to that I had accepted her with a matter-of-factness that one extends to familiar objects. She had moved silently about the house, serving us at every step, performing her drudgery with, as I now recall it, a quiet and self-effacing dignity. My illness, as it were, suddenly rent aside a veil from my eyes and I began to see her as a marvelous and magnificent creature who miraculously had turned up to save the family from its tragic plight.

"Mom," as we children used to call her affectionately, had a very beautiful face. It was smooth and round and her coloring was warm and red as a bloodbeet. Like all Indians, she had long, blue-black hair. We children found great pleasure when she allowed us to comb it for her. This admiration must have compensated her for the chaffing we directed against her big varicosed legs. With the unreflective cruelty of all children we mercilessly examined and discussed all her anatomic peculiarities. The dear thing did not seem to mind it at all, for she only smiled good-naturedly and shooed us out of the house. All in all, she was an exceptionally well-preserved woman, what with having been born and raised as a slave in the State of Virginia and having given birth to fourteen children. Unable to stand the solitude of her life, she would stay in rotation from six months to a year with each of her fourteen children. Most of the time she lived with my family because she was particularly fond of us. Of course we children loved Mom, perhaps mostly for the reason that she always bought us candy on the sly whenever Mother was away. We were just eaten up by curiosity to know how she got her money. We decided to watch her. But we could not penetrate her secret.

However, during my illness she suddenly revealed to us the hiding place of her treasure. When Mom saw the despair into which my parents were flung when they could not pay the doctors' fees for medicine and for food, she called the family together. Without a word she reached into her waist and drew out a little cloth bag which hung suspended from her neck between her breasts. My father, who sat watching, incredulous and spellbound, jumped to his feet and exclaimed:

"My God, where did you get that money from?"

Mom looked embarrassed because she did not relish the role of philanthropist she was about to play. In a hesitant voice she said:

"Before you were born I had already started saving my coins. I did it to make sure that my last years would not be spent in want, and that I would die with a roof over my head. Now I reckon that I haven't much longer to live anyway, and it's more important that little Gelo get well."

The joy of my parents was indescribable. My mother bent over me and whispered soothingly:

"Don't worry, Gelo, everything will be all right soon."

I was not unaware of what was happening. Children of the very poor become conscious of the problems of their parents long before they should. When there was no food in the house or the rent could not be paid or there were not enough shoes to go around to tide us children over the winter, a dark cloud descended upon us all. We read the anxiety in the faces of our father and mother and we too became anxious and went about brooding in silence.

During the time of my illness I began to see my father in a new light. While my mother was demonstrative in her affection for us, he acted in a constrained and absent manner. Worry had made his face prematurely lined. It was only when he smiled that the essential kindness of the man was revealed. But he rarely smiled. Then I did not know why, but now I do know that it was overwork, under-nourishment and the burdens of daily living which had made a broken man out of him, although still so young in years. His eyes were perpetually inflamed by the coal dust which also gnawed away at his lungs and made him spit out black sputum. This was no cause for wonder to me, as all miners had inflamed eyes, bent backs, coughed and spat coal dust. My father worked from ten to fourteen hours a day and sometimes during the night, for which he never received any extra pay. Every year that passed only increased the wretchedness of his condition and our way of living. Work as hard as he would, there seemed to be no way out for us. We were all walking in a blind alley, resigned to our fate and surviving physically, by what miraculous means I do not understand even to this day. My father was miserably treated by the mining company, but he had imbibed the false humility and meekness that the oppressors of his race and class had hypocritically taught him. He sought consolation from his torment in a touching devotion to his church, distracting himself from the sordid realities of his life and that of his family with dreams of the Reward Hereafter.

Mom's emergence as our fairy godmother had an extraordinary effect upon him. Usually despondent, he now became almost gay. He kissed me shamefacedly and spoke cheering words to me in the manner of a man not used to such things. The windfall of good luck seemed to excite him beyond its merits. He read in it an encouraging sign from heaven. His hopes rose high. He assured my mother, beaming all over, that Mom's money would carry us along for some time. He himself would make enough money to pay all the bills and get everything straightened out. He'd go down into the mine and dig coal like a man. We had nothing to fear. Good times were coming.

TWO

I WAS NOT THE SAME CHILD after I had left my sick-bed. I now looked out upon my little world with new and troubled eyes. My illness had drawn me closer to my family. Absurdly young as I was, I already began to feel a share of the general responsibility toward warding off the hunger and suffering which were driving my poor parents to despair. I fully understood now what it meant to be poor. My childish mind became greatly distressed. "Why are people poor?" I asked myself. But I could find no answer. Yet the squalor and wretchedness of my surroundings, in contrast with the lovely world of the whites outside, filled me with broodings far too morbid and grave for a mite of six. Baffled for an explanation, I found naïve consolation in the rapturous dream my mother used to weave for me about the Second Coming whenever poverty obliged us to go to bed hungry.

I recall how once, being the unreasonable child that I was, I burst into tears because there was nothing to still my hunger. It was then that all the protective tenderness that was in my mother flowed out to me. She tried to distract me with words of the following nature:

"A time will come, Gelo, when little children like you won't go hungry any more. That will be when our dear Lord and Saviour, Jesus Christ, will come again and judge the people. He will make the crooked straight and the sick whole, and He will feed the poor. There will be no more poor people, not even the blackest sinners, for our Lord will have mercy on all. Blessed be the name of the Lord, for His mercy endureth forever."

I listened breathlessly, and the music of her words entered into me. For the moment I even forgot my hunger.

2

One day I saw some white children at a game of marbles. Innocent of any evil thought or expectations, I joined their game. As my misfortune would have it, I shot all their marbles out of the ring. A white boy, livid with rage, called me a "nigger." "Nigger?" I repeated, not understanding. "What does 'nigger' mean?" The boys burst out laughing and I laughed with them good-naturedly. But the incident hereupon went beyond name-calling.

"Do you want to know what 'nigger' means?" asked the white boy spitefully. "Let me show you."

Together with the other boys he began to pelt me with stones and I fled for dear life. After a while, tiring of their sport, they let me alone. With feelings smarting more than did the bruises on my body, I turned in the direction of home. When I entered the house I ran to my mother, weeping. Between my sobs I managed to gasp the all-important question:

"Mother, what does 'nigger' mean?"

A look of pain and indignation came into her face. She wanted to know who had used that nasty word to me. When I had explained, she put on the sing-song voice that she always used whenever she read out of the Scriptures. She intoned the following verse from the Song of Songs:

"Look not at me so because I am black for the sun hath burned me, the children of my father were angry with me and they made me watchman of their vineyard, but my own vineyard I have not kept."

She went on to explain to me that because we Negroes sinned against God, against His only begotten Son, and the Holy Ghost, therefore He has humbled us in our pride and vanity; He has made slaves of us for the white man to oppress and to mistreat, so that we might learn to be obedient and to walk in His way, and sin no more.

Moved by her own words, she raised her beautiful voice in song as was her way when religion came upon her:

You can't hide, sinner, you can't hide!
Oh, tell me what you going to do?
You can't hide!
When the mountains start falling, you can't hide!
You can't hide, sinner, you can't hide!

As I listened to her, a deep sense of guilt came over me. To be sure, I must be a sinner too, and the fact that the white boys called me "nigger" must have been by the will of God. Already I felt as if by this act alone, by being humiliated in spirit and bruised in body, that I was expiating for the pride and the vanity which my mother charged against our race.

THREE

My father and mother showed a touching humility before learning. While they could only read and write and had managed to pick up only stray bits of knowledge from books, they regarded education as the highest possible achievement in life. It is no wonder, therefore, that my own thirst for knowledge came quite naturally to me while I was still a little boy. My brothers, who did not feel so strongly about the matter, used to razz me, saying, "So you want to become one of those high-falutin college boys, Gelo." But my sister, Lola Mae, who had a tender spot for me, would always rise to my defense. She gave my brothers a severe tongue-lashing and would try to point out to them how wonderful learning was.

By the time I started going to public school the financial difficulties of my family had increased tenfold. My father and mother regarded the situation with sinking heart. Sending their large brood to school was quite a costly matter, for books, paper, pencils and school clothes had to be bought for each child. Conditions got to be so critical that my two oldest brothers were sent away to live with relatives who had consented to take them in as an act of charity. The struggle my parents carried on to keep me in school was gallant as well as heartbreaking. To make possible my education, my mother uncomplainingly used to work Sundays and holidays in order to earn a few extra dollars.

Despite all the difficulties my parents experienced in keeping me in school, I proved a bright kid and always got my lessons with ease. I was fortunate in having for my teacher a certain Mrs. Williams, a Negro, whose extraordinary kindness and understanding exercised a strong influence on my early life. It was she who showed me the way to the principle of mutual aid and social responsibility. She did not teach it to me in so many words, for I was too young to understand, and I doubt if even she herself understood. Rather I got to understand this view of life indirectly, by the example of her actions and deep sympathy toward me and the other unfortunate children in the class.

When school hours were over she would ask me to stay behind. She urged me to be more aggressive in class, for I was very timid and tongue-tied. She had me recite various poems and made me read from books out loud. Her encouragement bore fruit. At the end of my first term I was skipped from the first to the third grade.

About that time we had a concert at school. I participated in the program upon the request of Mrs. Williams. I raced through several recitations with all the appropriate gestures; one was about Rumpelstilskin and the Dwarf and the other was "The Night Before Christmas." The latter was my big act. It was about ten pages long and I had to learn it all by heart. Needless to say, I covered myself with imperishable glory in the eyes of my proud parents and neighbors.

FOUR

Whenever I look back upon those days, tears come to my eyes when I recall the touching solicitude and helpfulness of my father to see me get on with my studies. Long even before I went to school he would sit down with me and make me write my name by imitation thirty or forty times. No matter how tired he was after work he would not neglect this ritual upon which he had set his heart: to make an educated man out of his son Gelo. The most curious thing about all these sessions was the fact that, unmindful that I was too young to understand what he was talking about, he would go into impassioned songs of praise of learning. Education, said he, was a powerful weapon with which to fight poverty and the handicaps of racial discrimination. Once he said to me in his soft quiet voice that he and Mother wanted me to become an educated man so that I could be of service to my people. Most earnestly he assured me that he was ready to make every sacrifice in the world so that at least one of our family would get an education and become a man among his own people. I was the family's choice for this great honor. Therefore, he begged me to take the matter very seriously. I was to mind my teacher and to do my homework very carefully each day.

This advice of my father will never be erased from my consciousness. Even to this very day it remains a spur and an inspiration to me—to seek knowledge and to widen my sympathies for suffering mankind.

2

Mrs. Williams was ever such a lovely and sweet soul. She was just like a mother to me and to all of my little schoolmates. She used to arrange parties for us at her home on weekends and never lost an opportunity to impress upon us how important it was that we be studious and diligent in our studies. At one of these parties she said that she was glad to say that all of us were doing fine in our studies. We got our lessons and were not so mischievous as some of her other pupils. But if we wanted to get all we could out of school we were not to be ashamed to tell her of any outside troubles that might be bothering us. She assured us with great warmth that she was our friend and wished to help us in every way she could. Therefore, we were not to hold back but to tell her frankly about the troubles in our families; she was sure that we had many of them.

"Now come on, do please tell me," she cajoled.

She beamed at us in such a friendly way that I could not help but be irresistibly drawn to her in confidence. I immediately sensed what it was she was referring to vaguely, yet not mentioning it in so many words. She was no doubt alluding to the fact that some of our parents had no money to buy us clothes and supplies for school. We were tatterdemalion and looked pinched and undernourished, and how we managed to survive physically still remains a deep mystery to me.

On an impulse I arose, nervous and stammering, and spoke up:

"You are very kind, Mrs. Williams, and therefore I will tell you about some of the troubles in my family. There are eight of us and it is very hard for my father and mother to keep us going. My father is a coal miner. He does not make enough money to buy us clothes and school books. Mother is a servant and she makes very little money. What both make is not enough to pay for food, gas, light and other expenses."

I sat down, overwhelmed with shame that I should have disclosed such intimate information about our family life before the others, but I sensed unconsciously that what I had done was the right thing, since it was intended to help my family whom I dearly loved.

The following day Mrs. Williams called on my father and mother and spoke very tactfully and with concern about their difficulties. Before she left she begged them to let me live with her. She felt that it was absolutely necessary because of the poverty of the family. She said I was a good and sweet child and that I deserved what she wanted to do for me. My father and mother thanked her very profusely in their simple gracious way. While they admitted that things were very bad for them, just the same they declined her offer, thinking that it was better to suffer with one's own kin than to go and live with strangers, no matter how kind they were.

3

On our way home from school, we Negro boys would frequently meet with certain white boys. As long as we ganged together these white boys did us no mischief. But whenever it was the misfortune of one of us to be alone they gave us a good shellacking. At first we did not fight back. We took to our heels, trying to get out of reach of the sharp stones they would throw at us. We had to run so fast and so frequently that we grew sores and callouses on our bare feet.

Once, when complaining to my mother about my sore feet, she asked me how it happened. I told her that after we left school that day some white boys hid behind houses and waited for us to approach. When we came near them, they began throwing stones at us and we had to run for our lives. One of our boys got hit in the head with a stone which one of the white boys threw at him. They chased us, but we finally got away.

My mother's concern gave way to grimness. Her eyes flashed fire.

"So you call yourself a son of mine, Gelo," she shouted at me, and then and there she began to lambast me, admonishing me that next time if I did not fight back the white boys I had better not come home again, if I knew what was good for me.

My mother did not content herself with this. She called on all my friends' parents and told them what had happened. Her visits proved very unprofitable to my friends, for they, too, were given a good trouncing. This treatment proved highly beneficial to all of us, for the following day when we met on our way to school we drew up a plan of battle, should the white boys try to attack us again. Before going to our classes we had the foresight to fill our satchels with stones. On our way home we fixed upon the following strategy. We sent before us several Negro boys. The rest were to follow discreetly behind. Should our vanguard be attacked, the rest of us were to rush up from behind and hand it to the white boys in good measure.

Things worked out just as we had expected. The white boys dashed out from behind the houses and began throwing stones at our scouts. When we saw this, we closed in on them from the rear. Our flank attack took the white boys by surprise. A pitched battle raged between us for almost half an hour. On the sidelines women screamed and men shouted threats but we heard nothing. Like true warriors we were only concerned with getting our enemies. Some of the white boys were struck in the head by stones and some came near having their eyes scratched out. For it was a hand-to-hand combat, no mercy was asked and no mercy was given. I covered myself with glory. I threw stones, pummeled, scratched, bit, wrestled and rolled in the gutter. Finally, I had used up all the stones that I had in my satchel. I reached down to gather up some more, and just as I laid my hand on the first stone I felt as if I had been hit on the head with a cannon-ball. Everything went black before my eyes. I slumped to the ground, unconscious.

I was laid up in bed for two weeks. There was a deep gash behind my right ear. I still have a scar as a souvenir of this famous battle. I must confess that I am not at all ashamed of it. . . .

As soon as I got well my mother took me in hand again. She pursued the practical lessons she was giving me in the art of getting on in the world. With a stern look in her eyes she admonished me this time to seek revenge on the wretch who had thrown at my head that almost fatal stone. And she warned me that if I did not obey her she would give me such a shellacking that by comparison it would make the wound from the stone look like a trifle.

Inasmuch as I always tried to be a good and obedient son I decided to do a single-handed job this time. I watched out for the white kid who had been my assailant. One day I saw him in a marble game with some Negro kids. With an innocent air I asked if I could join in, and they said no. I stood sulking around for a few minutes with my right hand clutching tightly at a stone in my pocket and just at the right moment I let it fly. He gave a shout and sprawled on all fours. I exulted over my victory and not very heroically took to my heels.

4

As I have already stated once before, I experienced the tragic impact of poverty almost as soon as I began to think. Prompted by a mysterious impulse, I felt a strong urge to assume my share of financial responsibility in the family. I constantly was plotting ways and means to earn a little money. An opportunity suddenly turned up when I had reached the age of nine. Mike De Costello, our grocer, who had taken a liking to me, offered me a job to make deliveries for him. He was a short, chunky fellow, with a full-grown soup-strainer mustache. He always sang his Italian songs in a rich, lyric tenor. He was full of fun, and when he laughed all the kindness of the man became evident. Half of the day I attended school; the other half I delivered groceries. Some weeks I would make three dollars, and even five dollars. Mike was so generous that he forced upon me food, fruits and vegetables to take home to Mother; gesticulating demonstratively, he refused payment as if it were a mere trifle.

Now that I think of it, despite his infectious gaiety, Mike was a solitary soul. A luxuriant Mediterranean plant from Sicily, he could not take root in the cold, impersonal soil of his new environment. Perhaps it was the warmth of my own Negro soul which struck a sympathetic accord in his expansive nature. At convenient intervals he loved to talk to me about his life in Italy. He was so moved by his own narrative as he reminisced about the past that tears often came to his eyes.

"If Italy was such a beautiful country and you were so happy there, why did you leave it, Mike?" I asked.

Mike looked sad.

"You see, Gelo, it was this way. I was a Socialist and the Italian government does not like Socialists, so I couldn't make a living. But that wasn't the worst part of it. They used to throw us in prison and they killed some of us. Well, you know how it is, Gelo, I got tired of the whole rotten business, and one day I said to my wife, Mrs. De Costello: 'Mrs. De Costello, what's the use of living so miserably. Let's take Josephine, Mario and John and go to America. Maybe the people there don't hate Socialists as much as they do here and will let us make a living and maybe even let us be Socialists too.' "

He tried very hard to make an impression upon me with the fact that he was a Socialist. But I had never heard of a

Socialist and therefore did not know what he was talking about. But somehow I got the idea that it must have been some sort of criminal like a burglar.

As I was a healthy and lively little fellow I did not find my job too fatiguing. My sense of duty was very strong and although I was frequently tempted to join the other boys at play whenever I passed them, I resisted the temptation by a great effort.

It was then that I fully became conscious of the inequalities in being a worker. It rankled in my young soul but it did not embitter me, for I was by nature full of gaiety and good spirits. However, I did not always succeed in carrying on in an unperturbed way. Sometimes I would suffer great humiliation at the hands of some of the white customers when I would make my deliveries. They used to refer to me unthinkingly as the "nigger boy" and sometimes would treat me with a callousness quite startling. If I knew what it was to be a "worker" I knew even better what it was to be a "nigger." The walls of race, color and class now rose between me and the hostile world outside. I wondered, in my confused, childish way, whether there would ever come a time when I would be able to scale them.

5

In 1922 my Uncle Jeremiah was ordained as minister in the Baptist Church. This event created a great sensation in the family and in our circle of neighbors. We Herndons expanded and strutted about like peacocks in our new family distinction. All my little playmates envied me and treated me with increased respect. I basked in the sunshine with full abandonment. "There was religion in our family."

Uncle Jeremiah was a thin, scrawny man with a prominent Adam's apple. Whenever he swallowed hard, it bobbed up and down. We kids watched it in tireless fascination. Despite his thinness he had a rich baritone voice which he used like an organ, now cajoling and exhorting in soft, wheedling tones, or threatening and thundering in a Day-of-Judgment voice. His holiness notwithstanding, he was as shrewd and clever as a fox. People used to say that nothing could ever get by him and that he was sure to get the best part of a bargain. For good reason, therefore, everybody used to call him "Old Reverend Fox."

After he had opened up a church I was taken to hear his first sermon. It was a great event, and the family occupied the front pew. I felt the importance of the occasion and followed every word and movement of my uncle raptly. After the feet-washing rite, for it was the annual feet-washing festival, and all had washed one another's feet, my Uncle Jeremiah mounted the rostrum, cleared his throat and began solemnly in this wise:

"Sistern and brethren, we are gathered here today to drink the blood of Jesus Christ and in our most humble way to do reverence to His Holy Name for the sacrifices and suffering He hath endured so that He might save us from sin and from the fiery pits of hell. We praise Thee, O Father, our King, Thou, Who rulest over man and beast, over the sea and over the elements. We are weak but Thou art strong, and whatever we do is only small in Thine eyesight. But O Lord, we do ask that Thou be with us this day to guide us and teach us, so that we will be better capable of teaching others who live in sin."

My uncle's gestures while delivering his sermon made a powerful impression on me. With his arms outstretched toward heaven and his head flung back, his eyes were fixed upon the ceiling of the church as if he and God were carrying on a very personal conversation.

At the close of the sermon the whole congregation broke out into cries and sobs. Everyone was swept away by religious fervor. Even I felt my excitement mounting. My heart beat violently. Women began to scream and to weep out loud. Some were even seized by hysteria and began to chant the following incantation:

"O Lord, one can't hold me. O Lord, two can't hold me. O Lord, three can't hold me—you will have to get a rope and tie me."

When Uncle Jeremiah saw what a furor he had made with his sermon, he became inspired and began singing in a very low voice, trembling with emotion:

"O blessed be the name of the Lord."

My mother could not contain her tears. She began to sing.

Soon one morning, death come a-creeping in my room,
Soon one morning death come a-creeping in my room,
O my Lord, what shall I do?

I too began to cry. I said to my mother: "I've got religion in me, Mother."

"How do you know?"

"I feel it, Mother."

When the shouting and the singing had at last come to an end, I crowded up to the rostrum with the others in the congregation and laid my hand in the big bony hand of Uncle Jeremiah. I said:

"Uncle Jeremiah I want to become a member of this church."

Uncle Jeremiah gripped my hand tightly until my knuckles pained. He transfixed me with a fiery eye and said:

"Angelo Herndon, are you sure you've got religion?"

"Yes," mumbled I, breathlessly, so excited that I thought my heart would stop beating.

"Are you sure you feel the spirit of Jesus Christ, our Saviour, in your heart?"

Almost inaudibly I murmured: "Yes."

Uncle Jeremiah now arranged to baptize me and several other converts in the pool which was in the yard of the church. I disrobed and my mother dressed me in a long white cotton nightshirt and led me, barefoot, to Uncle Jeremiah at the side of the pool. Around us stood the entire congregation, shouting encouragement to me and to my fellow-converts. I stood there trembling and stage-struck like an inexperienced actor. Uncle Jeremiah cleared his throat and swallowed so hard that his Adam's apple quivered. He rolled his eyes violently and intoned:

"In the name of the Father and of the Son and of the Holy Ghost, I now baptize you, Angelo Herndon, and accept you into the congregation of the Lord. You are now a member of the Church. I therefore call upon you to obey your father and mother and to follow in the path of righteousness as long as you live. Amen!"

"Amen!" chanted the entire congregation.

My Uncle Jeremiah seized me by the nape of my neck and dipped me into the water. I began to shiver and splutter like a fish because the water was icy cold and, worse yet, I had swallowed too much of it and was now trying to cough it up.

"Say 'Amen'!" commanded Uncle Jeremiah.

"Amen!" I gargled, with a mouth full of water.

On my way home I said to my mother:

"Mother, can you talk to God like Uncle Jeremiah?"

My mother reproved me sternly:

"Do not try to go too fast, my dear son. Just be patient. You will learn in time."

6

When we came home from church my mother and father spoke gravely to me. They told me that parents are responsible for the sins of their children only up to the age of twelve.

"Now, Angelo, that you're a member of God's Congregation, and nine years old, you are already responsible for your own sins. See to it that you do nothing wrong in the sight of God."

My father's words filled me with a sense of deep responsibility. I prayed with fervor upon the slightest pretext. Every night and morning I was obliged to read a passage from the Old Testament and recite verses from the Psalms. Frequently I recognized in their words a true description of the trials and tribulations of my own family. I was particularly moved by the following verses:

> Reproach hath broken my heart and I am full of heaviness and I looked for some to take pity, but there was none, and for comforters I found none.
>
> But as for me, my prayer is unto Thee, O Lord, in an acceptable time, O God, in the multitude of thy mercy hear me, in the truth of salvation.
>
> He shall judge thy people with righteousness, and thy poor with judgment. The mountains shall bring peace to the people, and the little hills, by righteousness. He shall judge the poor of the people, he shall save the children of the needy and shall break in pieces the oppressor.

My mother, as I have already indicated, was a devout woman. She sought every opportunity to instil in me a feeling for religion. Constantly she talked about heaven and hell, punishment for sin and reward for virtue. Her description of

Judgment Day was so excruciatingly vivid that many a night I lay awake tormented by a guilty conscience and the fear of the Day of Wrath when I would have to give a strict accounting of my evil ways.

On the day of my baptism my mother took me aside to give me saintly advice. She spoke to me in the following manner:

"The Lord gives us ample time to repent for our sins. Those who die as Christians will rest peacefully in their graves until Angel Gabriel will blow on his great trumpet. He will wake up the dead and make them rise from their graves, the clouds will swing low and as they reach the earth the angels of our Lord, Jesus Christ, will bend down and reach out their hands and pull on board all those who have served the Lord and who are His children in righteousness. But those sinners who have been the servants of Satan, the Evil One, they will be running from the fire to the ocean, from the trees to the stones, begging that they be killed, but the ocean and the trees and the fire and the stones will cry out and say: 'Depart from me for I know ye not!' The whole world will be set ablaze with fire that shall burn forever and as the clouds begin to swing upward with the children of God on board the angels will burst into hymns, flying upward while they watch the wicked sinners they leave behind burned to a crisp. And when the righteous will reach heaven all their troubles will be gone and over. They will serve the Lord with song and psaltery. They will enjoy all good things, they will eat honey and sip sweet milk and praise the Lord."

I looked wide-eyed at my mother and in a choking voice I said: "Mother, I will be ready when that great trumpet sounds."

FIVE

TRAGEDY OVERTOOK MY HOME. My baby brother, Frank Eliot, who was one year old, died of scarlet fever. It seemed as if all trouble was piling down on our heads at the same time. As my mother sat beside the body of her dead child I looked at her. Her eyes were filled with tears. Her face had a strange blue color. She seemed to have aged over night. We all tried the best way we knew how to console her. My father pleaded with her:

"Do not suffer so. It is the will of God. He knows what is best."

My mother's friends, Mrs. Tolbert, Mrs. Josephine, Effie and others arranged meetings of churchgoers to help raise money for the burial, for we were penniless and weak from hunger. The death of my little brother was highly untimely. Our neighbors all came to the funeral. They spoke to my mother and begged her not to weep over the dead. Mrs. Tolbert reproached her:

"Rejoice over those who die and weep over those who come into the world. So Scripture teaches us."

They tried everything to cheer her up, but it was a long time before my mother got over the shock.

2

Troubles came thick and fast. Only a few months after the death of my brother, my father took ill with miner's pneumonia.

It was in the year of my baptism. We somehow had come to regard our father as immortal. That he could ever fall sick never came to our minds. He was our provider and protector. Sometimes, when I thought of God and the role he played in the universe, I unconsciously thought of my father. He was the center of our little universe and like vines around a tree we clung to him. Now that he had fallen ill, it came as a shock to us all. Seeing him lying helpless and in fever made us grow silent and thoughtful. We children stopped our fooling, for we became troubled. Our naturally gay spirits were darkened. We tried very hard to walk on tiptoe and not to make any unnecessary noise.

It all had come so unexpectedly. It had begun innocently with a cold, which developed into the grippe and finally wound up in double pneumonia. Old Doctor Brown came to see him once every day. He was an elderly gentle Negro, exceptionally reserved but always with a professional air about him. He was very kindly but, now that I think of it, he never hesitated to ask for money if he but suspected that my mother had it, regardless of the hardships it would cause us.

My father's illness almost prostrated my mother. She hovered over him constantly. All night long she sat at his bedside patiently attending to his needs and wiping away the perspiration on his face. She cried all the time and her eyes looked swollen. Often I saw her covertly moving her lips in prayer. We children knew by this token that matters stood very desperately with our father.

No one went to school. My older brothers took care of the house. This made them feel very important and responsible. There were six of us then. Hilliard was nineteen, Leroy was seventeen, Milton sixteen, Leo twelve, Lola Mae was seven, and I was nine. Face to face with death, our thoughts turned to God. My Uncle Jeremiah had a lot to do with it. Daily he knelt in prayer before my father's bed and his rich baritone voice filled the room. We all felt overawed.

Father's lungs were terribly congested. He gasped for breath. All day and all night long he lay moaning till we could almost hear it wherever we went. I even heard it in my sleep and I would wake up with a sigh or a cry. My father couldn't hold any food. He vomited constantly. Because of his high fever he talked deliriously, but it was all incoherent. At times when his fever left him for a while he became conscious of what was happening to him, but he did not know the true nature of his illness. He thought he only had a bad cold.

Money was even scarcer now than before. We lived on black coffee without sugar and on a crust of bread, and we thought ourselves fortunate in having that much. Added to the torments that my father's illness had brought to my mother she now was distracted to the point of madness by the need of money for medicines and other absolute necessities. With our father rapidly dying before our eyes we felt that our last earthly prop was being snatched from us. I looked almost bitterly, in my own childish way, upon the face of Jesus that looked down on me from the wall opposite my bed. "Why don't you help us, Jesus?" I reproached him. But He only looked at me in His usual gentle, searching way. And my father grew only worse.

The time came when my father's condition grew so alarming that the doctor gave him up. My father knew that he was dying. One by one he called us in and took farewell of us. When my turn came I was choked with sobs. I hardly dared look at him. My heart pounded wildly and I then knew that I would joyfully die for my father if only he would be spared. Between gasps, his eyes eloquent with pain and regret, he said to me:

"Angelo, I am dying. You have always been a good boy and I want you to promise me that after I am gone you will continue to do what is right. Study hard, do your lessons well, mind what Mother says and try to make a man of yourself."

He moaned so piteously that I thought my heart would break. In conclusion he said to me, almost in a wail:

"Get education, Angelo, get education. Lift yourself above our condition. See what mining has done to me, so that now I am dying and will leave you all alone."

His pulse grew weak and his heart began to give out. I no longer could recognize him. He looked so emaciated, nothing but a bundle of bones and skin from which protruded his knotted veins and muscles. That same night he closed his eyes and never opened them again. And our tiny little home was full of weeping.

3

We had no money with which to bury our father. Again my mother was obliged to ask assistance from our friends, neighbors and relatives. As usual, Mrs. Josephine and Effie proved themselves true staunch friends. As little money as they had, they contributed their mite toward the funeral expenses. It was a real sacrifice for them. Mother felt abashed. She thought it was imposing too much on their good nature to ask so many favors of them. So she sent letters to her brothers and sisters, including Uncle Jeremiah, asking them for money. "After all, he was your brother," she wrote to them. "You must help get him a decent Christian burial." But all our relatives, with the exception of Uncle Jeremiah, pleaded poverty, and we got nothing from them. Uncle Jeremiah, strange to relate, despite his foxy disposition, had a generous streak in his twisted nature. He actually contributed five dollars for the burial, but with the instinct of a true pulpit showman, he withheld it until the time when he would be able to make a grand display of his good heart in public. Since time was pressing and my mother could muster only a fraction of the burial costs, dear Mrs. Josephine and Effie decided to hold another prayer meeting in our home.

Our house was overcrowded with the neighbors and relatives who came to the prayer meeting. Uncle Jeremiah looked magnificent in a long, black frock coat with shining silk lapels. He was officious and pompous and his voice was in magnificent condition. When all were assembled he cried out:

"Now let us all kneel down and pray for the soul of our departed brother Paul."

Thereupon the house began to resound with groans, sighs and lamentations. Some began to weep out loud. Only my mother wept silently, dabbing at her eyes with her handkerchief. When everybody was kneeling, Uncle Jeremiah cleared his throat and prayed. I recall it as being something like this:

'O Lord Jesus Christ, Our Saviour, You who are the only begotten son of God and who died so that we miserable sinners might find salvation, grant that divine forgiveness be given to our dear brother Paul for all his sins that he may have committed in this evil world. Grant, dear Lord, that he may rise with the dead on the Day of Resurrection and enter Paradise with God's dear angels. Yes, dear Lord, brother Paul was a good and righteous man. He always walked in Thy path and served Thee in Thy Temple. Forgive him his sins and lead his departed spirit into Glory Land. Amen!"

"Amen," we all cried fervently.

Then Uncle Jeremiah carefully put on his thick old spectacles, moistened his finger tips and began to page the Bible. In a sonorous voice he read Psalm 106, beginning with Verse 6:

We have sinned with our fathers,
We have done iniquitously, we have dealt wickedly.
Our fathers in Egypt gave no heed unto Thy wonders;
They remembered not the multitude of Thy mercies;

But were rebellious at the sea, even at the Red Sea.
Nevertheless He saved them for His Name's sake,
That He might make His mighty power to be known.
And He rebuked the Red Sea, and it was dried up;
And He led them through the depths, as through a
wilderness.

Uncle Jeremiah hereupon extended his arms in a mighty upward swing, threw back his head and rolled his eyeballs toward Heaven, saying with unction:

"Yea verily, brothers, the Lord will surely lead the soul of brother Paul through the depths, as through a wilderness, into the pearly gates of the Heavenly Kingdom."

"Amen!" chanted our neighbors and relatives.

Uncle Jeremiah now rose to his feet and with a magnificent gesture took out his black leather wallet. All eyes turned to watch him intently. He took out a five-dollar bill with a careless gesture, held it up and said:

"Sistern and brethren, let us all, to the best of our abilities, do our Christian duty to our departed brother Paul and give him a decent burial, for he was a good Christian man."

Uncle Jeremiah dropped his five-dollar bill into a plate which stood on the table. Everybody present dropped bills and coins, mostly coins, into the plate. My mother was too grief-stricken to notice anything. If she had, she would have been very much ashamed, for she was very proud.

4

During his lifetime my father had expressed the wish that he be buried in his home town, Birmingham. He also requested that all the children be present at the funeral. Unfortunately, there was not enough money to pay the train fare for all the children. My mother just managed to scrape together enough money for the barest funeral and for the train fare for herself.

My father's body was therefore taken to a funeral parlor, where it was prepared for shipment to Birmingham.

On the day of the funeral our house was in turmoil. All of us children were crying and begging our mother to take us with her to Birmingham. She pleaded with us, begged us to be reasonable, told us how poor we were, and that it was impossible for her to raise the train fare for all of us. However, she agreed to take me along.

That evening some friends came with two ramshackle cars and drove us off in grand style to the station. My mother was sedately dressed in a black satin gown. Her face was covered by a black veil. As soon as she started to get into the car she uttered a shriek and collapsed. General pandemonium followed. Everybody tried to help her at the same time, until Uncle Jeremiah raised his voice in authority and ordered everyone to stand aside. Someone brought a bottle of smelling salts. Uncle Jeremiah shoved it under her nose with solemnity, as if he were conducting a religious service. My mother finally gave a deep moan and came to. We carried her into the train and stretched her out in the back seat of the day coach. I have experienced many hardships and torments in the later years of my life, yet I must say that never was I gripped by such abysmal despair as when I looked upon the prostrate and semi-conscious form of my mother that day. I, too, felt that death had taken away our last and only friend in the world.

When the train was about to pull out my brothers and sister began to cry. But my brother Milton showed the greatest sense. He said:

"Oh, what's the use of crying! If God saw fit to take him from us, it is all His will. What right have we got to question it?"

We saw that he was right, and so we dried our tears.

The train pulled out of the station with a terrific clatter.

Every puff of the engine seemed to be shrieking, "Birmingham! Birmingham!" with an inevitability that constricted my heart. The thought came to my mind: "That's the last of my father, all right."

I began to pray an impossible prayer: that we somehow never manage to get to Birmingham.

5

A drunken white man lurched into the car. He almost sprawled all over us. My Uncle Jeremiah tried to push him off. Thereupon he let loose a flood of vile abuse. Suddenly he lunged forward as if to strike my mother. Her nerves already overwrought, she now let out a loud scream. The conductor came rushing in. He tried to move the drunken man into another car, but he refused to go. He kept on mumbling in his drunken way: "Dirty nigger, dirty nigger." When the train stopped at the next station he was put off.

Without any further misadventures we finally arrived in Birmingham. We were met at the station by a host of relatives. As soon as they caught sight of us they let out dismal howls of mourning. They wrung their hands and dabbed at their eyes. Their laments could have broken the heart of a stone. They again opened the floodgates of our tears.

We drove to the cemetery in some more battered chariots. "Style," is what we called it. Never in all my life had I felt so splendid as I did then. Arrived at the cemetery we gathered around the open grave which my father's body was to be laid in. The funeral sermon was delivered by the Reverend Johnson, a distant kinsman. He concluded with the following prayer:

"O Lord, bless our dear brother Paul's beloved widow and little children. I ask you, O Father in Heaven, to stick by her through all her trials and tribulations. Help her make Christians out of her children, so that they might be saved, and when the great Judgment Day will come around they will be sure to meet their dear father again in Glory Land. Amen!"

The Reverend Johnson had been very eloquent. He had moved himself to tears and the mourners into a state bordering on hysteria.

They lowered my father into the grave. I could hear my heart pounding against my chest. I listened to the crunch, crunch of the shovels of the grave diggers against the pebbly clay. It all seemed to take an eternity. When the coffin was already covered with a top layer of pebbles I started weeping all over again. I flung myself upon the heap and with my fingers tried frenziedly to dig my father up again. Unseen hands tried to pull me away, but I clung desperately to one of the tombstones. Sobbing, I pleaded with my mother:

"Please let me stay here, Mother. We cannot leave Father all alone here."

But my mother entreated:

"Come away from here, Angelo, come away, Father has gone bye-bye now."

SIX

Broken in spirit, we returned home. Our poverty was appalling. I was terribly distressed by my mother's helplessness. She was a house servant to rich whites. They mistreated her. We hardly ever saw her, for she left to work while we were still asleep. Sometimes she worked until midnight. Only on rare occasions did we see her, and the little affection that we got from her then had to suffice for a whole week's desolateness. She received ten dollars weekly for her wages and was never paid overtime. Her masters caused her endless wretchedness by grumbling ill-naturedly because she had taken time off during Father's illness and funeral. I knew that my mother was a servant, that she had a low position in the social scale, that she was black and despised, that she was poor and oppressed, but I never could see in this fact anything very extraordinary. I regarded her lot in life as if it were the most natural thing in the world.

Our situation became very acute. We were a large family left all alone in the world to die from starvation. To whom could we turn for assistance? Mom's romantic little hoard had melted away like snow in the sun. Uncle Jeremiah very reluctantly gave my mother a few dollars every week, but it was far from enough to keep us alive. My mother began to develop very strange ideas. She thought she saw a way out in marriage. But we children raised an awful hullabaloo. What! Mother marrying another man! That must never be. "I don't want any stepfather," I told her with finality. We assured her that we would all get jobs, and somehow we would make ends meet. We pictured for her a glorious vision of the life we would lead. I realize now how cunning it all was on our part and how hopelessly selfish. Fortunately, my mother did not allow herself to be swayed by us. She was still young. Her life was still ahead of her and she planned to get married just the same.

2

I spent few days in school now. All my family's and my own dreams of becoming an educated man had burst like a soap bubble. It seemed certain now that at best I could only hope to become a miner.

Once again my dear school teacher, Mrs. Williams, asked my mother to let me live with her. Mother thanked her again for her kind offer, but she told her with finality that she would never allow herself to surrender any of her children to a stranger, no matter how nice and estimable that stranger might be, and no matter how much poverty and misfortune should dog her.

The death of my father caused a deep change in me. It made me think of life in realistic terms. I was no longer a child in mind but one who knew what it meant to be poor and to struggle for sheer physical survival. I began to have ideas of my own on the subject. At night I could not sleep. I lay worrying and racking my brains until the early hours of dawn. I fully realized what a burden I was to my mother, and so I wished to do something to help support the family. To buttress this resolution I brought all my religious fantasy into play. I felt certain that my prayers would be answered; for were they not just and ever so humble and modest in their demands? With the pious air of a little minister, in imitation of Uncle Jeremiah, I said to my mother: "Rest assured, Mother,

ANGELO HERNDON AND HIS MOTHER

the Lord will come to our rescue; for don't we need Him now more than ever before?"

Every night before I went to bed I knelt in prayer. My heart now overflowed with bitterness and grief. "O Lord," I prayed, "what have we done to be treated as if we were not Your children? Help us live a decent life like true Christians. Now, Lord, I lay me down to sleep, put an angel at my head, and an angel at my feet, and if I should die before I wake, I pray to Thee my soul to take. Amen!"

Daily our difficulties grew in number and complexity. The burden weighed heavily upon me. I grew morose and gave up playing with the boys. My school chums, Isaiah and Rose, called for me from time to time. They did their utmost to reach me in my grief, but everything seemed unreal to me and fast slipping from me. I became emotionally tied-up in myself. An unscalable wall separated me from everybody. I turned away from my playmates. They, too, seemed unreal to me now.

3

One day I took a walk through the park. I saw white and Negro children swimming in a pool and making mud pies in the sand. The whole world seemed deeply immersed in peace. Only I felt heavy-hearted and a stranger to it all. I passed the playing children and made my way into the woods on the outskirts of the city. I sat down on a stone and sobbed unconsolably. I must have cried myself to sleep. I dreamed I saw little white seraphim and cherubim flying about me. They beckoned joyously to me to come and fly with them. They were like a cloud of brightly tinted butterflies. They were so beautiful that I thrilled at the sight.

But I soon awoke from my dream of beauty and radiance to find myself in the midst of coarse reality once more. When I returned home I knelt before the picture of Jesus which hung on my wall. And with the familiar gestures which my Uncle Jeremiah employed in the pulpit I addressed myself to God.

"Have mercy on me, Lord!" I moaned.

I knew I was a Christian and that I tried to be as good as possible. I recited aloud a few passages from the Old Testament that I remembered and again called on the Lord not to forsake me. I looked imploringly into the face of my Saviour on the wall. But He made no answer, only looked at me with His steady searching glance, until I thought I was ready to faint from anguish. I felt so small, so weak, so utterly alone! The whole world seemed to be closing in on me, and, because in my childish heart I was terribly afraid, I began to sing.

Down on me, O down on me,
Looks like everybody in the whole round world is down
on me.

I took my brother Leo aside and had a long conversation with him. I said to him:

"Leo, what do you think about the way we have to live? Mother is getting old and she does not make enough money to feed all of us. We are pretty much grown up and we ought to do something about it. What do you say?"

Leo answered: "I, too, have been thinking this thing over. I've also spoken to Hilliard, Leroy and Milt about it. They feel the same as we do. What do you say, Gelo, how about it—let's run away! Let's go to our relatives across the river in Covington. We can sneak out of the house before daybreak while everyone is asleep and get across the river before anyone will miss us."

My heart leaped with joy. I thrilled with the excitement of the adventure we were about to undertake.

4

Early that morning, while the house lay silent and dark, Leo and I slipped noiselessly into our clothes and tiptoed out of the house. By five o'clock we were already crossing the Ohio River. We tramped through the streets of Covington, looking for the home of our relatives. They were surprised to see us and looked genuinely pleased. My cousin Novella had two children. She was kind and sweet. Although her husband, Sam, was a poor, unskilled laborer, he received us with fatherly concern. He asked me why we came without letting him know beforehand. I told him that since Father's death matters had gotten worse at home. Mother worked hard, but she could not support all of us. We had not enough to eat and we always felt hungry. The children were without shoes and we could not buy school supplies and books. Leo and I felt that we ought to do something about it. So we had come here to look for jobs in order to help Mother out.

Sam beamed at us and patted us on the back.

"Good boys, good boys," he kept on repeating with relish. He assured us that we were welcome to stay with him as long as we liked. "Never fear, as long as there will be a crust of bread in the house we'll share it with you." When my mother ultimately discovered where we were she hastened to fetch us. We implored her to let us carry out our original plan to get jobs, but she said sternly:

"You're still kids and your place is home and in school."

We returned home without any enthusiasm, frustrated in our first effort at worldly self-assertion.

5

One morning in the spring of 1926, my brother Leo and I left home for Lexington, Kentucky. We went by freight train. People had told us a lot of money could be made in the Kentucky mines if we worked hard enough. Since there was no legally specified age limit for miners at that time, we felt sure that we could land jobs and earn enough money between the two of us to help keep the family going.

Luck was on our side this time. We landed jobs immediately. Nobody then seemed to be particularly concerned about having kids of thirteen, which was my age, work several miles deep in the ground from early morning until late at night. It was quite the usual thing, and it never occurred to anyone to question it.

Leo and I were given jobs as coal loaders. First the coal was cut by a machine and then it was shot down with dynamite, after which we loaded it into the cars. The compartments in which we worked were only from three to four feet high. We constantly had to stoop and hit our heads against the ceiling. We were paired off in twos in each room. The work was terribly hard. My back ached. My whole body was stiff and sore with strain and what made matters worse were the callouses on my feet and the blisters on my hands. Life was utterly unbearable. Fortunately for me I found comfort in Leo's company. We helped each other along and we felt that together we would overcome all difficulties.

Every two weeks an estimate of our work was given by the company. Together Leo and I cleared, after the usual deductions were made, approximately $35 for this period. We worked from ten to eleven hours a day and sometimes fourteen, but we received no pay for overtime. And that was during the prosperity era, at a time when wages were high! The fact that we were being cheated by the coal company did not strike us then as very significant, for we were still childishly innocent about the ways of the world.

I recall the night when Leo and I were first initiated into coal mining. Between the two of us we managed to load twenty tons of coal. The next day we felt indescribably stiff and sore. That night we were unable to continue our work.

Leo said to me: "Do you think you can stand it?"

I countered: "What about you?"

"Oh, don't worry about me," he replied. "All I want to know is whether you're all right."

"Of course, I am all right!" I lied defiantly.

The pain in my back was almost killing me, but I stubbornly refused to admit it. The dreadful thought of conditions at home stiffened my spine.

In addition to the strain of working from sunrise to sundown we were obliged to walk from three to four miles from the bottom of the mine to the surface. There was no mantrip for the use of the coal loaders. Only those who had "company jobs" (jobs offering fixed wages, in counterdistinction to our piece-work jobs) could ride the mantrip. On every pay day I found in my pay envelope an account of deductions which the company made. These usually amounted to from ten to fifteen dollars. They were for bath (which I hardly ever got a chance to take), for school (I was only thirteen years old then and certainly had no children), for medical and hospital service, for insurance and for supplies. All supplies, such as carbide, lamp, dynamite, fuses, picks, etc., had to be bought at the company store and nowhere else. Anyone who bought elsewhere was liable to immediate discharge from the company service.

One Saturday afternoon, as we were being paid our two weeks' earnings, we saw that most of the money had been deducted for the fantastic purposes mentioned above. Leo and I looked dazedly at each other.

But the company did not content itself merely with making deductions from our pay. Because the workers had no union they were systematically robbed. The company was like God the Father. It could do what it pleased and the worker who would have the temerity to protest would find himself booted out of the place. They robbed us with an undisguised brazenness over which I still marvel today. The check-weighman would have the motorman run the cars filled with our coal over the scales at full speed without stopping. In this way, on cars holding four thousand pounds of coal we never got more to our credit than seventeen hundred to nineteen hundred pounds.

One day at the weighing-in ceremonies, when I saw the company rob us of the fruits of our labor which we earned by the sweat of our brows and the ache in our limbs, I lost control of my temper which I was trying hard to restrain. Immediately there passed before my mind's eye a vision of Mother and the children crying for bread. My fighting spirit was aroused. I ran up to the foreman and found myself shouting into his face:

"You have no right to do that! I have four thousand pounds of coal in those cars and you are only giving me credit for seventeen hundred. This is a gyp and I don't mind telling it to you."

Livid with rage, the white foreman seized me by the throat and began shaking me. I was delicate and thin and almost a child. But what hurt more than the shaking I got were the words he said to me. They left an indelible impression on me. Sometimes in my darker moments I can still hear them ringing in my ears:

"You dirty little nigger, shut your trap and don't let me hear a sound from you again. You take what you get and be grateful for it. If you don't like it, get the hell out of here and see if you are treated better elsewhere."

I knew that he spoke the truth. Wherever I would go, wherever we Negro workers would go, we would receive the same treatment. I decided I could do nothing about it, and as it is written in the Bible, I "walked softly and spoke low." What else was I to do? The whole world looked dark for me.

After the coal was weighed, it was dumped out of the cars and searched for slate. For every can of slate that was found in the coal we were docked one ton. The company punished us this way, partly because it could cheat us and partly because it would make the coal diggers more careful of the way they threw slate into the car, thus saving the company any need of hiring extra men to wash the slate out of the coal. The slate pickers were also "company men." In order to keep their jobs they had to find slate from somewhere, so that we might be penalized, even if they had to pick it stealthily from the garb. There seemed to be no end to the company's inventiveness and cunning. We all could see through it, but as we were not organized, we could only find cold comfort in grumbling under our breath whenever the company officials did not hear us. A number of miners had even gone individually to complain to the mine superintendent. He promised to look into the matter, and tactfully dismissed them. He gave me similar advice once when I had gone to his office to complain about the coal that was stolen by his underlings from Leo and me. Needless to say, he never did anything about it, and we all grew more sullen and resentful as the weeks went by.

6

We lived in one of the houses belonging to the company. It was just a shack built upon wooden posts. The rent was exorbitant, fifty dollars monthly! It had neither water nor electricity. There was no toilet; the outhouse was used in common by fifteen families. It was the busiest part of the establishment. There were, of course, better houses that were equipped with all modern improvements, but these were designed for the superintendents, bank bosses and section foremen. What made life in these company houses particularly distasteful were the hired gunmen whom the company employed to patrol our quarters all the time. Although ostensibly it was only to protect us from harm, in reality it was to keep watch over us and to guard against our stealing company property. Somehow, their watchful presence made me feel creepy and guilty, as if I were plotting to commit some crime.

As Negroes we were segregated in a section set aside for a garbage dump. The stenches that rose in mighty waves from the refuse turned my stomach with disgust and nausea. It smelled like a slaughter house. But even slaughter houses are cleaned sometimes.

We seldom had decent food to eat. Our main diet consisted of beans, peas and rice. Occasionally we had a strip of fatback. On pay days we would even treat ourselves to a piece of pork, which cost a mint of money. We had to pay thirty cents a pound for the meanest pork chops which literally stank. The butcher in town was selling better quality chops for ten cents less. The bread we ate was moldy and the soup tasted like slop. A muddy, sour beverage, that made me twist my mouth, passed as coffee. All in all, our standard of living was pretty much subhuman. There was nothing unusual in it, for millions of workers throughout the country jogged on their existence in such hopeless wretchedness year in and year out.

Because of these conditions everybody fell into debt. Like buzzards around carrion, disreputable loan sharks and credit stores battened upon the simplicity of the men and hopelessly involved them in purchases and obligations which they could never meet. Most of the miners no longer were their own masters. They were irretrievably mortgaged to these heartless ghouls who preyed upon them systematically.

The safety conditions in the mine were scandalous. All escapeways were far from where we worked. Should there have occurred an accident under the surface, we would have been buried alive. There was never enough timbering to keep the rock from falling. Accidents occurred in some parts of the mine, almost every night. The company laid no value to our lives. The number of those killed and wounded was accepted by them as part of the ordinary routine of mining. But those who did not forget were the bereaved wives, sons and daughters of the men maimed and killed. . . .

One night, as my partner and I were working at breakneck speed because we had plenty of cars to load, the car that I had my shoulder against suddenly turned up against the roof and the tracks flew apart. My partner and I were thrown to the ground violently. All the skin and a good deal of flesh was ripped off my hand. The men rushed me to the doctor, who bandaged it. In order to avoid paying me any insurance I was given light work to do for a month. The superintendent said to me:

"All you have to do is to check in and check out for work every day and stick around the job, but I warn you, better be careful and see that this does not happen again, or as sure as you're alive I'll fire you!"

Segregation of the Negroes was not only an established practice in the company-owned houses, but it was observed during work hours as well. The Negroes worked on the north side of the mine and the whites on the south. We Negroes never had the slightest chance of ever getting any of the better-paying jobs. We could not become section foremen or electricians, surveyors, bank bosses, check-weighmen, steel sharpeners or engineers. We could only look forward to coal loading, to run the motors, to pick the coal and muck the rock and be mule boys like beasts of burden. We had to wear knee pants and work stretched out on our bellies most of the time.

One day, after I had been working in the mine for almost nine months, the company put up a notice on the bulletin board at the entrance to the mine. It read:

"Due to large overhead expenses we announce a reduction in wages from 43c per ton of coal to 31c per ton."

7

The entrance to the mine that day afforded a strange spectacle. The men refused to go down but milled around the bulletin board in great excitement, vocalizing their disgust and indignation with the ways of the company. Suddenly one of the miners shouted:

"God damn it! We shouldn't stand for it!"

Another man standing near by took up the cry:

"I have a wife and family and, as much as I love them, I'll be damned if I'll work for 31c per ton. I'd rather see them starve and I'd rather steal than take it, that's what I would do."

The crowd applauded him vociferously. Dynamite seemed to be packed in their anger. Just a spark would be sufficient to cause an explosion. By seven-thirty, at the time when we were supposed to have been at the bottom of the mine, the crowd swelled to almost a thousand workers. The superintendent, having gotten wind of the trouble, came down. He was surrounded by a bodyguard of heavily armed and vicious-looking company gunmen. He was pale and nervous, but he tried to put on a good show for us. He said:

"Now listen here, fellows, you know we are trying to do our darnedest by you. Sure I understand it's hard for you to accept this cut, but what are we to do? No one knows better than you that times are getting hard. I'll tell you what I'll do—I'll take you into my confidence because I know you are a bunch of hard working, honest and loyal men: The company is running the mine at a loss. If we keep it running it is only because we are sincerely sorry for you. We don't wish to keep you out of a job. If we reduce your wages it's because we have your own interests at heart. Now be sensible fellows, just let me ask you a question: 'What would you rather that we did, pay you what we have been paying and then be forced to close the mine or cut your wages a little and keep it running?' Think of your wives and children before you give me that answer."

Some of the miners seemed impressed. They said: "The boss is right." "The company sure does look out for us." "We've got no kick coming." Then shamefacedly they went down to work. Only a small group of us remained.

"Let's quit!" shouted an elderly man.

"I'm with you a hundred per cent," I piped up.

Unfortunately, the spirit was willing but the flesh was weak. Only a few of us stuck to our determination. The others returned to work. Crestfallen, we had to abandon our struggle. We did not know how to organize ourselves and how to make our demands effective. At this time I had not even heard of the existence of such a thing as a union. Some of the older men did, but they did not know what it was all about. The mine owners saw to it that none of us ever learned about it. The outside world was concealed from us by a thousand barriers.

We sent home all the money we could possibly spare to Mother, but our reduced earnings drove us frantic. One day I was so overcome by the thought of conditions at home that I burst into tears and lamented before my brother:

"Oh, Leo, why is life so cruel to us? Is it because of our sins? Is it because of the sins of Father and Mother? Are we not good Christians, all of us? Is it right for us to be singled out by God and to be punished this way?"

Leo tried to soothe me:

"Cheer up, Gelo. Take it easy. Since leaving home I've learned this much—what is right becomes wrong with different kinds of people. The company owns the mines and pays the wages. It's not for us to decide what's right and what's wrong."

"Then what shall we do?" I asked.

Leo answered: "There's no use going back home again.

There's nothing to look forward to there. So let's keep on moving. Maybe God will be good and we'll have good luck."

So again we packed up our few rags and wandered on.

8

We set out for Birmingham, where we had relatives, and where we were told there were plenty more mines. How bitter were my recollections as the train pulled into Birmingham! The scene of my father's funeral haunted me. I tried hard to shut it from my mind, but I could not free myself from it.

Our Aunt Catherine welcomed us. She was a very warm-hearted but talkative woman. She could rattle off ten speeches in the time it would take someone else to say ten words. She inquired about Mother and the other children. We told her all that had happened to us. When we had finished our story there were tears in her eyes. She told us we could stay with her as long as we liked and if we were unable to find jobs it would be all right with her too. She promised to keep us until we were able to shift for ourselves. I remember being very much touched by her words. I said to her:

"Thank you very much for your good heart, Aunt Catherine."

We lost no time and went out looking for a job. At first matters did not turn out as we had expected. We were but mere kids, and inexperienced. However, after a month of wearying job-hunting, Leo finally landed work in a mine. He became the bread winner for the two of us. I took it very hard, for I, too, wished to become independent. But Leo was a swell kid. He understood what was bothering me and so he tried to make my economic dependence on him as painless as possible. He gave me pocket money and bought me some clothes. I was a little bit embarrassed although he was my own brother.

9

In most Southern states there are so-called labor agents who prowl through the city streets like beasts of prey looking for laborers to work out of town. At that time I used to see such labor agents lingering around the railroad station in Birmingham. I also saw them on the street corners in the Negro belt on the lookout for victims. It was my misfortune one day to be accosted on the street by one of these scavengers. He was flashily dressed in a brown checked suit and brown derby. He wore patent-leather boots, had diamond rings on both hands as big as pebbles and a pearl pin in his tie. He was middle-aged, had a big belly and oozed prosperity and geniality. As he saw me he called out to me:

"Hey, buddy, want a job?"

"Sure!" I said, overjoyed in my innocence.

He told me confidentially that if I went out of town on a job that he would procure for me just because I looked like a nice fellow and he did not mind doing me a favor, I could earn forty dollars a month and get my board besides. This looked like a windfall from heaven to me. It did appear a little incredible to me that a kid like me could earn so much money, but as the wish was father to the thought I swallowed his words hook, line and sinker and believed that I must indeed be a wonderful fellow to have been chosen for such a distinction. We sealed our bargain with a handshake.

That night forty of us were loaded into a truck and driven toward our unknown destination. All on the truck were Negroes, ranging from old men to mere children. The old men looked battered, human factory refuse that had been discarded, too old to work, too old to make profits for the mine and mill owners. But what amazed me was the fact that they were hopeful like day-dreaming children. "Wait, some day we'll get a break," one of them said. All were ragged, few wore shoes, and these were dilapidated-looking, patched over and over again. Many looked sick and the rest were but a wretched lot. Some of the men had long whiskers because they were too poor to own a razor. I sat next to one old graybeard who aroused my interest. Though ragged and sick-looking he bore himself with great dignity and looked at me with grand-paternal kindness. It amused me to see that each of his shoes pointed in the opposite direction. They were full of gaping holes and anyhow each of them was on the wrong foot. He puffed away at a large cob pipe which he filled with cigar and cigarette butts that he had somehow picked up on the streets of Birmingham. His trouser pockets were stuffed with them. He kept on looking curiously at me. Finally, he addressed me in a kindly manner:

"Where do you live, son? Who are your father and mother? You sure look mighty young to be away from home." He stroked my face with his parchment-like hand. "You look just like a little girl," he teased good-naturedly. "Do you expect to do a man's job?"

I was deeply offended. "Girl! What do you mean girl? I am as good a man as you, mister."

The old man laughed heartily. But as I had no rancor toward him, I told him about my family and the circumstances that drove me out into the world to seek my fortune. He told me:

"As soon as I saw you I knew that you did not look like one from these parts. My boy, you will have to rough it a bit here because conditions are worse than rotten. God for everybody, everybody for himself and the devil take the hindmost. As Scripture says, a poor man is worse than a dead man, and why a poor, homeless sick old man like me wants to keep on living is beyond me."

His words depressed me but his friendly interest in me made me feel less lonesome. If the truth must be told, I was mighty scared at the thought of the unknown fate that was awaiting me, and were it not that I was ashamed to be called just a mere kid I would have burst out crying.

10

We finally reached the camp. It was called Lock 18 and was situated in a valley standing on the left bank of a river which traversed it. It was springtime and the weather was mild. Together with seven others I was led into a bell-shaped tent, one of an army set up in the woods. We were assigned double-decker cots standing one over another. The tent stank of filthy clothes, foul refuse and sweaty bodies. The men had neither time nor energy to bathe. The scene about us was ugly and dismal, a confusion of cranes, steam shovels and concrete mixers.

After we had deposited our belongings on our cots we were led into the company office. In a corner sat the doctor, looking contemptuously at us. He examined us all for venereal diseases. Later on I discovered that this examination was just a formality, for there were quite a number of diseased men working in the camp.

We were put to work on a dam which the company was constructing across the Alabama River. We worked in the broiling sun. I was perpetually thirsty and somehow it recalled to my mind the stories my mother used to tell me out of the Bible, about the Egyptians who put the Children of Israel to work building the cities of Pisom and Rameses, and how they groaned under the lash of the taskmasters. A whole army of company watch dogs ("floor walkers," we called them) kept guard over us night and day so as to prevent the possibility of our escape.

The first night I got into conversation with some of my tentmates who had been there for several months already. I asked them about working conditions. They looked scared.

One of them leaned toward me, first looking to right and left of him to make sure that no company underling was within earshot, and whispered:

"Shhh, we can't talk here. I'll see you later."

At an opportune moment he told me that the place was just like a prison, that the workers were not getting any pay and that it was impossible to leave the camp voluntarily. Some men tried to escape on their way to the mess hall but they were caught and beaten up to a pulp. He also told me that some men were caught trying to cross the wooden bridge to the other side of the river but were shot down by the guards. Their bodies fell into the river and they were never seen again. There was only one way to escape, he counselled me, and that was to work hard and make friends with the officials. If they liked me I might get a job driving a truck. That would afford me some chance to escape.

I listened incredulously to this story. I felt frightened. As I did not wish to be thought yellow I tried hard to smile. But I really felt a desire to scream and curse and fight. The instinct of self-preservation battled in me.

That night my seven tentmates and I laid our plans for escape. We knew we ran a great risk, for a "floor walker" searched all tents once every hour. We had no doubts that he would use his gun freely if he but suspected what we were planning to do. But we decided that it was far better to risk getting killed than to remain any longer in that hell.

11

It must have been after midnight when we stole out of our tents on tiptoe and crawled barefooted through the woods down to the river. At home I had learned how to swim. It now came in good stead. We leaped into the water and we were submerged by a mountain of waves. The river was wide but we swam alongside that part of the concrete dam that had already been constructed. From time to time we rested for a minute, holding on to some iron bar or pipe that jutted out of the dam. Once while we stopped swimming long enough to catch our breath, one of our number in a plaintive voice started singing:

Just help me across the river!
I'll make Birmingham all by myself.

I remember the words of this song had an energizing effect on all of us.

The bank on the other side of the river still looked distant and unattainable. My muscles were tiring. For a moment panic seized me. "Suppose I drown," I was thinking. Then there recurred to my mind the thought of all those at home. The vision of the death that was threatening made all our poverty and squalor look heavenly by comparison. At that moment I even loved Uncle Jeremiah. I wanted so strongly to live! Then and there I made a solemn vow that if I reached the opposite bank in safety I would work night and day to make a man out of myself, just as I had promised my father on his death-bed.

I swam with closed eyes, silently praying:

"Jesus, Saviour, save me!"

To my utter amazement and my joy, my feet struck bottom. I opened my eyes and peered into the darkness. The shore lay only a few yards away.

What greatly impressed me during our flight was the feeling of kinship between all of us. The stronger swimmers helped the weaker not only with physical assistance, but with words of encouragement as well. I then learned a valuable lesson in the ethics and practicality of mutual aid.

However, new troubles awaited us now. We had blundered into swampy land and I must have fallen into deep bogs at least a dozen times. We helped each other out of them and made light of our mishaps. A feeling of good fellowship united us all.

Suddenly we heard the sound of barking dogs. Terror seized us. One imaginative and slightly terrified worker suggested that the "floor walkers" must have discovered our escape and were after us with bloodhounds. Some advised hiding in the top branches of the trees. But others thought that idea was crazy because bloodhounds can smell men even up in trees. We ran on breathlessly. My heart beat wildly.

We had straggled along about fifteen miles when day began to break. We stopped on the highway and when a truck driven by some Negroes came by, we begged for a hitch and rode back to Birmingham, full of the exhilaration of men who had just escaped some terrible fate.

12

My brother Leo was overjoyed seeing me. After I had told him what had happened to me he put on a severe look, playing the role of the older and protecting brother. He advised me that I had better stay in Birmingham and find myself a job in the city instead of going out to God-forsaken places where fellows were being treated just like in a nightmare.

The search for work became an obsession with me. In my experience I have found job-hunting much more disheartening and devitalizing than the most difficult and most harassing work. I look back with horror at the anguish, the suspense and the humiliation which accompanied my job-hunting. I wore out my shoes, I spent all my car fare, I tried so hard to be as pleasing and as polite as an angel, I smiled until my face almost cracked although I was sick at heart, but as for a job, alas, none came!

One day, as I was passing an employment agency, I entered it on the impulse of the moment. I was signed up with a lot of others to do construction work for the Goodyear Rubber Company in Gadsden, Alabama. I paid three dollars for the privilege, if such it may be called. We were shipped off in trucks from Birmingham. The agency full-handedly had promised $3.00 a day, but when we reached Gadsden the superintendent of the company, a mealy-mouthed gent, told us that all we would be getting would be $1.75 a day.

I was bitter with resentment but I was by this time already becoming a veteran in the game of disillusionment. At first I decided that I would return to Birmingham but prudence finally became the better part of valor; I decided that $1.75 a day was better than nothing.

With some other laborers I was set to work on a concrete mixer. We prepared the foundation of the plant. There were day and night shifts, and often I worked one shift after another. We worked like mules, slept like dogs in stinking tents, and ate rotten food. The discipline was that of an army camp, and woe be to anyone who infringed any of the rules! We were given orders not to leave our tents after ten o'clock at night. We could not go to the city to see a movie or to indulge in any other amusement. Life here was only a little better than in that never-to-be-forgotten ghostly camp on the Alabama River from which I had escaped. I began to be overwhelmed with the painful certainty that all of the world was a prison and that man was born to suffer, suffer endlessly from the day of his birth to the day when they return him to the earth. I could see neither joy nor purpose in life and my young spirit, only fourteen years of age, was weighted down by a burden of weariness hard to imagine.

We worked like galley slaves, prayerfully looking forward to Sunday when we would be able to throw our tired bodies on our cots and sleep, do nothing but sleep.

When Saturday arrived we all lined up to get our pay. Dozens of uniformed company guards stood around the pay office. Finally, our foremen came out of an inner office and with an impudent leer said:

"Well, fellows, I guess there is no pay coming to you today. Your earnings this week have been deducted for transportation, food and housing."

We Negro workers flamed with resentment and anger. We howled like jungle beasts. We felt like tearing them limb from limb. It was our lives or theirs and we were in no Bible-class mood either. We rushed the guards. They melted like snow before us, but they soon re-formed and attacked us in a body with clubs, black jacks and drawn guns. Sullenly, we submitted to brute force and called upon the superintendent to send us back to Birmingham, but he refused. So we trudged all the way back, sore-footed and heavy-hearted. It was the beginning of my worldly education. I learned my lesson well, though slowly.

SEVEN

AFTER I RETURNED to Birmingham I again made the rounds of the mines. Unfortunately, I had great difficulty in getting a job. Regulations prohibited the employment of any worker under the age of 18. In order to get by that obstacle I brazenly lied. I said I was twenty-two years old. The Scottish superintendent of the Docena Mine, a subsidiary of the U. S. Steel Corporation, finally hired me, since he saw I was husky and tall.

My work for the Tennessee Coal, Iron and Railroad Company was somewhat different from that on my first job. The Company cleverly sidetracked the trade-union movement by establishing its own dummy company union. It even appointed the union's officials. The workers cursed under their breath. They knew they could not take independent union action without the consent and the control of the Company officials. The whole thing smacked of a stage farce. What made matters even more ridiculous was the fact that Negroes fell under the Jim-Crow ban and were prevented from joining this company union. However, due to the union's innocuous character, we did not lose anything by our exclusion.

I would sometimes work fourteen hours at a stretch at the bottom of the mine. Although the regulations prohibited more than eight hours of such work, the Company conveniently closed an eye to this irregularity. In fact, we were urged to load as much coal as we wanted to. We were assured that it would be all right to stay down until we were ready to come out. I needed the extra money badly to provide for the train fare between Birmingham and the mine and for my subsistence, which at its best was pretty wretched.

One year passed by this way. I became a veteran in endurance and in suffering. The world looked evil to me. As for myself, I felt like a leaf in the wind, without a will to guide my own destiny. The life I led might have brutalized me, were it not for the terrific resistance I offered against the influence of my environment. The men in their wretchedness grew brutish. They quarreled with each other incessantly. The merest trifle was sufficient for them to leap at one another's throats. The profanity that they used in their speech shocked me. I thought of my father and my mother and how hard they tried to bring me up in a decent way, and I hid myself from this sordidness in a protective mantle of revulsion. The men did not crave for anything better. Hard work, maltreatment, ignorance and a bestial atmosphere contrived to keep them blind as bats to their degradation. Every Saturday when they got their pay they went out on a drunk and awoke to their misery the following day more warped and embittered than ever.

"This is no life for a man and a Christian," I once confided to my partner.

He snorted savagely:

"There are no men—there are no Christians nowhere. Only pigs."

I knew that could not be true, for I had seen men kind and good under happier circumstances. My faith in the good in man never faltered even in my darkest hours.

As time went on I was transferred to surface work. I helped build transformation lines, cutting the right-of-way for wires. This work was infinitely more agreeable and healthy; I could see the sun and fill my lungs with fresh air, a luxury which I did not have before. Although I was supposed to be paid at the rate of $2.70 per day, the Company saw to it that plenty of deductions left me with fantastically little.

2

There was a certain Mr. Tucker. He was my section foreman. Prior to this he had been a plantation owner but having lost all his property he was obliged to get a job with the T.C.I. Company. He never could quite get over his illustrious past and always tried to vent his chagrin by taking it out of us in ruthless slave driving. He was a rabid Negro hater. But we were well matched; we hated him just as heartily. He would insist that we work overtime but without pay, but our nanny was up and when the time to quit work came we answered his curses and his threats with the downing of our tools and told him to go plumb to hell. This made him go apoplectic with rage, and he would try at opportune moments to avenge himself on us by devious and disgusting tricks. He was a master in the art of cruelty, particularly in little things. Needless to say, we paid dearly for defending our dignity, our human rights and our rights as workers.

One Saturday, when we were about to knock off work at the usual noon hour, he ordered us to continue working until three o'clock. Cries of anger rose from among the men. One Negro worker spoke up and said that we did not choose to work one minute overtime without getting paid for it. Mr. Tucker turned purple with rage. His long duck-bill nose, lined with little red and blue veins, looked as if blood was going to burst from it. He jeered at us:

"What's the matter with you fellows! Getting lazy? Trouble with you niggers is that you are getting fat bellies. Too easy life—too much money." Then clenching his fists and narrowing his eyes he yelled, "I wish I had you God damn niggers on my plantation, I'd make you sweat blood all day—Saturday and Sunday, too."

Something unaccountable happened to me, something exploded inside my brain; I became full of a searing flame. The first thing I knew was that I sprang forward and shouted in his face:

"Why are you so mean? You're only a worker like us. We know that you just lost your farm and everything else that you had. We know that you are trying to make a living just like us. I would like you to remember that you've got to talk politely to us. We are no longer living under chattel slavery. Negroes are free men. And as for your orders, I think I can speak for the men: 'To hell with you and your orders!' "

The foreman began to froth at the mouth. He ranted incoherently like a man bereft of his senses:

"So you niggers think you are free—oh, yeah! I'll show you whether you are or not."

And then he let loose a flood of obscenity, the like of which I have never heard in my life. A Negro worker grew wild with resentment. He seized a pick and was ready to brain him when some of the other Negro workers rushed up and took the pick from him in the nick of time. They shouted to him that Negroes were not murderers, that he ought to have it out with the foreman with his fists, that he didn't need the pick to beat him up anyhow.

The two men squared off and we Negro workers retired to the top of a hill near by. The outcome of the slugging contest was a foregone conclusion. The foreman was no match for our champion, whom we encouraged with whoops and cries: "Come on, black man—give it to the ——."

Never have I seen a man so mercilessly beaten before as was Mr. Tucker. His face was beaten to a pulp. The sight of blood streaming from his sores nauseated me. The fight at last came to an end, with the foreman nursing his bruises on the ground.

We did not pay any more attention to him, but showered congratulations on our man. Suddenly there was an outcry. While everybody's attention was diverted from him the foreman stole up behind his Negro opponent and tried to stab him with his knife. The two grappled. They fell to the ground and after a moment rolled into the lake, clutching each other. We enjoyed the fight tremendously. It was a field day for us oppressed Negro workers. For once we had the highly deceptive feeling of being strong. There was not the slightest danger of a lynch mob going after us. We were way off in the woods and our foreman was the only white man among us.

One Negro worker commented upon the incident:

"That's the trouble with us Negroes—one white man can lord it over a hundred of us. We're some heroes, alone in the woods with one white man! Now just show me how brave you are when there are a lot of white men around with a lot of guns and hickory clubs!"

This Negro's caustic remark disturbed me greatly. I readily saw the truth in what he said. It gave me much food for thought.

3

A short time after this incident occurred, an extraordinary event took place. It taught me more than anything else did hitherto that we Negroes could improve our conditions only if we stuck together and made a collective effort.

I had a work partner. I can now only recall that his first name was Jimmy. He was a young fellow of nineteen or twenty, a quiet and decent young fellow who was so meek that he could never bring himself to utter a word of complaint. He used to mutter prayers to himself as he worked, and when the foreman was not around he would sing spirituals in a voice full of emotion. At about that time the shielding on an electric wire had fallen down. Although we kept on reminding Mr. Tucker about it, he did nothing. One day, about two weeks later, my partner Jimmy, while working at terrific speed and soaking in perspiration, began handling some of the electric wires. He received a violent electric shock from the unshielded wire. He tried to get away but got tangled up in the wires. We made an effort to raise him with our hands, but we, too, got almost as much of a shock as he did. Our efforts were all in vain. After about three minutes his body had been burned to a crisp.

We tried to revive him. We gave him first aid, but he lay deathly still and limp. We left him lying uncovered under a near-by tree because we had nothing to cover him with. He looked unhuman, a mere stick of coal. I was sick with horror and thought I would faint.

All of us surface men did not go back to work that day. We called to the superintendent to explain "the accident." The foreman came to me and said:

"If the super asks you anything say that the shielding was up all the time and that ycur buddy was electrocuted because he was careless."

What he tried to do was the usual thing. He merely wanted me to whitewash him and the Company so that it would not have to pay any insurance money to the dead man's family.

Next morning when I was brought before the superintendent I spoke up without hesitation. The foreman turned red as a beet and the superintendent looked surprised. The latter asked me:

"What do you know? Did you see the accident when it happened?"

I answered boldly: "Yes, let me tell you the story. Two weeks ago I was almost killed by the same wire. My partner and I had been working for two weeks near the wire that had been left unshielded. Somehow I lost my balance and fell against the wire. I received a shock, but I was fortunate that

I could jump back in time. I immediately told Mr. Tucker about it and warned him that the wire needed shielding up. He said 'All right,' but he never did anything about it."

The foreman nudged me and in an undertone hissed at me, "Shut up!" Out loud he said: "Now listen here, nigger boy, you're talking too damn much!"

I paid no attention to him and went right on with my story.

The superintendent was obliged to fire Mr. Tucker. Eventually, my dead partner's family received some compensation. It wasn't much. The T.C.I. Company saw to that. Usually in similar cases, no redress or compensation is ever given to a worker's family. If partial justice was given by the Company in this instance it was not because of its high conception of ethics but because it feared adverse publicity, for it saw in the rising anger of the workers a threat to possible trade-union organization.

4

As I left the super's office I said to my fellow-workers who were waiting outside:

"Did you notice how they tried to hush the thing up? If it were not for the fact that we were all pulling for one another, that Mr. Tucker would still be keeping his job and my buddy's family wouldn't get a cent. Those white people surely must be hating us because we talk like we do, but I'll bet that they know now that we are free Negroes!"

My fellow-workers agreed heartily with me. They said:

"That's right! That's right! We colored folks can make them treat us much better if we just stand up for our rights. We've got to show them that we've as much right to live as they."

In a curious way this incident furnished my first lesson in the need of organization. What, no doubt, stimulated my thoughts in this direction was the pressure of events. Everywhere things were happening. Mines and factories were closing down; businesses failed, banks crashed. Workers who had never been out of jobs before, suddenly found themselves tramping vainly in search for new employment. Those who still had jobs found themselves getting microscopic wages. Often was the time when on opening our pay envelopes we found nothing but blank strips of paper which indicated that the Company had made deductions from our wages for supplies, food advances and for less legitimate purposes. Our anger was laughable in the extreme. It was like that of a puny man shaking his fist against the sky.

EIGHT

My encounters with Mr. Tucker, although they awakened in me an impelling desire to fight for my rights as a worker and for the rights of the Negro people, nevertheless did not succeed in crystallizing my attitude as to how I was to go about it. But my experiences with Jim Crowism hastened the process. At first I had accepted it as I did the sunrise and the sunset; it evidently was all a part of a pre-established plan of things. Fortunately, my mind became stimulated by forces outside of my control. The more I reflected upon the grave injustices inflicted upon my people the more the spirit of rebellion surged up in me.

One morning some eight years ago (that was in 1928 when I was fifteen years old), as I was riding home from work on the train, I noticed that a certain Negro worker had fallen asleep out of sheer exhaustion. When the conductor came around to collect the tickets he did not try to wake him up. Instead his face became distorted with rage. He pounced upon him and began to hit him with his fists. The poor Negro, startled from his sleep, did not know what was happening to him; he looked amazed and terrified and made no effort to defend himself, but hid his face between his hands and received his beating like a child, whimpering softly. The conductor in an unnatural voice was shouting:

"So you think you'll get away with paying your fare, pretending you're asleep. I'll show you – – – – you black —."

The conductor continued pounding away, trying to reach the Negro worker's face all the time. Blood began to trickle from the latter's nose into his mouth. There were only Negroes on the train. They sat fuming and sullen and glared at the conductor, yet no one said a word or made a move to defend their fellow-worker. I watched in horrified fascination. I asked myself wrathfully:

"Why are so many strong Negro men afraid of one white bully?"

Then there flashed across my mind the incident out of the Bible which I have always read with terrifying emotion, of the suddenly aroused Moses killing the Egyptian taskmaster who was mercilessly beating a Jewish slave, crying:

"Why do you beat my brother?"

I, too, felt the urge to tear the white conductor limb from limb, but I thought of my fifteen years and of my physical frailty and I cursed this misfortune. Never in my life did I want so much to grow up quickly in order to show the might and spirit of the Negro people to our white oppressors.

After the conductor left the car, excited voices were raised.

"If I could only lay my hands on his lousy white throat I'd choke the hell out of him!" ranted one Negro.

"I could eat his heart and enjoy it!" boasted another.

I grew angry and said:

"Smart guys! Why didn't you help this man when the conductor beat him? I think we're all yellow, otherwise we would never have allowed this to happen. When that white conductor beat this fellow he was beating us, too, but we never said a word. Shame on us all!"

An old Negro sighed and said:

"That's the trouble with us Negroes. We don't stick together. One white man can bulldoze a hundred of us black men. Why, if we only got together what a shellacking we could have given that ——."

Later I asked the beaten Negro why he didn't fight back. He hung his head shamefacedly and said:

"I have a wife and three children to support. The white man is always right where we Negroes are concerned. If I struck him back I'd not only lose my job, because the T.C.I. owns the railroad, but I would also find myself in the coop."

2

I saw many incidents in which Negroes were horribly mistreated. I once knew a Negro worker who was almost lynched because of the vicious atmosphere white exploiters have created about the Negro character as a further excuse to oppress my race. This Negro was working for a rich white woman who lived in an exclusive white neighborhood. One day some white people, strangers to the place, who happened to walk by saw him going into the house. Suddenly they got a lunatic idea to yell on top of their voices that a Negro had raped a white woman. A lynch mob formed in the shake of a lamb's tail. As soon as the lynch rumor went abroad all Negroes in Birmingham disappeared from the streets. They hid in their houses and waited in terror until the affair would blow over. Fortunately, the police arrived in time and arrested him. It was only when they discovered that no white woman was raped, that, in fact, this Negro was working for the rich white woman, who even gave him a splendid character, the police and the lynch mob left.

I know many stories about Negroes who were lynched on no more just provocation than this. Sometimes the lynch mobs need neither provocation nor excuse to carry on their bestial orgies. Often I used to read with horror about the lynching of some Negro worker in the South. The most gruesome, the most disgusting lynching story I ever heard was that which concerned Hayes and Mary Turner, Negro sharecroppers in Georgia. They were pauperized and their landlord had tried to rob them of everything they had produced on their land with the toil of their hands and the sweat of their brows. The sharecropper was man enough to stand up for his rights. He demanded that the farm products be divided equally, as had been agreed upon at the beginning of the year. The landlord grew violently abusive. He threatened him and said he would "fix" him.

Terrified out of his wits, for he knew that his landlord would not stop at anything to revenge himself, Hayes Turner tried to make a quiet getaway. But his landlord had not allowed grass to grow on his track. He quickly organized a posse of hooligans and the most disreputable elements in the community and gave chase to the runaway. The posse, led by the County Sheriff, caught up with Hayes Turner at the fork of the road near Barney. They strung him up on a tree at the wayside where he hung for two days. Hysterical and grief-stricken, Mrs. Turner was heard to remark that she would have the lynchers arrested. When the lynch mob heard of her determination they decided they were going to teach her a lesson for such presumption. Although she was in the eighth month of her pregnancy, they strung her to a tree and broke her neck. They hanged her by her feet and poured gasoline over her. As she burned, the mob howled with glee. Then one maniac, wielding a hog-splitting knife, ripped her belly open and the little infant fell out. One of the lynchers stamped the infant with his hobnailed shoes into the earth. Then the mob, driven wild with bestiality, began to howl like wolves and in their criminal sadism fired hundreds of bullets into her lifeless body.*

When I heard of this monstrous story I felt like moving heaven and earth to bring the guilty to justice. Again I recognized my own puny strength and grieved over it. This inci-

* For a more detailed account of this lynching, read *The Crisis* of September, 1918.

dent has been a topic of frenzied discussion among Negroes to this very day. Some Negroes even started buying ammunition and guns with which to resist the Ku Kluxers and the American Legionnaires who used to parade very frequently and provocatively in the Negro neighborhoods of Birmingham. I, too, went about in the very greatest excitement and spoke to anyone who would listen. I argued that if only the Negroes would unite, if only they would pluck up fighting courage and lay hold of stones, pistols, pitchforks and anything else at hand, they could lick the Klan and the Legion to a frazzle. After that they wouldn't dare parade any more in our segregated neighborhoods!

I recalled how my father and mother used to counsel me never to get excited, always to be humble and patient in the face of white brutality, to turn my gaze to the Lamb of God and to forgive those that trespassed against me. And I saw how wrong and impossible was my parents' teaching. I was no longer among those who could honestly turn the right cheek when the left was smitten. Rather, my own moral code now was to return two blows for every blow I got, to take two eyes for one taken from me, to defend my rights as an upstanding man, to defend the elementary dignity of the human being in me against all aggressors.

My parents, so they said, were hard-boiled Republicans. They often told me that it was the Republican Lincoln who had freed the slaves, that the Negroes would have to look to the Republican Party to protect them against racial injustice. Was it not the Yankees from the North led by Lincoln who had delivered the Negro from the damnable system of chattel slavery? But now it seemed very strange to me that the Republicans, the inheritors of Lincoln's traditions, who ran the government at Washington, were keeping stony silence about lynching and discrimination against Negroes. They made no effort to enforce the laws which guaranteed Negroes equal rights and protection. Everywhere in the South we were being Jim Crowed and segregated. It was even dangerous for us to walk on the sidewalks when a white man passed by. A reign of perpetual terror had been instituted against the Negro people while the Federal Government winked roguishly and looked away. Laws were being passed by state Legislatures depriving us of our barest Constitutional rights. All this I read in the newspapers and these were my deductions which I made from the facts themselves. How could I come to any other conclusions? My thoughts streamed into one mighty torrent of bitterness and hatred toward white men and their cruelty. It required courage to renounce my mother's teachings of Christian meekness and forgiveness. I no longer could find explanation and consolation in the imitation of Christ, my Saviour. I turned from it with contempt and indignation, for I realized now that it was only designed as a trap and as a distraction from the true realities of our lives. I now made a solemn resolve with all the ardor of my youthful spirit that no longer would I peacefully submit to the persecution and the exploitation of my people. I would fight against all aggressors and all aggression. I would speak to all my relatives and all my friends and all those I would come in contact with. I would call on them to unite with me and together free ourselves from white terror. Not by prayers and the intercession of the Saviour, but by our own determined wills.

3

On my way home one day I got on a trolley. I sat among the Negroes in the Jim Crow section in the rear. Iron bars separated us from the whites. As many of the latter kept coming on we were shoved back into the rear behind the bars which were movable. I felt like a monkey in the zoo. I knew I was going to lose my temper upon the slightest provocation. I had been sitting on a bench right behind these bars wher some white boys in front of me asked me to move back. This made me angry. I said:

"What do you mean? I paid my cold cash to ride on this car just as you did and you can bet your sweet life I won't budge."

Meekly the other Negroes on the car began moving back, urging me to do the same. I felt so ashamed of them! A Negro preacher sitting across from me came over to me and whispered in my ear:

"Please, son, for the Lord's sake, don't do that. You'll only cause trouble for yourself and for all of us. What need is there for it? You know you don't own this car. White people run things like they want to, and it's not up to us to tell them what to do."

Revulsion seized me, and I said to him:

"Dear Reverend, will you please go and take ten steps to hell!"

The conductor finally came back and rudely asked me to move over. I rose from my seat and said to him:

"You white people are so civilized that you seem to think that you can afford to behave worse than savages toward us defenseless Negroes. I know you hate us, but it strikes me awfully funny that you are ready to accept money from a black hand as well as from a white. Now understand me clearly, I've paid my fare to ride this car and I won't give up my seat to any white man until hell freezes over!"

The conductor said to the white boys:

"Leave him alone—he's crazy."

4

Was it at all unnatural that I should begin to think how I could be of use to my people and to work for their social and economic liberation? True enough, I was only sixteen years old then and a little childish, and worse yet, terribly confused about the Negro problem and its possible solutions, but I was earnest and all of me was yearning to put into effect the ridiculous ideas I then had. It probably will sound incredible to many, but the role of deliverer for the Negro people, which I now wished to assume, was as a detective—yes, as a detective. The reason for this being that as a detective I would be able to move practically unnoticed among the Negro people, to discover those who were ready to unite and to fight against white mistreatment. It would also enable me to ferret out all our enemies. My idea was to organize some kind of a secret society that was to arm itself with guns and ammunition and retaliate against the Ku Klux and the American Legion.

Naturally, the correspondence school understood the psychology of romantic young detectives and supplied me with all the finger-print instruments and the other mysterious paraphernalia. I constantly went snooping about with my little magnifying glass looking for clues. Unbeknown to them, I experimented on my relatives and friends. Also I had not failed to devour every word of Sherlock Holmes. I grew very enthusiastic about scientific sleuthing. It had the elements of magic in it for me. Toward the end, my relatives and friends very unkindly began razzing me. They called me in derisive voices the "little detective." But what provoked me most was their question:

"Now, Angelo, that you have almost finished your training, when do you get a job?"

I was very evasive.

The detective agency in Chicago which sponsored the correspondence courses had presented me with an engraved certificate, promising that upon completion of their courses, as soon as there would be an opening, I would be given an important assignment to trail people down in various states. At the time, comically enough, I actually believed that by taking these detective courses I was fulfilling my parents' dream of having an educated son. I was hopeful and convinced that I was going to be a rip-roaring success as a detective. Contrary to what others might expect, when I think back upon all this, the comical character of the whole business does not make me laugh. I become grave and sad, for there is no tragedy to compare with the pathos of inspired confusion.

One day my talkative Aunt Catherine said to me:

"Better leave this detective work alone, Angelo. Some day you are going to go and get yourself killed. You know, white people will not stand for this nonsense!"

I found her advice gratuitous and I did not hesitate to tell her that. I made her understand that I was no mere child, but a man, and that I could well take care of myself.

5

It was on a sultry evening in June, 1930. I was coming home from work with a friend when some soiled handbills, upon which people had trampled, caught my eye. I was startled by its headline, which read: "Would you rather fight or starve?" My friend and I sat down on a house step and began reading it. We read it over and over again, not believing our own eyes, as if we had been living in an evil dream all the time and suddenly awoke to reality with a bang. The writing on the handbill discussed unemployment, hunger and suffering of both Negro and white workers in Birmingham and throughout the whole country. It called upon all Birmingham workers to attend a meeting under the auspices of the Unemployment Council that afternoon.

Conditions were so bad that many people believed that the only way they could ever get better was to start a new war. As I read the handbill I very naïvely was under the impression that the Unemployed Council was calling all Negro and white workers to a new war. I said to my friend, my eyes suddenly dazzled by the blinding truth: "It's war, all right—war is the only thing that will make times better. We might as well get into it now as later."

My friend looked puzzled and hesitated, but out of friendship for me he agreed to accompany me to the meeting. I was full of excitement in anticipation of all the glory I was to cover myself with in the course of such a war. I saw myself dressed in a magnificent uniform, resplendent with many medals on my breast. I wore a long sword at my side like an officer and at its hilt dangled gold tassels. I saw myself returning home triumphant from this war with people throwing flowers in my way, with bands playing and the mayor making a speech of welcome befitting a hero.

NINE

It was three o'clock that afternoon when I walked into the meeting hall. It was a large and stuffy room, full of cigarette smoke and that indefinable electricity which radiates from a large body of tense and excited men. Outside were gathered hundreds of policemen, looking grim and ready for action. They surrounded the building on every side. I was puzzled to understand the presence of police officers in such large numbers. But I began to have an inkling of understanding when I looked at the audience. It was composed of both white and Negro workers. A feeling of astonishment and incredulity came over me when I looked at them. I could hardly believe what my own eyes were seeing. I thought something was wrong somewhere. Suddenly I recalled that eloquent prophecy which most Negroes cherish:

"And the day shall come when the bottom rail shall be on top and the top rail on the bottom. The Ethiopians will stretch forth their arms and find their place under the sun."

A white worker came over to me and said: "Won't you have a seat?" I was touched by his courtesy, which I had never experienced before from a white man.

Finally the speaker of the evening was introduced. He was Frank Williams, the organizer of the Unemployment Council in Birmingham, a white man possessing a dynamic personality and great strength of character. The following is a transcript of his speech that night:

"Friends and fellow-workers: It is estimated that throughout the country there are 17,000,000 unemployed workers. Most of these people are able-bodied men and women who are willing and anxious to work if only they could find jobs. Through no fault of their own, they have been thrown out of the steel mills, textile factories, coal mines and other industries to lead a wretched and tragic existence, while the Wall Street bankers and coupon clippers are wallowing up to their necks in wealth, wealth that you and I have created. And particularly here in the South, conditions are even more deplorable. The living standard of the workers is almost similar to that of the Chinese coolie. Negroes are discriminated against. They are given the worst and dirtiest jobs and are paid less for the same work done by a white worker. They are segregated into such disease-infested neighborhoods as Tittersville, East Birmingham, the South Side and others. They are denied the rights of citizenship; they are lynched and terrorized in open violation of the United States Constitution.

"Why must this be? The bosses tell the white workers that they are superior to Negroes, but can't you see that your conditions are the same as those of the Negro people? Thousands of white workers are today unemployed and suffering just as the Negro. Can't you see that those who teach you about white superiority are not only the exploiters of the Negroes, but they play one worker against the other and rob you and starve your children? If you want to improve your conditions and receive unemployment insurance to be paid by the Federal Government and the bosses, your ranks have to be united. If you want to maintain your human dignity instead of being looked upon as vagabonds and paupers, there is only one way to do it, and that is to establish unity among all workers, Negro and white. You have been told that the Reds are dirty foreigners and 'Nigger Lovers,' but why have you come to this meeting today? Is it because you have been told that you must love somebody or is it because of your desire to improve your living conditions? I assume that you have come for the latter. That's why we Reds fight for political, economic and social equality for Negroes, not because we must express hypocritically our love for anyone, but because the bosses have our backs against the wall and all of us alike will be threatened with the same danger of pestilence, hunger and untold misery. Remember the slogan of our forefathers in the fight for independence, 'Either we hang together or we hang separately!' "

I said to my friend with the greatest excitement:

"He's right! He does nothing but tell the truth. He's the first honest white man I've seen. Have you heard of another white man who has the courage to publicly tell the truth about the conditions of Negroes?"

The speaker's eloquence had overwhelmed me. Others must have had a similar stirring experience, if I was to judge by the reactions of my friend. I saw now what a ridiculous error I had made in believing that we were going to fight a war, although in another sense it was to be a war, but one against oppression and exploitation. The prospects of this fight so thrilled me that I had almost no regrets seeing the beautiful vision of myself as returning hero go up in smoke.

The next speaker was a Negro steel worker. His name was John Lindley. He was short and thin and his face was marked with toil and suffering. He spoke very slowly and with much effort; obviously he was a sick man. But his words rang true and convincing and they flowed into us like balm. He said:

"For eighteen years I worked at the Ensley Steel Mills, with the T.C.I. Company and now when I am no longer able to speed up and work like I used to, they have decided to get rid of me by throwing me out on the streets to starve, but I am one of those who will not take it lying down. I am going to fight for my rights, no matter how dear the price may be.

The bosses have already tried to run me out of town because they say I am an agitator. I have lived here all my life and I do not know any other place and before I would let them run me out I'd rather see myself killed fighting for what I know is right. There is only one way for us to free ourselves from the wage-slave system and that is by uniting both Negro and white workers into one fighting alliance. If you do not believe what I say, then why do they molest Negro and white workers when they meet together? Why are Negroes Jim Crowed and lynched? It is only because the bosses are afraid of black and white workers getting together. That's why they drive the wedge of discrimination between us. The government can take care of all of us if we will fight hard enough. Let's unite today and live today because tomorrow is not promised to us."

At the end of the meeting I went up to the platform and said to the white organizer:

"I'm with you with all my heart and I would like you to put me down as a member."

Strange, only once before had I walked up to a speaker who had moved me so deeply and been converted. That was the time when my Uncle Jeremiah preached his first sermon and I had gone up to him, extended my hand and piped in my nine-year-old voice: "I know religion is in me, Uncle Jeremiah." The emotional motivation in both cases was identical, but what a difference in their nature and in their aim! The change of my viewpoint was almost fabulous, emerging from the urge to escape the cruelties of life in religious abstractions into a healthy, vigorous and realistic recognition that life on earth, which was so full of struggle and tears for the poor, could be changed by the intelligent and organized will of the workers.

I urged my friend, who was with me, to join up also. But he was a timid soul and raised doubts about the wisdom of such a step. I argued with him and tried to convince him that he must become a member of the Unemployment Council. When he could find no argument to resist my persuasion he took refuge in a cynical objection:

"Well, you don't know anything about these people. For all you may know they are just out to collect our hard-earned cash. White folks, Angelo, have fooled the Negro many times before and they will do it again, you can bet your sweet life."

I persisted:

"Maybe you're right, maybe they are fakers, but you will certainly have to hand it to this white man who has had enough courage to stand up like a man and speak the truth about us as he did. I don't care what you say, I like the way he talked. I'm going to follow this thing down and see what's in it."

It suddenly struck me as very curious that it wasn't at all necessary for me to go snooping around with a magnifying glass looking for friends of the Negro people; in fact, they sought me out. I was determined not to let such a golden opportunity pass by without a thorough investigation.

2

That night when I went to bed, I couldn't fall asleep. My mind was too excited by the events of the evening to calm down. Something very important had happened to me, I knew, and I lay with wide open eyes staring into the darkness of my room and thinking that it was at last necessary for me to revise my attitude toward white people. I had discovered at last the truth that not all white people were enemies and exploiters of the Negro people. In fact, the same vicious interests that were oppressing Negro workers were doing the same thing to white workers, that both black and white workers could solve their problems only by a united effort against the common enemy: the rich white people, they who owned the mines, the mills, the factories, the banks. I began to reason in the following way:

The Negro leaders tell us that the poor white workers are responsible for our sufferings. But who controls the powerful weapons with which to spread anti-Negro propaganda, with which to vilify us and spit venom upon us? Decidedly, it could not be the poor white workers who had all they could do to keep themselves alive. Therefore, it could only be the rich white people who were our oppressors, for they controlled the churches and the schools and the newspapers and the radio. They were the ones who had the corrupt clergy preach white superiority, that God's intention was not to make the Negro equal to the white. It was funny to me that although there was supposed to be only one God and one church, yet Negroes were segregated even in church and were made to feel that they were God's stepchildren. The schools and the newspapers, also controlled by the rich white people, deceived and distorted and molded the minds of the young in unjustified hatreds and in the creation of differences that were imaginary. And the real reason for this was that in order that the exploiters might secure their profits from human sweat and brawn they fall back upon these wicked methods of "divide and rule," divide the white workers from their Negro brothers.

Wherever I went I bubbled over with my enthusiasm and discovery of the Unemployment Council. I talked to my relatives about the meeting and told them what the speakers said about Negroes and whites fighting together against their bosses so that they might live like human beings. They looked aghast and warned me very solemnly that I had better stay away from those Reds who were wicked people blaspheming against God.

3

I began to attend all of the meetings of the Unemployment Council regularly. Never was my mind stimulated to such an extent before! I eagerly listened to the ideas on social, economic and political problems that the various speakers talked to us about. I felt like a man from Mars entering into a new world, a little bit puzzled, a whole lot confused, but tremendously thrilled with the sheer adventure of it. I felt like a Columbus sailing an uncharted sea of ideas, each day lured on by some new and exciting discovery. I heard Earl Browder, William Z. Foster and Bill Dunne speak about Communism as the only emancipating force for the workers. I was very anxious to understand all the fine things they were saying, so I began reading every piece of literature they wrote that I could lay my hands on. I also read a pamphlet on the Gastonia Textile Strike and I could see that the methods of exploiters and sweaters of labor were the same everywhere and that our problems were their problems.

I remember reading about a meeting in Southern Illinois at which Bill Dunne spoke. He had been asked by a white heckler the following question, designed to embarrass and floor him:

"Would you want a nigger to marry your daughter?"

Bill Dunne replied, "Listen, mister, my daughter will marry any man she likes whether white, Negro or Chinese. That will be her affair, not mine. But one thing you can rest assured of: I would rather that she jump into a lake than to marry such a yellow-bellied Negro-hater like you."

This retort of Bill Dunne's became famous throughout the South. It was the subject for very lively discussions among white workers, particularly in Birmingham.

One white worker gave me the Communist Manifesto to read. I read it over and over again with painful concentration.

It took me at least a month before I could understand what it was all about. For my own edification I analyzed it paragraph by paragraph, reading passages over and over many times. I wrote a simple account of it in my own words for my own private use. Marx and Engels' statement "The history of all hitherto existing society is the history of class struggles" impressed me as a very profound truth. Life and history approached in this light assumed a new and startling significance. It dazzled me beyond words with its truth. To quote a passage from this composition which I still have in my possession:

"The worker has no power. All he possesses is the power of his hands and his brains. It is his ability to produce things. It is only natural, therefore, that he should try and get as much as he can for his labor. To make his demands more effective he is obliged to band together with other workers into powerful labor organizations, for there is strength in numbers. The capitalists, on the other hand, own all the factories, the mines and the government. Their only interest is to make as much profit as they can. They are not concerned with the well-being of those who work for them. We see, therefore, that the interests of the capitalists and the workers are not the same. In fact, they are opposed to each other. What happens? A desperate fight takes place between the two. This is known as the class struggle."

The idea seemed so self-evident now that I scolded myself for having been so stupid as not to have recognized it before.

As I remarked before, my ideas were hopelessly scrambled at this time. I still had a lot of confidence in the big Negro leaders, such as De Priest and Du Bois. However, I did not know then, as I know now, that these self-appointed Negro leaders are lined up on the side of the capitalist class, and that they help in every way that they can to perpetuate the slave conditions under which the Negro worker is forced to live. On the one hand, they pretend to fight for Negro rights, on the other, they become the tools and the lickspittles of the white ruling class. Their right hand pretends not to know what the left hand is doing. They speak with the sweet voice of Jacob, but they extend the hairy hand of Esau. However, it was not very long before I freed myself of my childish faith in them. It happened in a manner which I shall now relate.

4

There was a big Community Chest drive on in Birmingham for the unemployed. Both whites and Negroes were appealed to for funds. Some gave willingly, believing that their money was really going to help feed the unemployed. Many workers were forced to make contributions by their employers. Those who refused to make it "voluntarily" had it "involuntarily" taken out of their wages. When the relief was handed out it was very meager. It wasn't even enough to maintain an animal. What galled me most was the fact that discrimination began automatically. Negroes received only about half of what the whites got. The Unemployment Council, ever vigilant against injustice and discrimination for the Negro workers, launched a vigorous fight for cash relief, for aid to single men, and for equal distribution of relief among both Negroes and whites.

A protest meeting was called in Capitol Park. About five hundred unemployed workers of both colors gathered around the Confederate Monument. It was amusing as well as distressing to notice the fright we gave the City Fathers. About one hundred cops turned out to "maintain order." After the meeting the workers marched to the Community Chest headquarters. Mr. Simms, head of the drive, came out to speak to us. He was a short slender man with graying mustache and thin white hair. He was very shrewd and very polished. His ability to pour oil on troubled waters filled me with a sort of negative admiration—a born diplomat!

Mr. Simms told us with almost a sob in his voice that he realized in what a terrible situation we jobless were in. Heaven was his witness that he was doing everything humanly possible to help us! But what is a fellow going to do? He wasn't President of the United States! He was only a harassed, overworked relief subordinate. As for us, we simply had to be patient and considerate. We just had to give him time, for an important thing like this could not be rushed. To us Negroes he gave the following advice:

"Go back to the farms where you came from. That's the kind of work that's best suited for you. With plenty of potatoes and bacon you won't have to worry about jobs."

The crowd listened patiently and courteously to him without any interruption, but after his speech it became uneasy, even angry. A Negro up front shouted:

"He's a liar."

The cops in the rear took this as their cue. Clubs in hand they rushed up. But the crowd was orderly and refused to be provoked by the shoving from the maintainers of law and order.

Frank Williams, our leader, next spoke up. He was full of biting sarcasm and each sally stirred the crowd to laughter. He said something to the following effect:

"Fellow-workers: I've listened with deep interest to what Mr. Simms had to say. I will now take the liberty to advise the speaker in case his knowledge fails him, that going back to the land for the Negro is like jumping from the frying pan into the fire, for the tenant farmers and sharecroppers in the cotton fields in the Birmingham district are starving just the same as the workers in the cities. They are losing their land and stock. Hundreds are drifting into the cities in the hope of getting work. You can see them everywhere in Birmingham and you can recognize them by the rags that they wear, by the hunger in their eyes and by the hopelessness of their walk. Sure, fellow-workers, let's go back to the farms and live on milk and honey."

Our spokesman then demanded from Mr. Simms a definite statement as to his intentions about the unemployed workers under his charge. He warned that we would not allow him to confuse us with catch phrases and fairy tales.

The men cheered Frank Williams when he was through speaking. His fighting words made them all feel as one. After he had spoken Oscar Adams took the floor. I knew all about him, and I was worried. As editor of the Birmingham *Reporter*, a Negro newspaper, he exercised considerable influence locally. There was something disconcerting and disagreeable about the man as he spoke. He was a big beefy man with a booming voice. In turn he cajoled and threatened us. He tried to cotton up to Mr. Simms with an obsequiousness that only a social climber belonging to a despised race can employ. "Soul of a slave!" I thought to myself.

He became vituperative and abusive when he dwelt on the subject of Frank Williams and the Unemployment Council. He characterized them as a bunch of "furriners" who had come thousands of miles to Birmingham, paid by Moscow and Jewish gold, to stir up trouble among the Negroes of the South. He assured us that the only real friends we Negroes had, whenever we were in need, were the rich white people of the South. He concluded with a plea that we ignore the Unemployment Council and their crazy ideas of social equality for the Negroes. "We do not need it, and what's more, we don't want it!"

I was boiling over with indignation, but there was nothing I could do, for I feared to make a mark of myself in public; the police would be sure to spot me. But I thought to myself:

"Oh, Oscar Adams, for thirty pieces of silver Judas sold his master. You, too, are selling your people for a mess of pottage and the rich white man's condescending smile. Fortunately, we Negroes are not all degraded yet. We will fight on until we have secured not only social equality, but every other kind of equality. To this end I will dedicate my life until the day I die."

5

A few days later there was a police raid on the office of the Unemployment Council, which occupied the second floor of a stucco house in the poor downtown section, across the street from the Court House and the County Jail. It consisted of a large room. The walls were dilapidated; the plaster was falling off in strips but the floors were clean, for the workers took a great deal of pride in their headquarters and kept on mopping the floor all the time. There was nothing very impressive about the office. It looked poverty-stricken and not so efficient, as is the case with all offices that are run exclusively by volunteer help. There was no telephone, and the electric lights were dim. There was nothing in its appearance to boast about. However, when the raiding party got through with it, nothing more desolate or wretched could be imagined. They smashed up the desk, the table, the chairs, the two old typewriters and the heroic little mimeograph machine. Worse yet, they arrested Frank Williams and our other leaders, and with much abuse and pummelling led them off to jail across the street. Our literature was thrown out of the window and trampled under foot by hostile, laughing crowds who stood outside being entertained by the merry goings-on of the police.

One morning, shortly after, I went up to the office, hoping it would be open. I found the doors locked, but as I went down the stairs I was halted by six detectives. They asked me my business. I told them I was looking for the leaders of the Unemployment Council. One said to me:

"We've got them all locked up, son. Better get the hell out of here before you get into trouble. These 'Nigger Lovers' are only trying to get you niggers killed, believe me."

I hurried across the street to the County Jail. I asked the jail-keeper if I could see Frank Williams. He told me curtly that I couldn't. I pretended not to know the reason why he was locked up and with an air of innocence asked him what the nature of his crime was. He answered me something like this:

"Young fellow, if you know what is good for you you'll keep away from these dirty foreigners. They'll only get you into trouble."

Some of us got together and decided to communicate with the Unemployment Council in the North. Aid was promptly given; our friends in New York furnished the bail for the prisoners, who were released.

6

My education, as I have made clear in this narrative, was practically nil. Throughout all my struggles and vicissitudes I hungered for learning, never forgetting for a moment my vows to my dying father. But life was too much for me. I was a poor Negro lad and an orphan with no one to help. What could I do? But a new force now entered into my life. It created a revolution in it. The education I longed for in the world I had expected to find it, I surprisingly began to receive in my new Communist circles. To the everlasting glory of the Communist movement may it be said that wherever it is active, it brings enlightenment and culture. Rather than break down or discard the cultural traditions of the past, it is the only force today which battles with might and main to preserve the light of civilization and humanity among the great masses of the people against the anti-cultural and reactionary policies of the society in which we live.

Every meeting of the Unemployment Council became a classroom for me. I never left one of them without bearing away with me the discovery of a new idea. Of course, I did not always understand everything that I heard or read, but what of it? It was enough that I understood that they were on the right track.

Much water had run under the bridges since I walked up to my Uncle Jeremiah at the end of his first sermon in church and shook his hand, saying: "I've got religion in me, Uncle Jeremiah."

Come to think of it, only eight years had passed. I had travelled much during that period. Life had robbed me of my innocence and illusions, but I had found something more satisfying, a realistic recognition of the world and the rational plan of scientific socialism with which to create order and harmony out of the human chaos.

Now, as if by a miracle, a new world had unfolded itself before my eyes. It, too, was a part of the white man's world, but it did not leave us Negroes standing like beggars outside in the cold. Welcoming brotherly hands were outstretched to us. We were called "comrades" without condescension or patronage. Better yet, we were treated like equals and brothers. No longer did I feel like everybody's stepchild or scapegoat. At last I had found my true friends in the world and I was happy. My new white friends, my white fellow-workers gave me courage and inspiration to look, not back at the past, but at the radiant future. How good it was to live, I now felt! Life was more beautiful, more worth while, more exciting and full of meaning. The bitterness and hatred which I had formerly felt toward all white people was now transformed into love and understanding. Like a man who had gone through some terrible sickness of the soul I miraculously became whole again. Never before was I so full of determination, so fired by the fighting spirit. No, my discovery of Communism did not bring me religion, or a mystic faith; it gave me a purpose in living, in doing, in aspiring. Rational and scientific in its base, ethical in its motives, it is the only philosophy of living worthy of a thinking civilized man.

Up to the time I had met the Communists I did not know how to fight the lynching of Negroes and Jim Crowism. I was bewildered, grief-stricken and helpless. All of a sudden I found myself in an organization which fought selflessly and tirelessly to undo all the wrongs perpetrated upon my race. Here was no dilly-dallying, no pussyfooting on the question of full equality for the Negro people. The Communist position on this question was clear-cut and definite. Early in the history of the Communist Party its white leaders had been advised that if they would abandon their demand for social, political and economic equality for the Negroes, thousands more of white people would join the movement. But the Communist leaders, true to their cause and to their class, refused to compromise. They spurned the advice of "well-meaning friends."

What I have written here concerned me most vitally. Some people may, perhaps, accuse me of preaching or making unnecessary propaganda here for the Communist cause. After all, they might say, this is only the story of my life and does not call for evangelical outbursts. To this I will answer in all earnestness that the story of my life without my reactions to my own problems and to the problems of the world with the Communistic viewpoint as its key and guide, without my fervors and indignations, without my hatreds and without my loves, would remain an untrue and distorted narrative, without blood and without entrails.

My bosses and the Negro Uncle Toms, like Oscar Adams, had warned us to keep clear of the Reds because they were foreigners and trouble makers and that the Communist program could never work in the South. But as I got to know them, the leaders of the Communist Party and the Unemployment Council seemed like the people I had always wished to know. They were workers and spoke to us in direct and heartfelt words; they spoke to us in a language we understood, the language of men who toil and seek a better life.

My new Communist friends carried on their activities under the most trying conditions. We could not work in the open, for, as I have already recounted, our headquarters were raided and closed by the police and our leaders thrown into jail. Despite our Constitutional rights, we had to forget that we were living in the country in which the Revolutionary War had been fought. We were driven underground. Did we feel like conspirators or criminals? Quite the opposite. We knew we were carrying on in the spirit of the truest American patriots and Revolutionary Fathers, who, too, had to fight against the same reactionary forces in their day. I saw Frank Williams, Earl Browder and William Z. Foster as the spiritual descendants of Thomas Jefferson, Thomas Paine, Patrick Henry, Frederick Douglas and John Brown. I felt it a privilege to be working with them toward the same noble goal.

To carry on our organization work proved very difficult. We had so little money. Constantly we were harassed by the need of funds. If I were in need I'd rather starve than impose on anyone. But how differently did I react when it concerned the collection of money for the movement! It was no longer a matter of pride or dignity. If I asked someone for money, it was not as if it were a favor to me; quite the contrary, I felt and made the approached person feel as if I were conferring the greatest privilege and honor upon him, a privilege and honor that bore with them possibilities of social usefulness.

With our few pennies that we collected we ground out leaflets on an old rickety mimeograph machine, which we kept concealed in the home of one of our workers. We were obliged to work very quietly, like the Abolitionists in the South during the Civil War, behind drawn shades and locked doors. We always posted a lookout for spies and police. With the same secretiveness and caution we distributed our leaflets at night from door to door. Our members who worked in factories and steel mills smuggled them in there, too, and distributed them among their fellow-workers. Necessity sharpened our wits. We fell upon the following stratagem for holding meetings on the streets that otherwise would have been forbidden to us; we would issue a leaflet calling for a meeting in half an hour, from time of issuance of this leaflet, on a certain street corner. When the people would assemble without loss of any time, a speaker would jump upon an improvised stand and in a few well-chosen words would drive home his message to his listeners. While he would be speaking, others would circulate rapidly in the crowd passing out pamphlets and leaflets. In case the police would come running up to see what was happening, the meeting would already be ended and the crowd would have dissolved like mist.

Our dramatic and successful ways of doing things scared the bosses. The Ku Klux Klan and the American Legion now got busy in Birmingham. They paraded up and down the streets, especially in the Negro neighborhood, night after night. They were dressed in their full regalia, like spooks in the funny pictures, with nightgowns and pillow cases and flaming torches. Everywhere they went they howled in unearthly voices the warning that Negroes better keep away from the Communists or . . .

TEN

About a month after I had joined the Unemployment Council of Birmingham it elected me as a delegate to the National Convention of Unemployment Councils in Chicago. During that month I was very active. I threw myself into the work with unbounded enthusiasm. My mental and nervous energy had at last found an organized outlet. I was not, as hitherto, merely sowing with the wind, but harnessed in systematic and well-disciplined activity.

Up to that time I had been living with Aunt Catherine and her husband. Good souls that they were, they nevertheless were under the influence of those Negro misleaders, De Priest and Du Bois. It has always been so: the unthinking fall prey to so-called respectability, to those "who belong" and exercise worldly power. With the longest faces imaginable and with a look of genuine grief they issued an ultimatum to me. If I went to the Convention with those "Red hoodlums" they never wished to see my face again. Needless to say, their attitude pained me greatly, for I was genuinely fond of them.

The very morning I was to leave for Chicago I found a leaflet lying on our doorstep. It had been placed there by the Ku Klux Klan and read:

"Communism must be wiped out. Drive the foreigners back to the North and Russia where they came from. Alabama is a good place for good Negroes, but a bad place for bad Negroes who want social equality."

This open threat did not deter me from going to the Convention. If it was going to be merciless warfare, I was ready to take my chances. I rode the rods to Chicago as I did not have enough money for train fare. The twenty other members of our delegation rode the same way. We had an inelegant but grand time, singing and discussing seriously many vital subjects all the way. We were united by a feeling of good fellowship and, above all, by a common aim.

Just before the Convention opened, an unusual demonstration was staged by the workers in Union Park. It had unforseen consequences. Although the city had given us the right to meet in the park, this right was suddenly revoked at the very last minute. The Police Commissioner issued orders that all those who assembled in the park were to be driven out This, however, was not going to be such a simple matter as he expected. The resentment among the thousands of working men, women and children, both Negro and white, rose high. They stood their ground with smiling stubbornness. The tension visibly grew. At any moment we expected trouble to break out. From past experience we knew that the police would deliberately provoke us, in order to justify their use of violence against us. But it was not in the nature of our workers to slink away like rats. They were determined to stand their ground peacefully, and to resist only in self-defense.

Suddenly the children spontaneously formed a line and marched up and down singing the following song:

Empty is the cupboard, no pillow for the head.
We are the hunger children who fight for milk and bread.
We are the workers' children, who must, who must be
be fed.

A worker then mounted the ladder and began to speak. This furnished the right cue to the police. Sirens began to blow. They almost split our ears with their terrifying shrieks. The cops then formed for the attack and swooped down upon the speaker. They wielded their clubs left and right. The cries of those struck rent the air. The workers stood their ground. With their bare fists they struck back at the attacking police sluggers. Some of the policemen, inflamed by the sight of blood which they spilled, and drunk with a sort of gory pleasure looking at the smashed-in skulls and prostrate forms, lost their self-control and emptied their revolvers into the crowd. By deliberate pre-arrangement, Negro cops swung their clubs at the heads of white women workers and white cops tried to bash in the skulls of Negro women. This time, strange as it may seem, when it came to the crushing of workers' skulls, no race prejudice was in evidence. Even little children were smashed down by the police clubs. I saw one little white girl of ten savagely knocked down by a cop. She screamed in terror. Her tiny face smeared with blood, she turned toward him a pair of tear-stained eyes, mutely begging for mercy. The policeman, having whipped himself into a frenzy, with a well-aimed blow cracked one of her fragile legs. With a low moan she crumpled up in a heap.

The streets were literally dyed red. Many were taken away to the city morgue. Others were sent to the hospital and eighteen were thrown into jail. In this way did organized law and order preserve its power and majesty among those of its citizens it was duty-bound to protect.

The following morning one newspaper carried the headline:

TWELVE THOUSAND COPS QUELL RIOT
OF TWENTY-FIVE THOUSAND REDS

I cursed out loud, for I knew the tragic truth only too well. But what did the prostituted press care for the truth!

2

The Chicago Convention marked the beginning of a new chapter in my life. I got my first broad view of the workers' movement there. I talked with delegates from almost every state in the Union and was cheered by the knowledge that what we were trying to do in Birmingham was being duplicated by hundreds of similar organizations throughout the country. For the first time there dawned on me the knowledge of the potential strength of the working class. There were not only our few militants in Birmingham, but hundreds of thousands of others banded together in one irresistible movement, sweeping like a tidal wave from coast to coast.

How thrilled I was by the brotherly handshake of my white fellow-delegates! White and Negro workers fraternized. There was not in evidence the slightest vestige of race consciousness, not speaking of race prejudice. The color line was ignored, indeed forgotten.

The speakers at the Convention were the late J. Louis Engdahl, General Secretary of the International Labor Defense; Bill Dunne, the labor journalist, and one of the leaders of the 1919 Steel Strike; and Nels Kjar, leader of the Unemployment Council in Chicago, who later was arrested by the Immigration Authorities and deported to Sweden as reward for his loyalty to the American working class. It was he who made the most powerful speech at the Convention. He called upon the workers of America to resist with all their might the imposition upon them by the capitalist class of hunger, unemployment and hopeless poverty. The delegates leaped to their feet cheering wildly. It was not merely that we were swept away by a strong emotion. The ovation we gave him was only an expression of our full understanding of what we were facing, and of our determination to achieve our just goal.

ELEVEN

ONE DAY, shortly after my return from the Convention, I made a round of visits to the mines together with a friend. Our intention was to induce the workers to join the National Miners' Union. I had many friends among them. This, I suppose, was because I've always liked people very much, and sensing that, they are not at all unfriendly to me in return. Therefore, I had no difficulty in gathering together about twenty-five of the miners I knew for an informal chat. I talked to them about their conditions and how to improve them when suddenly an automobile filled with company gunmen drove up. They pointed their guns at us threateningly. Their leader shouted:

"Stick 'em up! You are under arrest!"

As the men began to frisk us for concealed weapons I asked their leader:

"Why are you arresting us? You have no right to do this. You are not cops and you've got to have warrants to arrest us."

The gunman fairly snarled at me:

"Shut up you dirty nigger! Get in this car. You'll damn soon enough find out what we want you for."

It seemed that the Company gunmen had a definite program of action. Before lodging us in the Birmingham jail, they took us to all the mines owned by the Tennessee Coal, Iron and Railroad Company, so that all their crews of armed blackguards could look us over and keep us in mind for future reference.

On our way the car stopped in Pratt City, a little coal town owned in its entirety by the T.C.I. The gunmen roughly told us to get out. While we waited they talked matters over. I got the impression that they were undecided what to do with us. One of them, a cruel-faced individual, approached me and said in a threatening tone of voice:

"You God-damn black son-of-a-bitch! Tell me what you know about those —— Reds!"

"Nothing," I answered.

"Well, you're going to know something before you leave here. I'm going to take you out into the woods and beat hell out of your black hide until you talk."

But he never carried out his threat.

I recognized the sheriff of the Docena Mine standing in the group of gunmen. He knew me very well, so he walked over and said to my tormentor:

"Oh, I know this fellow. He's a very nice boy. He's the guy that had an accident some time ago; he had some fingers smashed."

The man who threatened me retorted:

"Well, it's just too bad for him now. He's got himself mixed up with those God-damn Rooshian heathens and Jews."

In the end we were locked up in the Big Rock Jail in Birmingham. Although we still had jobs with the T.C.I. Company, a charge of vagrancy was trumped up against us. Despite all our protests, bail was fixed at $3,000 for each.

2

I was locked up in what was called solitary confinement with another Negro prisoner. He had been there for seven weeks, he told me. I could well understand what this period of solitude had done for him. There was a wild, haunted look in his eyes, and he almost clutched at me for sheer joy when I was put into his cell, for it came as a merciful relief to the terrible silence he lived in. He looked like a nice and quiet worker in his late twenties. I was unstrung watching him pace up and down the cell in a depressed and listless sort of way like a caged animal. It was a habit with him, he told me, and he could not stop. Later on I discovered for myself that many prisoners suffer from this compulsion. There was a murder charge against him, and with tears in his eyes, as if justifying himself before me would help clear him before the whole world, he pleaded that he was innocent—that he had been framed by the police, and if there was a God in heaven he would surely come to his aid. I tried to console him as well as I could, but he was not listening. There was a far-off look in his eyes. Was he already seeing the electric chair?

One morning, it must have been about three o'clock, and together with the rest of the prisoners in the solitary-confinement block I was fast asleep, when I was awakened by a bloodcurdling yell. I leaped off my cot and heard my cellmate shrieking in an unearthly voice. He looked stark mad. I asked him to tell me what was the matter. He blurted incoherently that he had been dreaming in his sleep that he was back at home having a good time with his friends and family. But suddenly he had awakened. Uncomprehendingly he had looked at the iron bars around him. His thoughts had gotten all tangled and twisted so that he could not make out just where he was. The dream had been so vivid that he was sure it was real. Now he became quite frightened when he saw that he was not at home, and he went out of his mind. It took me some time before I could calm him. Dazed, he sank back on his cot and fell into a sort of stupor.

After a few days, I, too, began to feel that the deadly spirit of the jail was getting me. I saw the prisoners beaten and maltreated in a barbarous way. I heard their wild screams at night, and I trembled with anger and grief. I said to myself:

"When they strike the helpless and the weak they strike me."

Helpless myself, I began to brood on this insane business of living. For the first time I clearly saw that the white man's boastful civilization was a fraud. The few battened on the many and when the underdog dared question his evil lot he was beaten down without mercy. If there was violence at all in the world, it certainly was not being employed by the workers. Quite the contrary, it was the ruling class that was doing it in a conscienceless and bestial sort of way.

One night the guards, cursing furiously, dragged out a prisoner from the cell next to mine and began beating him up. It was a part of the routine of their jobs. Ostensibly punishment was being meted out to the prisoner because of his infraction of the rules. But as the Biblical injunction runs: "Seek and thou shalt find," they had no difficulty in finding such infractions. The poor wretch howled with pain and I stuffed my fingers into my ears to shut out his piteous cries. The guards knocked him down repeatedly to the steel floor every time he tried to raise himself. They jeered at him. It was a huge joke to them. One of them shoved his foot into his mouth and began lashing him on his naked body with a bull whip. Long red welts appeared. The whip cut deeply into the unresisting flesh. Blood trickled to the floor in rivulets.

What my thoughts were all this while I cannot well describe. I turned sick inside of me. I held on to the bars of my cell for I thought I was going to faint. Uppermost in my mind was the certainty that they were going to do the same thing to me. Why not? I was no better than the others in the estimation of our jailers. And so to give myself courage I kept on repeating mentally:

"Don't weaken, Angelo, don't weaken! You've got to survive!"

3

Much to my surprise, the guards left me alone. After seven days I was brought before Judge McDermott. At first my comrades in the Unemployment Council had difficulty in securing a lawyer for me. The man who would have dared defend me publicly in court would have been ruined professionally as well as socially. Finally, a Mr. Rosenthal agreed to defend me. He was a very curious character. Externally he made a very agreeable impression. Short and fat, he was always pleasant, always smiling, oozing good nature and self-confidence. But what made him appear a little ridiculous in my eyes was his apologetic boast to me that in his young and idealistic days, that was way back in 1919, he had been a Socialist; but now, thank heavens, he was through with such youthful folly and voted as a straight Democrat.

When the Prosecuting Attorney presented his case the court room was packed to suffocation. Everybody had come to take a look at that freak monster, a *Negro Red.* How they popped their eyes at me! And although I squirmed, for there was something cruel and depraved in their curiosity, I stared back at them unflinchingly. I tried to accept it with the same resignation that I would an attack of colic. It was equally beyond my control.

What the Prosecutor said in his argument before the court I do not clearly recall. But he ranted and raved and flung his arms about like flails. He glared and snarled at me and went through forty-nine acts of convulsions. He talked vaguely and bitterly about bewhiskered devils that carried bombs in their pockets and threatened the virtue of every white woman. He referred to Communists and Bolsheviks as if they were two separate kinds of radicals and talked about Russians as if they were all Jews. Finally, tiring of his circus acrobatics, he dramatically pointed a finger at me and at my friend who had been arrested with me, and demanded that society protect itself against such horrible creatures by giving us the fullest punishment under the law.

Throughout the trial I was distracted most unpleasantly by the sight of the Chief Kleagle of the Klan, who sat in the front row surrounded by his henchmen. They behaved in a rowdy and revolting manner. They laughed noisily, mimicked in exaggerated ways the speech of our Jewish lawyer, and every time Mr. Rosenthal demanded that we be acquitted, they all raised the chorus:

"The bastards should be lynched!"

Old Judge McDermott, with an amused smile on his ruddy, well-fed face, smiled at their antics. In my innocence, I was outraged. Judge McDermott was amusing himself throughout the trial by revolving round and round in his swivel chair and squirting tobacco juice on the floor and walls. It seemed to me as if he were deliberately trying to avoid spitting into the cuspidor at his feet.

When both sides rested, the judge in a drawling sleepy voice delivered sentence:

"I find that both of you are guilty. I am only sorry that we haven't got an insurrection law here in Alabama as they have in Georgia so we could have your necks broken in the court room without delay. I, therefore, now sentence both of you defendants to twelve months on the chain gang at hard labor. You are also to pay a fine of $500 each. Sheriff, take them away."

Flabbergasted, I held up my hand just as I did when I was a little boy at school and protested in as polite a way as I could that the sentence was unjust. The judge's ruddy face grew even ruddier with anger. He squinted his eyes at me and threatened to cite me for contempt of court.

"Shut your trap and sit down!" he bellowed at me.

With dragging feet and with all the spirit taken out of me, I was led back to my cell.

4

Fortunately for me, when Mr. Rosenthal appealed, the Circuit Court threw the case out, but my experience had made a changed man out of me. I now had a few illusions less about the capitalist world, and those I had left were soon dispelled by the action of the mining company. They put me on the blacklist and warned me that if I did not want my head knocked off I'd better keep clear of all Company property. This meant that I could not get a job in Birmingham again.

The time was ripe at last. The logic of events drove me to take the step. I joined the Communist Party. In my spare time, and I now had plenty of it, I worked as a volunteer organizer for the National Miners' Union. I was the first one to do such work in Jefferson County. It goes without saying that my seventeen years could not cope with the power, the trickery and the terror employed by the mine owners. Their armed thugs served as a sufficient restraint against the organization of unions. They kept careful watch over the men, searched and intimidated them at every step. If there were any workers' organizations in town they were only company unions, transparent shams to deceive the workers into the belief that they actually had a union.

My youth, instead of proving a handicap, turned out as a great boon. My ideas made some impression on the men. However, I did not deceive myself about the magnitude of my task. There were more than ten thousand miners in Birmingham, of whom about seventy-five per cent were Negroes. The difficulties I faced in organizing them were insuperable, so it seemed to me at the time. But after a while my efforts began to bear fruit. Within a few months I succeeded in establishing union locals in four of the mines. There were approximately thirty-five Negro and white workers in each local. But each of these members was easily worth ten of his unorganized fellows. They were tried and true men, intelligent and questioning, full of spirit and fight. I felt that with such men one could move mountains. But the authorities bore heavily down upon us. Our union locals were therefore obliged to carry on secretly in underground ways, just as the Revolutionary Fathers did under the English yoke.

My livelihood during this period was very precarious. I received no fixed salary for my work in the Union. Occasionally I was given a few dollars. It probably would have gone badly with me were it not for the fact that I was living with coal-miner friends. They were an elderly couple, decent, refined and hard-working. They were Communist sympathizers and regarded my work in the Union as a sacred task which they were ready to support in a personal way with food and lodgings, as much as they could. They treated me with the greatest solicitude and upbraided me for neglecting myself, something I could not avoid, for I was mobilized like a soldier in a war, and the battle was on continuously.

One of the happiest experiences in my life took place at this time. No, nothing happened to me. The excitement was purely mental. After meetings I would go home and try to make myself comfortable. Then, while the whole household was asleep, I sat before a kerosene lamp reading the works of Karl Marx, Frederick Engels and Lenin. I felt like Columbus discovering a new world. True enough, my education was limited. But I was fortunate in being able to read and write. Nature was not unkind to me; it had endowed me with a certain amount of curiosity about people and ideas. What I had not learned from books I derived from experience. To my surprise I discovered on reading the books of the great working-class leaders that my own experience was just the right background and preparation I needed to understand their ideas. The mental stimulation I received from my reading lifted me sky-high. I walked on thin air and repeated to myself the words:

"I'm becoming an educated man, Father!"

5

I could not go on living the way I did on the bounty of the old couple I lived with. The food stuck in my throat when I saw how poor they were and how they lived from hand to mouth. So I made frantic efforts to get a job. I was overjoyed when I landed one in a restaurant kitchen. I peeled potatoes, sliced onions, scoured the pots and pans, emptied garbage pails and swept the floors. On occasion I assisted in waiting on the customers. I was comparatively well paid. I received $13 a week. Everything went on hummingly well until one day my boss, happening to be out of humor, called after me:

"Hurry up, nigger!"

I dropped everything I was carrying in my hands. I was trembling with rage.

"You'll have to take that nasty word back, mister!" I said. "Otherwise you and I won't be seeing much of each other."

At this my boss picked up a butcher knife and raised it as if he were determined to slash me with it. A look of hatred distorted his face. He repeated with great emphasis:

"All right, nigger, hurry up!"

I rushed into the kitchen and seized the biggest butcher knife I could find. In justice to myself I must say that I am far from being a bloodthirsty individual. I abhor violence from the bottom of my soul. It was no mere savagery on my part that made me pick up a knife against my boss. My common sense told me that violence can only be countered with a display of violence, that if I did not fight my boss with his own weapons I would remain in his eyes a "nigger" ever after. My own pride and the honor of my race demanded that I stand up and resist him. Returning to the restaurant where many customers were waiting to be served, I said to him quietly:

"Pay me off now because I see we can't get along."

Both of us were standing behind the counter with butcher knives drawn on each other, ready for the attack. The customers stopped eating. They were pleased with the prospect of an unexpected entertainment. My boss, however, stood his ground and said:

"You are a nigger and I'll call you a nigger any time I like. What's more, I don't want to pay you off now."

Throwing his head back he laughed loudly. His humor was infectious. The customers laughed too. Only I did not feel like laughing. My boss was forcing my hand and I knew there was no turning back from the messy job.

"I'll teach you, Mr. White Man, how to respect a human being, black, yellow or red," I cried.

Thereupon, with an air of great determination, as if I really meant business, I started toward him with the butcher knife. He visibly blanched. He did not expect such a desperate advance.

"All right, all right!" he now hastened to say in a voice of assumed friendliness. "What's the idea of getting so excited? Like a good fellow put your knife down."

But I refused to do so until he had laid his own knife down.

He paid me what he owed me, and I walked out, much to our mutual relief.

6

We were preparing to celebrate Labor Day in as festive a mood as possible. Although few in number and surrounded by a hostile and threatening world, our gallant little band of Communist Party members, of the Unemployment Council and of the few militant unions in Birmingham, decided to demonstrate the workers' strength on this day. Despite all their efforts to spoil our plans, the police were obliged to grant us a permit for an open-air meeting in Capitol Park. Our enemies left no stone unturned to break up our meeting. The Ku Kluxers, Legionnaires and the city police, all being the self-appointed guardians of law, order and one-hundred-percent American patriotism, mobilized all their forces for a carefully laid attack upon us. Although extra-legal organizations, the Ku Klux Klan and the American Legion behaved as if they were the legally constituted authorities of the city. The police gave them that outrageous recognition. Altogether they regarded us as interlopers, criminals, foreigners and creatures utterly without rights as American citizens. We boiled inside, but we dared not give public expression to it. We well understood that our enemies were only looking for such a provocation in order to attack us physically with guns, tear-gas bombs, riot sticks, brass knuckles and blackjacks. My friends advised me not to attend the meeting. The police would surely be on the lookout for me. I might get into trouble. But I would have felt deeply ashamed of myself if I had listened to my friends. There was a limit to caution and timidity. A time comes when a man has to assert himself and live according to his principles, even if he is threatened with injury.

As I passed the post office on my way down to the park for the meeting, some plain-clothes detectives closed in on me and told me to steer clear of the park. I put on an air of innocence.

"What's wrong? Why can't I walk through the park?"

"There are a lot of those Communists and Reds up there."

"So what?"

"Why, they are trying to get you niggers killed. We've arrested them and we're going to run them out of town."

"Well, if you've arrested them what are you worrying about? Why can't I go into the park?"

The detectives thought the nigger was getting too smart. So one of them asked me for my name and address and made me get into a police car. They drove me in to the park to the spot where the meeting was supposed to have been taking place. No sooner did we get there when I saw Tom Wilson, the district organizer of the Communist Party, standing surrounded by the police. He certainly was not in an enviable spot. The police had "mussed him up," clapped handcuffs on him and were shoving him into a car. I pretended I did not know him and betrayed no sign of emotion although I was ready to run out to his defense.

The cops then began to question me.

"Do you know that nigger, Angelo Herndon, the Red who was sentenced to twelve months in jail and was given a fine of $500?"

"Who? Never heard of that guy before."

The Ku Kluxers began gathering around the car I was in. The Kleagle pushed his way through and pointed a menacing finger at me.

"I know that fellow—that's Angelo Herndon. I was present at his trial."

The cops grew angry. They asked me if I knew the Kleagle. I answered:

"No, I've never seen this man before. He must be talking out of his head."

A detective said:

"That's enough. Shut up, nigger! None of your wise cracks."

I was taken off to the jail, finger-printed and questioned again. They evidently took me for a nitwit when they tried to trap me with an assumed friendliness and solicitude for my welfare. Of course, they did not wish to see me go to the chain gang, where I would have to wear a ball and chain and convict stripes. "My, but isn't he a good-looking lad. I bet he is a regular lady-killer." This bit of choice flattery not making any impression on me, one of the detectives began making me a speech:

"Of course, I realize how you must feel about your people. Their going is hard, sure. But just the same they live pretty good, don't they? Almost as good as white people, no? Look here! Haven't they beautiful houses to live in out on Indian Ridge, Smithfield and other places? Now, I live in one of the best houses of the city, and although I don't say that you have to live in as good a house as mine, just the same if you behave yourself and play square with us you won't have to worry about anything. We'll fix you up all right, all right. But you must first promise us that you won't have anything to do with those Reds."

Trying hard to suppress a smile, I answered:

"I'm very much obliged to you, mister, for telling me this nice fairy tale. But you see that I'm young and although life is hell for me, I'm determined to face it in my own way."

The detectives were a little taken aback by my answer. Their friendliness disappeared just as fast as it was put on. They spoke in angry voices now. It was clear they were going to give me the third degree. It was also clear to me that they had something else in mind. They were after certain "information."

"Do you know Mary Dalton and Tom Wilson?"

"Sure I know Mary and Tom."

The expression on my questioners' faces became savage.

"They are white people, aren't they?"

"Yes."

"Do you call them Mary and Tom to their faces?"

"Sure, why not?"

"Listen, nigger, we are white men and you're a nigger, see? Now you've got to say 'Yes, sir,' and 'No, sir' when we talk to you."

As they looked menacingly at me I thought a little contemptuous hypocrisy would be the better part of valor and I answered:

"Very well, 'Yes, sir,' Mr. Detectives, if it will at all make you feel superior to me because I'm a black man and a prisoner in your hands."

When they asked me for my address I gave them a fictitious one, in the other end of the town. That night I was transferred to the County Jail. This was very fortunate for me, because when the detectives discovered that I had given them a wrong address they came to beat me up. Luckily they could not remove me from the jail because it was out of their jurisdiction.

7

The following morning my lawyer, Mr. Rosenthal, brought me a letter from Tom Wilson.

"September 2, 1930.

"Hello, Gelo:—I just got back in town this morning. I saw you yesterday when they were driving me off. They took me about twenty-one miles out of town and all the way there they burned me with live lighted cigarettes and kept nudging me in the side with their pistol barrels. They kept saying to me, 'So, you're a nigger lover, eh? I suppose you would want a nigger to marry your sister? Well, we are going to finish you this time.' As we drove through the hills of Shady Mountain, I looked back at the city and felt sure that it was my last ride. However, I told them, 'You can do what you will with me, but you can't stop the Communists from organizing the workers here in Birmingham.' They put me out near the river and asked me if I would rather be lynched or drowned. I, of course, replied that it didn't matter, one way or the other. If it meant death, I had no choice in the matter. After some hesitation, they robbed me of my money and cigarettes and told me that if I was seen in town again, I would be shot on sight. I had to take a freight back into town and stay up all night. I am sleepy as hell now, but I wanted to find out what had happened to you before going to sleep. This morning, on my way to the lawyer's office, I saw them, but nothing happened. Keep up your courage. We will have you out in a few days.

"Your friend,
"Tom Wilson"

For eleven days they kept me in jail and most of the time in the "dog house." The "dog house" is the place where they keep the insane prisoners. Sure, they thought I was crazy. Why not, wasn't I a Red? There were no mattresses, no bunks in the "dog house." Nothing but the cold concrete floors that were flooded with water. We had to sleep on the floor. There were no toilets. The foul odor of excrement made me violently ill. Despite my natural cheerfulness and resolve to survive in order to carry on the battle for the workers' liberation, I must sadly confess that the anguish of living so overwhelmed me then that I prayed for death. All night long the poor insane people raised an unearthly howl. Sometimes they even attacked me. My eyes filled with tears. I could not be angry with them in their terrible misfortune. Yes, they were crazy. Perhaps I, too, was crazy in resenting the human nightmare, in striving to change the world so that justice, enlightenment and humanity should be practiced among men.

8

My case was finally reached on the Court Calendar. County Judge Abernathy presided. He was an elderly skinny man who bore a slight resemblance to former Mayor Jimmy

Walker of New York. He was well primed for the occasion. A big fat cigar was stuck in the left corner of his mouth. At the same time he was vigorously chewing on a plug of tobacco. He rarely opened his mouth to ask a question. If he did, it was merely to spit tobacco juice.

I had a foretaste of what was coming in the way the judge handled a case that preceded mine. A young Italian fellow was being tried for non-support. The girl in question who brought the charges against him, and who was the mother of his baby, begged the judge to be lenient with him. All she wanted was financial support, but she did not want to see him punished. The judge listened with a concentrated expression on his face. I could see he was becoming interested, even excited, for he was furiously puffing at his cigar and spitting brown juice. Finally, there came an outburst from him. He addressed himself to the prisoner:

"What do you mean by going around here messing with these women? I could send you to jail forever but I'll tell you what, for the sake of the girl I'll be light on you this time."

Then the judge called the wretched Magdalene to the witness stand. She looked frightened to death and had her eyes cast down. The judge looked her up and down. He wetted his lips pleasurably.

"Are you sure that your baby is his?" he asked her.

Almost inaudibly the girl murmured, "Yes."

"Did you ever have intercourse with him?" he asked, laughter in his eyes.

The girl flushed and answered: "Yes, I did."

"When?"

"The first time was on July 15th; the next time on July 29th, and twice a month thereafter."

"Did you consent every time he asked you?"

"Yes, whenever he told me that he loved me."

"Do you mean to tell me that you didn't have sexual relations with him when he didn't tell you that he loved you?" asked the judge with a knowing wink.

The girl hung her head still lower and answered nothing.

"All right," said the judge, "that will be enough." Then pointing his finger threateningly at the young fellow, he said to him:

"Now I'm going to be as light as I can with you this time. You go to jail and stay six months and see to it that when you get out you take care of that kid of yours and report to me once a month or else I'll see to it that you are tucked away for good."

After the man was led back to jail, the court attendant bawled:

"Is Angelo Herndon here?"

I was amused by his question, for they had locked me up in a little cage with barbed wire around it and I could not help being there, whether I wanted to or not.

"Yes," said I. "I'm over here in the cage."

The people in the court laughed.

I was led out of the cage, and to tell the truth, it made me feel like a monkey in the zoo. The sensation I got from it was more funny than tragic.

Then the judge asked me:

"How do you plead, guilty or not guilty?"

"Not guilty," I answered.

He scratched his chin reflectively.

"What are the charges against you? Now, let me see. You were charged with vagrancy."

I was amazed. "No, your honor," I protested. "I am not charged with vagrancy. The charge against me is that I am a Communist. I cannot see why the court should be so hypocritical about the charges they have against a prisoner."

The judge interrupted me angrily.

"All right," said he, "that's enough, I want no speeches from you. What I want to know is whether you'll work if you'll get a job?"

"Yes, your honor, if you have a job to give me I'll surely work."

The judge wrote something on a piece of paper and sealed it in an envelope. Hardly suppressing a grin he handed it to me with the words:

"There you are, young man. Take this to the person to whom it is addressed. Also report to me once a month for a period of one year."

The instinct of self-preservation in the hunted becomes very acute in times of crises. The judge's overt friendliness in giving me a job so readily and the sly smile which accompanied the letter when he handed it to me put me on my guard.

No sooner had I walked out of the court room when I tore open the letter and saw that it was addressed to the Kleagle of the Ku Klux Klan. It read as follows:

> "Dear Mr. Murphy:
>
> "I'm sending Angelo Herndon to you. He was arrested for vagrancy a few weeks ago and wants to work. Will you please take care of him?
>
> (Signed) "Judge Abernathy."

I immediately re-addressed the letter and mailed it to the *Daily Worker*, the Communist newspaper in New York, which played it up prominently on its front page. Upon publication I clipped the story and autographed it for the judge with the following words:

"Compliments. Yours truly, Angelo Herndon."

A few days later I collided with the judge on the street. There was no avoiding him this time. As soon as he saw me he grew red as a beet, and glared at me furiously.

9

One evening on my way home I met a cousin of mine on the street.

"Hello, Angelo! How's the detective work coming along?" he asked banteringly. "It sure is unusual for a detective to go to jail."

I said: "Listen, don't you try to flatter me. I've now graduated from a detective to a Communist. I'm much better at that than at the silly Sherlock Holmes business."

Time and time again I was now picked up on the street and arrested, heaven knows for what fantastic reasons! I became reconciled to the idea of being arrested with almost fatalistic calm every time I left home. Inevitably I would walk straight into the dragnet the police set for me. It got to be such a habit that every time I looked at a policeman I knew "it" was coming.

However, there was a bright side to this. Every time I went to jail, every time I was brutally tortured and given the third degree, I felt myself bound closer and closer to the Communist movement. That was most natural. I remember reading in the Book of Martyrs of the early Christian Church that the greater and more cruel the trials of the saints of old, the more obstinate they became in their resistance to the authority of the Roman Empire. Although I was then only seventeen years old, I had the conviction that only death could stop me from working for the social revolution in America. My elders thought I was too impetuous. Was I trying to be smarter than the wisest men of the nation? Did I think that my ideas were better than those of the President of the United States? Sure, they said, I was full of youthful energy. It was only natural that I should want things to move fast, yet I must not forget that old people are for counsel and young people are for war. At the risk of being called impudent and a young whippersnapper, I nevertheless insisted that there was no earthly use in counsel if it was not coupled up with concrete action. The old folks gave me up as a bad job, saying: "The Communist bug has got him all right."

It looked as if things were getting too hot for me in Birmingham. My comrades were disgusted. What was the use of my staying in town if all I did was to get into jail and out again. I was like a suburbanite commuting, only it was less pleasant for me. So it was decided that I could be more effective for our cause elsewhere, in a place where they did not know me, where every cop and detective would not be on the lookout "to haul me in." I was therefore engaged by the Trade Union Unity League to go to New Orleans as its representative. A strike of seven thousand Negro and white longshoremen had just started and every bit of assistance was needed from the outside. The city police and the ship owners were whooping it up merrily in an orgy of repression and brutality.

It seemed as if my frequent arrests had drawn to me some attention among workers outside of Birmingham. For when I arrived in New Orleans I was embarrassed to find myself at a special reception that had been arranged for me by the striking seamen and longshoremen. Speaking to them I stressed the importance of solidarity among all workers, and in the name of my organization, the Trade Union Unity League, I pledged its wholehearted support to the strikers in their fight for better living conditions and higher wages.

As usual, the leaders of the International Longshoremen's Association were playing a double game. It seemed as if they were getting ready to sell out the workers who trusted and honored them to the Steamship Association. Much grumbling was being heard in the ranks of the strikers. They sensed something was going wrong somewhere. Whether they could hold out much longer proved a vexing problem. Money and relief were urgently needed to continue the battle. I aided in the collection of money and food among workers and sympathizers throughout the city. Food, clothing and bedding were also being sent from Mississippi, Georgia, Alabama and from other states in the South. The strikers were heartened by this display of unity and began to act more militantly from day to day.

Let it be understood that a strike of resolute and red-blooded longshoremen and seamen is no Sunday-school picnic. Despite all opposition and provocation from the police and the company thugs, the strikers engaged in mass picketing of the docks night after night. The steamship companies had succeeded in rounding up hundreds of bad characters and even worse workers. The latter were paid sixty-five cents an hour to scab against the longshoremen who were merely fighting against an outrageous twenty-per-cent wage cut. Backed by the police and their gangs of armed gunmen, the Steamship Association was on the lookout for an opportunity to show its full might to the strikers.

One night when the strikers picketed the docks en masse, the Association's plug-uglies opened fire without warning. One hundred and eighteen strikers were shot. Some were killed and a number died later in the hospitals from their wounds. The hired murderers had used machine-guns as well as sawed-off shotguns and many of the workers had been riddled with bullets like sieves.

The heroic struggle of the workers, alas, was nullified by the "silk-hat" leaders of the International Longshoremen's Association. The rank and file workers felt that they had been betrayed and grew disheartened. "Better luck next time," they consoled themselves grimly.

10

My own part in the strike was far from pleasant. I, too, fell a victim to property rights. One day, as I was distributing the

Marine Workers' Voice to some German seamen who had just arrived on the *S.S. Luckenbach,* some scabs threw themselves upon me and began beating me up. Then they called the police.

When the police captain arrived on the scene, he looked at me furtively. He could not make up his mind just what charges he should bring against me. First, he thought he would turn me over to the Federal Authorities. Then he suddenly changed his mind and decided that he would make a perfect job of it; he was going to go the limit and make it a combined city and federal case!

I was locked up in an old prison that had served in pre-Revolutionary days as a French fort. The place was dismal and unsanitary. But by this time I was already a veteran in the matter of prisons. I looked it over with a professional eye and decided, come what may, I was going to come out in good health from the wretched hole.

Every night the jail took on a festive character. What occasioned such celebration was the fact that the cops brought in hundreds of prostitutes from the red-light district. The poor women were drunk and blatantly noisy. Perhaps it was better so. It helped make things more endurable for them. At first I was amazed at the large number of women that were locked up every night. Finally I discovered that it was just a degrading local racket. The women were arrested in order that filthy tribute might be exacted from them. Upon payment of this ransom their pleas of "not guilty" were accepted.

Finally, my case was called, after four wretched days of moping in my filthy cell. The charges against me made me laugh when I heard them. They were too ridiculous for words. They were for "violation of the Federal Injunction, inciting to riot, dangerous and suspicious, distributing circulars without a permit, and having no visible means of support." The judge, whose mind seemed to be on other matters, was hardly listening. He dismissed my case with an air of weariness.

As I was being given my release papers I noticed that the Court Clerk was staring at me and not in an unfriendly way either. Much surprised, I looked at him questioningly. He carefully looked around him to see that no one was there to hear him. Then he said to me:

"Buddy, I was once a seaman, and let me tell you I was a good union man in good standing. I'm glad to see you fighting for the boys. Good-bye and good luck, and continue distributing those dandy circulars. Stick to it and the union will win in the end."

11

Toward the end of March, 1931, news of the Scottsboro Case appeared in the New Orleans papers. All of them headlined it on the front page. One carried the account with a caption printed in box-car letters:

NINE BLACK BRUTES
RAPE TWO LITTLE WHITE GIRLS

It appeared from these accounts that nine Negroes, ranging in age from thirteen to nineteen years, had boarded a freight train between Paint Rock and Scottsboro, Alabama. The car into which they climbed was then occupied by two white hoboes and two white girls. The Negroes, finding strength in numbers, immediately proceeded to throw the white boys off the running train. Then they threw the girls to the floor and raped them in succession. One of the girls offered fierce resistance in defense of her womanly virtue. The Negroes subdued her only after one of them had knocked her over the head with the butt of his revolver. In the meantime the two white hoboes who had been thrown off the train hurried back to Paint Rock and notified the authorities. When the train pulled into Scottsboro, it was met by the local police, who arrested all the nine boys and lodged them in jail on the charge of rape.

The story was altogether transparent, even to my inexperienced eye. Immediately I jumped to the conclusion that it was a frame-up. It had all the unmistakable earmarks of one. Of late, mill and mine owners had developed the rape charge against militant workers into a fine art. Just a few days before, a Negro longshoreman, participating in the New Orleans strike, had been arrested on the charge of raping a white girl. What made the trial proceedings ridiculous was the fact that the Steamship Association pressed the charges. It obviously was an attempt to discredit the strikers and to deprive them of any public sympathy in their fight. Fortunately, the case the Company built up was so flimsy that it was thrown out of court. It was as clear as daylight to me that the Scottsboro boys were also being made scapegoats. A lynch atmosphere was carefully being generated in the South in order to break up the labor organizations which white and Negro workers had established after so much trouble. The industrial interests had been gunning for labor organizations a long time already, and no means was too sordid for them.

The reaction to the Scottsboro incident was pretty much the same everywhere among union and fraternal organizations: It was a frame-up, and no mistake about it. Indignation ran high. The all-important thing now was to harness this emotion into a powerful mass protest. I decided that it was my job to make the first move in defense of the poor frightened Scottsboro boys. I spoke to Harry Hines, the white secretary of the Marine Workers' Industrial Union. He readily agreed that something should be done immediately, and he called a meeting at union headquarters.

Five hundred longshoremen and seamen turned up. What added special significance and interest to the meeting was the unexpected presence of a number of German sailors from the *S.S. Luckenbach*. They were a bunch of husky, stalwart Nordics, independent and upstanding in their manner. The German seamen have ever been a militant lot, and my respect for them has been very great. No sooner did the German contingent arrive in the hall than sparks began to fly. When they clapped their eyes on the half-dozen cops who guarded the meeting against heaven only knows what, they threw themselves bodily on them and flung them out through the door. Our amazement was indescribable. Never had we seen the likes of it before. One member of our union, a German-American, with a look of pain and amazement written on his face, addressed the *Luckenbach* heroes in their own tongue. He begged them to desist. It finally turned out, much to everybody's amusement, that in Germany no cop was ever allowed inside a meeting hall and that it was a standing tradition that if one dared cross the sacred union portals he was to be thrown out on his ear. The *Luckenbach* sailors were only trying to be obliging to us. However, at our urging they allowed the cops to come back. The latter looked meek as lambs when they returned. We all felt relieved, for the incident could well have been turned into a serious provocation against us.

First Harry Hines spoke. He roused the meeting to a fervent pitch. Following him a German seaman explained to his compatriots all the facts and implications of the Scottsboro Case. If anything was needed to forge Negro and white solidarity, he pleaded, it was the defense of the Scottsboro boys. Money was collected in the audience and telegrams and resolutions were dispatched to Governor Miller of Alabama, demanding the boys' release. We all felt bitter about it and were determined to carry the fight into the enemy's camp. This was not merely going to be a war of defense against capitalist aggression. We were determined to take the offensive and to expose the rottenness and the corruption of Southern justice before all the American people.

Later I induced the Order of Esther and Ruth, the Elks and Odd Fellows to hold a joint meeting. There were prominent white and Negro speakers. I, too, spoke. Before and during the meeting the cops had threatened that they would not allow us to congregate. Ostentatiously they stood on each street corner swinging their clubs and looking fierce. But New Orleans citizens know their constitutional rights as well as anybody else. They packed the meeting hall to suffocation and the cops looked glum.

The contagion of protest among New Orleans Negroes spread rapidly. The Methodist and Baptist Churches hurriedly called special church meetings. Blistering sermons on lynch justice were heard in every Negro pulpit. It was the consensus among Negroes that if the Scottsboro prosecution were to succeed it would expose all Negroes to the same unhappy fate. One clergyman, in exhorting his congregation to rise to the defense of the nine prisoners, ended his address with the following appeal:

"'Am I my brother's keeper?' asked Cain of the Lord Jehovah. Yes, my sistern and brethren, we are the keepers of our poor unfortunate brethren, and all the trouble that happens to them happens to us too, for we are their brethren."

The Provisional Committee for the Defense of the Scottsboro boys, representing tens of thousands of New Orleans citizens, resulted from this general mass indignation. More money was raised; the Governor was deluged by thousands of telegrams, letters and resolutions from organizations and individuals. One of the most touching activities of this Committee was a specially organized correspondence with the nine lads in prison. Every week different organizations would send letters of encouragement to them. Remarkably enough, as a result of this unified activity among Negroes, all political differences were sunk among the various groups of participants; even personal hostilities were ended for the time being. Once even at a meeting a man, who I knew was a steadfast Republican, rushed toward me and, clasping my hand, said, his eyes shining:

"All for one and one for all!"

Evidently the plan of our racial and class tormentors had miscarried. Instead of dividing and suppressing us, as they had intended, it had the very opposite effect; it only fused us together in a manner that hitherto had seemed impossible.

12

The first All-Southern Conference for the Scottsboro Defense had been called for May 31, 1931, in Chattanooga. Together with three white seamen I was elected a delegate. The Conference was charged with electricity. There were delegates from Alabama, North and South Carolina, Georgia, Tennessee and Kentucky. It was a strange gathering of shabby and undernourished sharecroppers, and of miners and mill workers who fraternized without any self-consciousness with well-dressed white and Negro middle-class liberals and intellectuals. I had never seen anything like that before and thought it to be the eighth wonder of creation. I could well understand white workers taking our part, but for middle-class whites to take an open stand on such matters astonished and heartened me very much.

All the comedy at the Conference as usual was supplied by the Chattanooga Police Department. When it learned that it was to be a "mixed" conference and that leading Communists from the North were to speak, it mobilized its entire force for the occasion. The cops threatened and fumed and tried to browbeat us. We refused to let them provoke us and went through with our business as if they were not there at all. We could see that our scornful indifference riled them very much, but sad experience had made us expert in strategy and as long as they did not attack us bodily we were confident that we could outsmart them.

The leading comrades from the North who addressed the meeting were Robert Minor, Harry Haywood, B. D. Amis and Tom Wilson. I was very much thrilled to hear Minor, who loomed very large in my imagination as a heroic working-class leader. He had just been released from prison for his part in the historic unemployment demonstration in Union Square, New York City, on March 6, 1930, which started as a peaceful gathering, but which was transformed by police clubs and tear gas into a bloody riot. Mr. Minor, in the name of the Communist Party, called on all Negro and white workers to organize and fight for the release of the Scottsboro boys. He pledged the whole-hearted support of the Communist Party, not only for them, but for the self-determination of Negroes in the Black Belt of the South.

"What better proof for the need of self-determination does the Negro people need than this vicious Scottsboro Case?" he asked.

Perhaps the most eloquent address of the meeting was made by B. D. Amis, the Secretary of the League of Struggle for Negro Rights and the Editor of *The Liberator*. He brought both whites and Negroes to their feet cheering loudly when he said in a voice choked with emotion:

"I call upon all Negroes wherever they may be to fight for the lives of the nine Scottsboro boys—to fight with the same might and determination as did Nat Turner, Frederick Douglas and other Negro heroes in the days of slavery."

So great was the enthusiasm and militancy of the audience that the cops looked scared. With their usual obtuseness they imagined that our anger was directed at them. To their surprise and relief they discovered that we had no interest in them at all. Maybe they felt offended by it, because when the Conference adjourned, as Robert Minor, Harry Haywood, B. D. Amis and Tom Wilson were standing in the corridor pleasantly chatting, the police swooped down on them and arrested them. Yes, for blocking traffic! After paying ten-dollar fines, they were released.

13

That same evening William Pickens, the National Field Secretary of the National Association for the Advancement of Colored People, was scheduled to speak at a Negro church in Chattanooga. I would not have missed hearing him for anything in the world. The situation was indeed very dramatic, for Pickens had demanded publicly that something be done about the Scottsboro Case.

At first Pickens uttered red-hot words which warmed the cockles of my heart. He took a very positive stand and pledged himself to do all in his power to help free the Scottsboro boys. But as he went on, his speech grew anemic. It bristled with conditions, qualifications and exceptions. Why was he hedging all of a sudden, I wondered. Then to my great surprise, and I believe to everyone else's, he opened a frontal attack on his audience:

"The trouble with you people is," said he, "that you do not know how to fight. All the noise that you are making with your demonstrations, telegrams and resolutions won't do the Scottsboro boys an ounce of good. It will only prejudice the country against them. If you were really smart people you would give your money to me and let the NAACP lawyers take care of this thing for you."

No sooner had Pickens ended when I jumped to my feet and asked for the floor. Now it happened that the meeting was being held in the church of which the Reverend Bowens was pastor. So he naturally served as chairman. When I asked for the floor he grew angry and rebuked me in true pulpit style, as if I were about to desecrate the altar.

"You can't speak here," he shouted.

Pandemonium broke loose in the audience. A chorus of yells and catcalls greeted the reverend gentleman's rebuke to me. Many called out:

"Let him speak! Let him speak!"

The Reverend Bowens lost his head completely. Pointing a reproving finger at the audience, he said:

"You can't run my church for me! Who paid for it, you or I?"

"You didn't pay for it," said a mocking voice. "The workers paid for it."

The audience rocked with laughter, and Reverend Bowens grew red in the face. Then a friend of mine rose and also demanded the floor.

"Sit down!" bellowed the clergyman.

Suddenly changing his tone, to my surprise, and in a voice dripping honey, he addressed himself to the audience:

"There are two nice-looking young men in the audience who are anxious to speak about something they seem very much interested in. Now they look like good boys to me. I believe they have our blood in them, or don't they? It seems to me they should be given a chance to speak for a few moments. Now, young men, will you be patient and wait until we have taken the collection?"

The strategy of the reverend gentleman seemed clear to us. He readily saw that if we were allowed to talk, the meeting would end in a fight. He, therefore, wanted to play safe and pocket the collection first. However, we decided to do the sporting thing and give him all the advantages. We agreed to await his pleasure.

In the meantime Mr. Pickens thought that retreat was the better part of valor, so he left by the back door. We suddenly noticed Reverend Bowens speaking in excited whispers to a man who then hastened out of the church.

"Smells like foul play," said a friend to me, and, getting up, followed the man out into the street.

He saw him enter a telephone booth and heard him call for the police. As my friend was no weakling, he grabbed the receiver out of the informer's hand and, seizing him by the collar, forced him to return to the church.

The Reverend Bowens, seeing that the meeting was no longer his, compromised with the reality and said to me cajolingly:

"I'll give you one minute's time to speak, young man, but I ask you to be nice, behave yourself respectably and, for heaven's sake, don't start any trouble."

I remember I had grown cold from head to foot. I was so upset emotionally that my voice trembled. Coming immediately to the point I said:

"The trouble with so many of our Negro leaders and with you, too, dear Reverend Bowens, is that you are all a bunch of lickspittles and self-seekers. To please the white lynchers you are ready to go crawling on your bellies and to betray our human dignity and our rights as men. Furthermore . . ."

But at this point my voice was drowned out completely. The most startling thing happened. The Reverend Bowens had decided to turn Napoleon. I admit his strategy, although a little unusual, was superb. What he did was to have about twenty-five "respectables," prominent Negro professionals and pillars of local Negro society, who had been sitting on the platform, come down into the audience, and, forming a circle round me, do an Indian war dance. I was so astonished by the strange performance that I could hardly utter a word. The "Indians" yelled and whooped and yodelled and drowned out my voice completely. Not only this, but they pressed close to me on every side and hid me entirely from view. The whole place was in an uproar.

Finally I fought my way through the circle, and, since I could not finish what I had to say, I threw bunches of leaflets about the Scottsboro boys to the audience, which was clamoring for them.

Then my friend tried to speak. The "Indians" did a war dance around him too. Our efforts were fruitless, for most people hate rowdyism and they hastened out of the hall as soon as they could. However, we were not at all displeased with what we had accomplished that night. We had definitely proven to the Negro people that those whom they regarded as their leaders were morally bankrupt. They now were able to see who really were their true friends.

Late that night I took the train back to Birmingham. I felt so hopeful about finding a solution to the Negro problem that I sang all the way.

TWELVE

SHORTLY AFTERWARD the League of Struggle for Negro Rights convened in St. Louis for its first national convention. The Scottsboro Defense Conference sent delegates to this convention, but I was not among them. More experienced, older and better-known workers were chosen. The decisions of the convention, however, impressed me very much because they were clear-cut and courageous. Such militancy was quite unheard of, for formerly both Negro organizations and white liberal groups had been playing puss-in-the-corner with our tragic problems that cried for energetic action. The League of Struggle for Negro Rights did no hemming and hawing on the burning issue of lynching. Its slogan on this matter rang out like the blow of a sledge hammer:

"Death Penalty to Lynchers!"

It also adopted a bill for Negro rights and for the suppression of lynching. It read in part:

"Be it enacted by the Senate and House of Representatives of the United States of America in Congress assembled that because the rights of the Negro people, although guaranteed by the Constitution of the United States of America, 13th, 14th and 15th Amendments, have been and are being systematically violated, as shown by the denial of rights of citizenship and equality, the denial in many sections of their right to vote, to serve on juries and to enjoy equal rights in the courts of law, the system of peonage and slavery and chain gangs widely practiced in the South, the wholesale frame-ups against innocent Negroes and other such oppressive practices, the fact that during the past fifty years, more than 5,000 lynchings have taken place in the United States and with very little effort on the part of the police and judicial authorities to apprehend or to punish the guilty parties; therefore, it becomes necessary to adopt special measures to suppress the practice of lynching and secure for the Negro people the full and free exercise of complete equal rights as for every other section of the population."

The Communist Party in Birmingham did everything in its power to publicize the decisions of the St. Louis Convention. Its principal aim was to involve as many Negroes as possible in a struggle for their constitutional rights. Nevertheless, we were obliged to practice patience as a virtue. The downright chicanery and selfish class-interest of our Negro demagogues and two-faced leaders made our progress painfully slow. But we felt confident we would win in the end, for humanity and justice were on our side.

2

It seemed as if my life were taking on new importance from day to day. Exciting events crowded in, one upon the other. Nothing was uninteresting, nothing humdrum. Everything had significance and social importance. When I looked back upon the drab monotony of my past life as a miner and contrasted it with the vital and constructive activities of what I was now doing, I first began to realize how far I had traveled. No day passed without something new and dramatic taking place.

It was in June of that year that I received a letter from a Negro clergyman, the Reverend Hamilton of Camden County, Alabama, inviting me to address a meeting of sharecroppers in his church with regard to their organizing a union. I responded to the invitation with enthusiasm and rode down to meet the minister in his little community.

I found him to be a man of substance. He had a big protruding stomach and prosperity oozed out of his every pore. He acted in a very friendly manner, a little too friendly, I thought to myself. With a few well-turned compliments he asked me to speak first to the children in his class. He told me he was the only teacher for Negro children in several counties. Oh, no, it wasn't the money he got from it—he was a big landowner—he loved children and he wished to do something for his Negro brethren. I was somewhat puzzled by the fact that such a large geographic area that was so closely populated with Negroes could boast only one school class. I then realized more fully than I ever did before how backward the South was and how deliberately it aimed to deprive the Negro people of any possibility of education. The Reverend Hamilton told me without any sign of perturbation that the reason his class was so small was because very few Negroes could afford to send their children to school. The distance was far too great to cover. Those children who attended school came only mornings. The rest of the day they broke their little backs picking cotton or doing other manual labor.

I spoke to the children. My heart went out to them. Despite all the sweetness of childhood on their faces, they looked so pinched, so stunted and sickly from neglect and undernourishment, that I felt there was little I could say to them that was proper for their young ears to hear. For I was choked with bitterness and anger at the society which deprived them of their right to health and happiness and to the joys of childhood. I was startled for I found myself talking to a group of little old men of six and of seven and of eight. How well I understood them, I who had never been a child myself!

I commended and thanked the Reverend Hamilton for his interest in his people, especially for the little children. By teaching them, I assured him fervently, he was planting imperishable seed for the liberation of his race. He smiled self-appreciatively and words of eloquence flowed from him in a golden torrent. I was quite overwhelmed by it, for I had never heard anything like it before.

I must confess that his conduct puzzled me. I could not make out what manner of man he was. Everything he said and did sounded false and seemed unreal. Maybe he was trying to take me in? Certainly I was suspicious. How could I be otherwise? My experience with human beings, even with members of my own race, had been very disillusioning. If my own interests were only involved, I probably would have behaved like a lamb, and in my innocence he would have shorn me. But because the interests of poor, underprivileged Negro folk were concerned, all my senses became alert. Danger ahead!

When the Reverend Hamilton introduced me to the meeting of sharecroppers in his church, he let loose the floodgates of his oratory. He seemed inexhaustible and I was becoming impatient. Perhaps I was mistaken, but I thought that punctuating his flattery to me was an ill-concealed sarcasm. He emphasized the "Mister" in Mister Herndon a little too unnecessarily. Whenever he said it he screwed up his eyes and looked cunningly out of their sharp corners, as if to say: Look what I've dished up for you for your evening's entertainment!

I was thoroughly on guard. I spoke cautiously, with great deliberation, and weighed every word I said. The reverend friend of mine was not going to find me napping in case he had something comical up his sleeve. At this point, I must say, that I always find it repugnant to behave in a shrewd manner. Above all things, I have worshipped simplicity and sincerity, and the need to match wits with sly people always makes me groan inwardly. But what else was I to do?

But as I addressed myself to my audience of Negro and white sharecroppers and peered into their faces and read in them such deep suffering and helplessness, I flung all caution to the winds and spoke to them what was on my mind. I assured them that the only possible solution to their problem was complete unity between black and white sharecroppers, in short, a militant union which would fight for the improvement of their lot.

My words awoke only a faint echo in their breasts. Life had been too hard for them. Perhaps I was one jump ahead of them in my ideas? Their misery seemed to be too pressing and immediate to look as far ahead and as searchingly as I did.

When I had finished speaking, they crowded around me and asked me how things were in Birmingham. Did I think they could get jobs there? Why did they wish to leave where they were, I asked. In answer, they told depressing stories about conditions on the farms. The price of cotton had sunk very low. The landlords in their greed were conveniently shifting their burdens upon the half-crushed croppers and tenants. They were hogging all the government loans. One of the croppers said to me with a rueful smile:

"A lot of us have borrowed money from the government to help us along with our work, but we never see any of it. When the mail brings the checks, the postman delivers them directly to the landlords, and that's the last ever heard of them. Into whose pockets they go, I'll let you decide. Well, I thought I was going to write to the government about it, but what the hell is the use? It will only get me into trouble. My landlord would fix me all right because I have no other place to go. So please, Mr. Herndon, as you are an educated man, won't you please help us out and write a letter for us to the President and tell him how we are robbed of our money?"

"Sure," I said, trying hard to sound convincing and reassuring. "Sure, I'll write that letter for you. I'll be glad to do anything I can for you."

It seemed that what my address had failed to do, the informal discussion of the sharecroppers after the meeting, when they poured out to me and to each other their bitterest grievances, succeeded in doing in an infinitely better way. For before leaving the church we drew up a plan for a huge gathering, two weeks later, of all sharecroppers in the surrounding counties. To my agreeable surprise, I observed that the usual apathy of the sharecroppers had now given way to a mild sort of enthusiasm. It brought the heartening reflection to my mind that no matter how crushed and prostrate a man may be he is never entirely without that human dignity and will to improve his lot. I suppose this quality in man can best be described as his capacity for good.

3

One of the sharecroppers volunteered to put me up for the night. When we got home he ransacked the house for some food for us. The poor man turned crimson. He could offer me nothing but coffee. I felt famished and would gladly have gone out to buy myself some food; but what was I going to do, embarrass the man? So I assured him I was not hungry and it really did not matter anyway.

Very hesitantly my host apologized for his poverty; there was not a bed in the house. What difference did it make? I shrugged my shoulders. We could sleep on the mattresses which lay on the floor. So I stretched out in my corner and tried to compose myself to sleep. But my nerves were so overwrought by the events of the day that I could not fall asleep. I lay prone on my back in the darkness, listening to the broken snoring of my host. Poor fellow, he had gone hungry to bed and mercifully found the poor man's principal solace—sleep.

The ceiling of the room was full of big cracks. I looked through them and beyond them and watched the stars tranquil in their crystalline light. All nature seemed to be immersed in devout peace. The frogs croaked their raucous music in a pond near by and the crickets chirped their monotonous evening song. The night lay still in revery about me. Only I felt in discord with the whole plan of the universe. The tragic destiny that was pursuing my fellow-men weighed down my spirit.

The wail of millions of hungry children and of men and women now reached me. I saw the despairing faces of those miserable dumb-driven sharecroppers I had addressed that night. And I now knew that their burden was my burden, that their anguish was my anguish. I knew that henceforth I was to have no peace and no rest until the day of their liberation would come.

The following day, with as good grace as possible, I wriggled out of my host's hospitality, fortunately, without offending him. I got myself a room at the only boarding house in the town. Starved beyond description, I devoured the breakfast my landlady placed before me. It consisted of a baffling kind of stew in which floated some chunky pieces of fat. It tasted like "nine days old." After that I was served some stale biscuits and a cup of coffee that tasted like dish water. I admit I was rash. I had enough of a forewarning of the consequences and I should not have eaten. A half hour later, as I was on my way to visit some sharecroppers, I felt a griping pain in my stomach. I literally began to see red. Before I knew it, I fell unconscious by the roadside. I lay there until a sharecropper came by. He raised me up and half carried me to his house.

4

Suffice it that I did not let grass grow in my tracks. I distributed pamphlets on the Negro question and quietly went about speaking to Negro and white sharecroppers. I proved to them that the only way they could possibly better their wretched conditions was to organize into a union. I was gratified to see that I was planting my seed in the right kind of soil. The response of the sharecroppers was almost child-like in its directness and simplicity.

"What have we to lose?" said one gloomily. "It's far better to be dead than to continue living the way we do."

But the gods of capitalist society were not going to permit my activities to go unchallenged. A trap was being laid for me. They expected that I would be fool enough to walk into it like an obliging fellow. It happened in the following way:

One morning, while I was on my way to meet with some of the sharecroppers, a smooth expensive car slid up beside me.

"Stop!" a familiar voice called out.

I wheeled round and looked at the occupants of the car. I saw a hatchet-faced individual, a Negro, who was a complete stranger to me. But sure enough, next to him sat my old genial friend, the Reverend Hamilton—only now he did not look so genial. In fact, he looked scared and guiltily at me. He blinked his eyes out of sheer nervousness. In the reflection of his expression I saw much trouble brewing for me. So I steeled myself for any eventuality.

"That's him!" The clergyman pointed a short pudgy finger at me. His voice trembled a bit.

I shot at him a questioning, puzzled look.

The strange Negro, glaring rudely at me, then spoke up:

"Young fellow, if you know what's good for you, you will clear out pretty damn fast."

Then showing me his Department of Justice badge, he continued:

"See? I am a government man. I could arrest you if I only wished. And you know damn well what would happen to you in the next fifteen minutes."

Drunk with power, he burst out into an arrogant laugh.

Immediately I saw a vision of a lynch mob, and I grew cold inside of me.

Then bending out of the car toward me, with what I thought was a friendly smile, the detective said to me in an undertone:

"As one Negro to another, who wishes you only good, let

me advise you to get the hell out of here before those white lynchers get wind of what you are doing. They'll get you if you don't."

I regarded him steadily for a moment without saying a word. I saw that he was not altogether bad. The man had a conscience of a sort. So I said to him:

"Mr. Detective, your interest might be with the government, but surely you can t forget that you are also a Negro. How can you stand by and say nothing, do nothing, when your people are chained down to the soil as slaves?"

"What's wrong with our people?" asked the Reverend Hamilton with feigned surprise at my question. He rolled his big cow-like eyes at me as if he thought my question preposterous. "All I know is that I myself am happy and comfortable."

Then turning comical, and mimicking my tone of voice, he said:

"I didn't wake up this morning with chains around my legs. Chains! What are you talking about? The man's crazy!"

The detective became impatient and, turning sternly upon me, said:

"Enough of your gaff, young fellow! If you know what's good for you, you'll leave the county immediately."

With these words he started his car and rode off.

All the indignation that I was capable of welled up in me at this display of ruling-class violence. Should I allow myself to be intimidated by brute force? Could I successfully pit my sense of right and my free intelligence against all the brutal forces of capitalist society? Fortunately, I was not left undecided for long. My mind was being made up for me at the moment by others over whom I had no control. A white sharecropper, a meek, crushed soul, with sad haunted eyes, rattled up in an old flivver. Breathlessly, he said to me:

"For God's sake, get out of here as soon as you can! The landlords are organizing a lynch mob over there, ten miles yonder. Here's some money. Take the next train out. It's the only one that stops at this station today. I reckon it'll be around in about two hours. Here's hoping that your train will come faster than the lynch mob."

Reaching out his hand, he clasped mine and said hurriedly:

"Good-bye and good luck, brother. We'll do what we can to continue your good work here. God bless you." *

5

I sat down on a log near a railroad shed and tried to compose my nerves, which were slightly shaken by this time. These last few years I had been mentally preparing myself for just such an emergency as this. I fully realized that my good friend, the sharecropper, was correct in his advice. My only chance of escape was to board the train. If I tried to run away or hide myself in the woods they would be sure to call out their bloodhounds and start a man-hunt for me. I had to be reasonable. Constantly I kept on repeating to myself the magic words:

"I must not lose my head! I must not lose my head!"

Instead I grew strangely calm. I recalled with considerable comfort a story by Tolstoy, which I had but recently read, about a young revolutionary in Czarist Russia mounting the scaffold with smiling face, and as the noose was tied around his neck, his face began to radiate like the sun. Tolstoy was lost

* My visit marked the beginning of a militant struggle of the sharecroppers against the landlords. Several months later the latter organized a lynch mob to square accounts with their rebellious tenants. While the croppers were meeting in the woods at Reeltown to protest against the landlords' punitive decision to deprive them of food allotments, the posse attacked without warning and fired pointblank into the crowd. Many croppers were killed that day and a large number wounded. A sad commentary on the treacherous conduct of our Negro "respectables" was the surrender to the lynchers by Dr. Moton, the former Principal of Tuskegee Institute, of one badly wounded cropper who had sought refuge at the Negro institution. He was later put in prison and, being denied medical aid, died of his wounds in solitary confinement.

in wonder contemplating this serene approach to death. What was it which made the revolutionary go to his death so joyously? The author answered his own question:

"It was his abiding faith that lent him the necessary strength —faith, that by his death he was serving mankind."

Funny, but I too began to feel like that revolutionary in Tolstoy's story! What if I had only two more hours to live—what if after that time I was to be dragged by a lynch mob howling like a pack of wolves to the woods, there to be stripped, to be beaten, to be tarred and feathered, to be tortured and mutilated until my body lay still? What if they did? The possibility of such a fate brought to me neither dread nor despair. Instead there passed before my mind's eye, the grave strong faces of Robert Minor, B. D. Amis and other fighters for the working class. The mere thought of them suffused my heart with a warm glow. I was not alone! Everywhere—everywhere where there was suffering, persecution and exploitation there were men like myself, thousands upon thousands of them, fighting resolutely for a new world order. And if I died, all these, my brothers everywhere, would pick up the loose threads of my unfinished labors and continue the advance to ultimate triumph. I felt sure my life had not been wasted. Few though my years may have been, I had succeeded in crowding them with significance and beauty, not outward beauty, for my worldly condition was wretched and drab, but with an inner beauty, a moral grandeur of which no exploiter could rob me, which gave me strength to sing defiantly in adversity and which now left me tranquil in the face of possible death.

5

I was still sitting on the log by the railroad tool shed. The sun was setting, when a Negro cropper riding furiously on a horse came roaring into the station enclosure. Seeing me, he bulged his eyes in amazement and cried out:

"They're coming, they're coming!"

"Who's coming?" I asked, smiling.

"Why, you blasted fool, the lynchers are coming for you."

"So what am I to do? Would you like me to hide under your bed?"

He looked at me as if I were mad and rode off shaking his head in great disapproval.

I never felt so sane in all my life!

The train finally rumbled in and I boarded it with a feeling of immense relief. The snapping of the tension under which I labored brought me into a state of happy lunacy. For, as I was hoisting myself into the car, I broke into that absurd stuttering war song, popular among our soldiers during the World War:

"K-k-k-Katie, beautiful Katie."

My jolly mood, unfortunately, did not last very long. For no sooner had I stepped into the coach when I was transfixed by forty pairs of hostile white eyes. I was the only Negro on the train. I could understand the excitement of the white passengers. But rarely were they privileged to see a Negro sharecropper on a passenger train. It goes without saying that if a sharecropper has no money for food, he will hardly indulge himself in the luxury of riding a passenger train. What if an emergency arises when he is obliged to travel? Then he will trudge the highway in his bare feet until they blister and he is ready to drop from fatigue.

When the train pulled into Selma, our first stop, I noticed on the station stands a local newspaper bearing a shrieking headline across the front page:

MULATTO NEGRO STIRS UP TROUBLE BETWEEN WHITES AND BLACKS IN GOVERNOR MILLER'S HOME TOWN

I bought a copy of the newspaper and as I had to wait for the Birmingham train, I decided to take a walk across town. I was afraid that I would be recognized if I exposed myself too prominently in such a public place as the railroad station.

The streets of Selma were choked with people. Along every road that led into the town flowed a stream of sharecroppers, come to do their shopping. They came in ox-carts. They came on horseback, on rusty bicycles, on rickety, ramshackle wagons. What a depressing sight it was! Hungry, cadaverous faces, hunched backs and consumptive chests, inflamed eyes and dragging feet. Worse to look upon were the children. Stunted, ragged and prematurely old, with spindly legs and swollen stomachs. Going to town was no mean event in their lives. They came only several times a year. With a joyless sort of pleasure, the children scampered through the streets holding on for dear life to their parents' hands and licking greedily away at ice-cream cones and huge red sticks of candy.

No sharecropper regards his expedition to town complete if in a final flourish of celebration he does not buy himself a cheap, rank cigar that costs five for a nickel. He puffs away at it with unsmiling gravity. On one street corner in Selma I heard one sharecropper grow highfalutin and recite a poem of his own creation as he blew smoke rings from his penny cee-ga-r:

Cee-ga-rs come but once a year
And when they come
They bring good chee-ar.

Another cropper standing near by winked an inflamed eye at me.

"That's our sharecropper poet-to-be," he kidded him good-naturedly.

I felt a painful constriction around my heart as I watched them in their "happiness." Poor children of my race! How long would they remain content to continue in their blindness? When were they going to discover the true nature of their oppression and the identity of their oppressors? Sentimental? Yes, I was being sentimental. Anyone with red blood in his veins, with a mind that reflects and a heart that feels cannot possibly watch the utter degradation and wretchedness of his fellow-beings without becoming incensed and embattled. It is true that at the moment I was intent with all my senses and wits to save my own hide from the white lynchers. Yet when I looked upon the human misery that passed in procession before my eyes all thought of my own danger disappeared.

A deep graveness fell upon my spirit. There was a throb in my heart and a tightening in my throat. I felt that that moment was one of the most solemn in all my experience. The sharecroppers before me became a living symbol of my life purpose. That day, standing before a cigar store on a street in Selma whose name I have forgotten, I re-consecrated myself to the complete social and economic liberation of my people. Moved by the ideas that came to me I scrawled the following few words on a postcard to a friend up North:

"Now, more than ever, I am fully convinced that my people will be free only when they themselves will rise from their centuries-old sleep and strike a mighty blow against the system which is destroying them."

Again the train whistle shrilled its disturbing music into the night air. I sat in a corner of the car buried in my own thoughts and marveling over the strange turns of human destiny. Faster and faster the train sped on, continuing its memorable ride, carrying me back into the world I knew—to enjoy what I in self-irony called the pursuit of life, liberty and even greater unhappiness than hitherto.

THIRTEEN

THE TRAIN PULLED into Birmingham station. But no sooner had I alighted when I walked straight into the loving arms of two police officers. They gave me a mock welcome, as if I had been a long-lost brother to them.

"Well, well—if this isn't dear old Angelo himself! How are yah, boy? We sure did miss yah for a long time! But now we'll see to it that we won't be lonesome for yah any more. The warden in jail will sho' give yah a big hand when yah come back."

The two policemen chuckled with delight over their little joke.

I looked at them with unseeing eyes. I smiled inwardly, for I knew that they, their cruelty and their legalized vengeance could never reach me.

Joking all the way, the detectives led me to the police station. For two interminable hours they gave me a verbal third degree. I was amazed at the ignorance and stupidity of the questions they put to me. One burly cop, who seemed to take great pride in his wide knowledge of political affairs, looked sternly at me as he popped the following question:

"Now, *Mister Herndon*, as you no doubt are on the executive committee of the Comm-u-nist Party of America, a big shot, by crackey! perhaps you'll tell us when that Rooshian Jew agitator Laynine is coming here to organize the steel mills?"

For a moment I was nonplussed. My hesitation received an odd interpretation from the detectives. They looked triumphantly at me and admiringly at their clever, learned friend who knew everything—as if to say: "Now you've got him in a tight corner all right."

"Well, why don't you answer?" prodded my interrogator. "When is Laynine coming?"

I scratched my head reflectively and replied:

"On Resurrection Day."

The detectives looked black as thunder.

"Stop your fooling, nigger!"

"I'm sorry, but I can't make him come before—he's been dead for seven years."

The intellectual detective turned red with self-consciousness and, trying to cover up his embarrassment before the others, made a gesture as if he were going to strike me, but finally thought the better of it.

I was released. As I left the station a detective called after me:

"Think you're a wise guy, eh? Wait, we'll get yah yet, dagnab it!"

2

The following day the Communist Party held a meeting in the Negro section of the town. Two white workers were present. But no sooner had the meeting gotten under way when we heard a terrific uproar outside. Someone looking out of the window saw uniformed and plain-clothes policemen piling out of seven large police cars.

"Well, we are in for it now!" cried the chairman with grim humor. "Now, all of you comrades will please sit down and keep perfectly calm. There's no earthly use in trying to escape. The building is surrounded on every side."

However, what seemed to worry all of us Negroes most

was the presence of the two white workers. We understood that they were in greater danger than we, for if Southern "gentlemen" hate "niggers," they hate even more what they call "nigger lovers." Foolhardy as it may have been, since nothing else could have been done, we advised the white workers to hide, and the rest of us were to await calmly the consequences of the raid.

One of the white workers slid under the mattress of a cot in a corner; the other shut himself in a closet. Despite the gravity of the situation the absurd humor of it did not escape any of us. As we heard the police pounding up the stairway in full gallop, one of our Negro comrades who was a little bit of a wag bawled through the closet keyhole in a simulated feminine voice to the concealed white worker:

"For Gawd's sake, hide! I hear my husband coming up the stairs—and I hate to think what he's going to do to you."

Just as he finished speaking, the door was flung open and the detectives and policemen with drawn guns piled in. As we were still laughing over the ridiculous piece of horse play with which we were being entertained, the head of the raiding party shouted:

"Wipe that laugh off your face, you —— What in hell is so funny about this?"

Then, spotting me, he said:

"Well, well, look who's here, the nigger who thinks he's as good as a white man! Say, did I tell you, or didn't I, that you were to leave this town? You seem to think we're just playing a game of peek-a-boo with you. Answer me, what the hell are you still doing here?"

"That's none of your business!" I answered. "As a citizen of the United States I have a right to come and go wherever and whenever I please."

My retort made some of the detectives laugh.

"Nigger a citizen! Phooey!"

Everybody laughed.

But the head of the raiding party lost his temper and cried out:

"You God-damn black yellow Red!"

With his heavy hob-nailed shoes he aimed a kick at my stomach. But I dodged, and instead I received the blow on the calf of my left leg.

"I didn't hurt you, did I?" asked my assailant with feigned solicitude.

I was writhing with pain. I made no reply.

"Why don't you answer, nigger? A white man is talking to you. Answer!"

But I sealed my lips tight and looked down at the floor. One of the detectives then pressed the burning end of a cigar against my neck. I stifled a cry of pain.

"Answer, or I will break your dirty black neck, you —."

Fortunately for me, at that moment one of the raiders had sat down on the bed and a look of amazement came over his face. He jumped to his feet and began examining the bed.

"Something is funny about this bed! It poked me in my — when I sat down."

Then, lifting the mattress, he discovered the already half-stifled white worker. Despite the fright that we all experienced, the scene was so comical that we shook with laughter. Then began a systematic search of the house. They found the other white worker in the closet and handled him very roughly. The two white workers were finally handcuffed and shoved into a corner. They next tied us all up with a long thick steel chain and led us off to jail.

It would be difficult for one who did not see us to imagine the weird spectacle we made as we staggered along in caterpillar fashion through the principal streets of Birmingham. People everywhere stopped either to gape or to taunt us. I had a curious mental association as I listened to the jeering crowd. Their eyes were filled with bitter mockery and hatred.

"Christ jeered by the hoodlums of Jerusalem as he dragged his cross to be crucified on Golgotha," I thought with a shudder.

At the police station we went through a grueling examination. They tried to pin down on us some technical infraction of the law. But they could find nothing against us.

"Too bad I can't make a public example of you Reds, Russians, Jews, and niggers," said the Police Commissioner. "That God-damn Legislature of ours—it won't enact the criminal-anarchy law I recommended against you bastards! If it were up to me alone I wouldn't be treating you as leniently as the courts do. Trials should be only for Americans and not for such Red trash as you. You've been agitating far too much and stirring up trouble among our steel workers and coal miners. If I had my own way about it I'd line you all up against the wall and shoot you down like dogs."

We were all released. But as we left the station-house we were filled with forebodings. We saw dark storm clouds gathering over Birmingham. In all these police persecutions and provocations we recognized the hand of the industrial bosses of the city. We workers were all of one opinion: The war was on and our bosses would not rest until they succeeded in crushing our revolt. They were going to stop at nothing to achieve this end. They would pass laws that would hound us from pillar to post. They would blacklist us so that we and our families could not live. They would blight our lives and those of our wives, children, mothers, fathers, sisters and brothers. And where the law would be insufficient to aid them, they would take extra-legal measures. They would fan into flame the ever-serviceable lynch spirit and hang our mutilated bodies on the limbs of trees by the wayside to terrorize our class brothers and to discourage disobedience to property and governmental authority.

I walked home with dragging feet and a heavy heart. I fully understood the nature of the terrors that lay ahead of the working class in Birmingham.

FOURTEEN

To THE CHRONICLER of our times, August 3, 1931, will go down as marking one of the most tragic events for American Negroes. That day three white girls were shot in Shades Valley, an exclusive white suburb of Birmingham. The shooting occasioned tremendous excitement throughout the city, which buzzed with all sorts of rumors. No one knew who the shooters were. Therefore the wildest speculations were concocted. It stands to reason that the criminals would be only—Negroes. Who else but Negroes were criminals? The lily-white myth of Nordic virtue had somehow to be sustained.

Quite by accident it happened that that day I was forty miles away from Birmingham, organizing coal miners. When I returned home I found that my house had been broken in. The furniture had been smashed with an unnecessary brutality. Every bit of printed matter I possessed had been thrown out of the window. Passers-by had trampled on my beloved books that I had purchased with my hard-earned pennies. I almost wept when I saw my precious copy of Lenin's *What Is to Be Done?* lying half torn and soiled in the gutter. It was as if an old friend had been mutilated and wounded by unmentionable degenerates. That single book for the moment took on the symbolic character of all culture and enlightenment, and what the vandals had done to it represented to me all that was evil, dark and of the jungle.

No sooner had I entered my home when friends arrived

hurriedly to warn me against remaining there. They assured me that I would be arrested, for the police were determined to "get me" by hook or by crook.

"And if someone shoots someone in Oskaloosa, I suppose Angelo Herndon did it while the same Angelo Herndon was in Chicago playing the piano." I attempted to deride their absurd fears and reasoning.

That crazy I did not believe even the police could be.

However, it turned out that they were that crazy. But there was a system to their madness. And come to think of it, it really was not so mad after all—only brazenly unscrupulous and corrupt.

Early that morning as I lay fast asleep I was awakened by a furious knocking on the door. Startled, I sat up in bed and saw the dark shadow of a policeman in the window.

"There is no need of your coming into decent folks' homes through their bedroom windows when you can come through their doors," I remarked angrily.

"Stick 'em up!" commanded the detective. "We've got you this time, you ——."

The detective climbed through the window and ordered me and my hosts out of bed. For mystifying reasons he demanded that we show him all our clothes, and choosing those that pleased his fancy he ordered us into them. Then he handcuffed us and for good measure kicked us in the shins.

My friend's mother came running into the room and demanded to know why we were being arrested.

"Shut up, you nigger wench!" the detective bellowed, and began pummeling her with the heavy butt of his gun.

We raged and we fumed, we exhorted and we threatened that he let the poor old woman alone. The detective laughed spitefully. He seemed to be getting a great deal of pleasure out of beating up "niggers." We looked on, powerless to do anything, handcuffed and tied to each other.

2

The police drove us to the Birmingham County Jail. When we arrived there we were informed that we were being held as suspects in the shooting of the three white girls. Now I realized how naïve I had been in believing that the police, corrupt and brutal as they were, were still incapable of doing certain things.

That morning about 9 o'clock the fun began. We were led out of our cells and conducted into a large room. There we were put through the third degree by a group of hard-faced detectives. Across the table from where I sat, a detective with a rubber hose in his hand glared at me. The hatred with which he regarded me made me sick to my stomach. The violence that lies in a brutal face often is as painful as a physical blow. To cow me, he began playing a game of cat and mouse with me. Several times he told me:

"I'd like nothing better than to put my two hands around your dirty little black neck and choke the damn life out of you."

Each time I refused to say "Yes, sir," or "No, sir," he struck me violently across the head with the rubber hose, shouting in a bestial voice:

"You black ——! We are real white men and you've got to say 'Yes, sir' and 'No, sir' to us, or else . . ."

Again the rubber hose swung and I bit my lips to stifle a cry of pain. Whatever was going to happen I was determined not to give my tormentors the satisfaction of betraying any sign of pain under their brutality.

To all their persistent questioning I kept a stubborn silence.

Then they cooked up another plan. They led me out of the jail and into a waiting automobile. After driving to a place about twenty-one miles out in the woods, the car suddenly stopped. One of the detectives, while shoving me out, asked me in a significant tone of voice whether I had my thinking cap on.

"For what?"

"You'll find out damn soon."

The detectives held a consultation. One suggested that I be chained to a tree. Another thought that my handcuffs should be taken off. It was as clear as daylight to me that I was in for an eventful beating. Would I emerge out of the incident alive, I wondered.

They finally decided to chain me, handcuffed, to a tree. I offered no resistance. Mentally I had made my peace with the situation. The whole thing was inevitable and beyond my control. It would have been in vain to struggle. I had only one devout hope: that they would beat me fast and get through with it. Would I get through with it, I wondered.

"I will get through with it!"

I almost shouted within me:

Their leader finally began to address me:

"Now, listen here, Angelo Herndon. We don't give a hoot and damn about your little old Communist Party. You can take it and—— What we want to know is: Who shot Nell Williams and the other two white girls? If you didn't do it yourself you know damn well who did. Now come across and pipe up or else you won't leave here alive."

In as calm a voice as possible, I answered:

"I know nothing about the shooting. I have nothing to confess."

"Oh, you don't, don't you!" shouted the leader. And turning to the others he commanded:

"Beat the hell out of him!"

Two of the detectives pulled off their coats and rolled up their sleeves. One of them drew a piece of rubber hose which he had concealed in one of his trouser legs. He began to beat me across the head. The first blow he struck almost knocked me unconscious. As I struggled instinctively to ward off the blows, I strained hard on my steel handcuffs. They cut deep gashes into both wrists until they bled. Every time the rubber hose swished through the air my heart leaped up in anguish. Down, down it came like a great sharp steel knife, slashing vengefully to reach my brain and crush my skull.

Rightfully they understood that the seat of my resistance was in the brain. So if they could only batter their way in and punish it for its defiance they would at last make me do their will.

I felt that my eyes were bloodshot. Foam and blood were flowing from my lips. There was a roaring sound in my ears, as if all the winds in the universe had gathered to shriek their fury into them. From a very great distance, it seemed to me, I heard one of the detectives say:

"You God-damn Reds aren't supposed to tell anything. You think you are smart, don't you? Well, before you leave here you are going to tell plenty, you dirty ——."

There now buzzed in my ears the shouting of many voices. The detectives, carried away by the sight of blood and brutality, went wild. They shouted in unearthly voices their encouragement to the detective who was beating me:

"Come on, John! Kill the dirty nigger! Smash his skull! Knock his brains out and make him eat 'em!"

But that same brain that they tried to bash in offered mighty resistance. Inside of me I was strangely calm and collected, although physically I was on the verge of collapse. Every time I felt faint my brain issued its imperious command to the body:

"You are not going to faint! You're going to survive! There's still a lot you can do. The working class needs you! You're now fighting in its defense. You are being beaten for its sake. You will survive for its sake, to see and to rejoice in its triumph!"

A most extraordinary thing happened. If anyone were to have told me before that such a thing was possible, I would not have believed him. As the flogging continued, at the time when I suffered the greatest physical torture, there suddenly flashed across my mind, like on a movie screen, the faces of Karl Marx and Frederick Engels, of Stalin, of Lenin, of Bob Minor and B. D. Amis, and of innumerable comrades in the workers' movement whom I had learned to love and to believe in. Now, in my hour of greatest need, they appeared to me in spirit to aid me. They were the source of my strength and my consolation. They would sustain me through the terrible ordeal inflicted upon me.

My mind seemed to have become full of light. My will was as firm as steel.

"Beat on! Beat on! Miserable creatures! Beat my body, but you cannot reach my mind!" I challenged defiantly inside of me.

It must have been a half hour that the first detective had been beating me. By that time he was utterly exhausted and wringing wet with perspiration. He had been striking me with all his might, and yet to his chagrin and that of the others, I was still standing up under the rain of his blows. In anger he bent over me and almost snarled in my face like a wild beast:

"So, you think I can't hurt you enough to holler? Well, I am going down into the woods and I am going to get good and mad there and then come back, and so help me God if I won't lynch you with my own hands!"

The other detective then picked up the hose and brought it down on me with all his might. His face was purple with rage and determination, and as I looked helplessly at him with my own blood half blinding my eyes, I gasped through my clenched teeth:

"Stop beating me! If you have to kill me, shoot me! Don't torment me this way!"

"Shooting would be too good for a black dog like you! We'll take it out of your hide for sure this time!" answered the leader.

Beyond that stage my memory is dim. The rubber hose rose and fell with a hiss, rose and fell again in tireless monotony. I no longer listened nor heard what my tormentors were saying.

By the time my second tormentor was worn and wilted because of his exertions, the other detectives had tired of the whole business. I was unchained from the tree and half-unconscious I was flung into the car.

All the way back to the jail they kicked and pummeled me. They threatened me with lynching and with perpetual beating for a whole week unless I confessed that I had shot the three white girls. They then locked me up in a filthy solitary confinement cell without water or food or a mattress to sleep on.

Huddled on the floor of my cell I fell into a sickly slumber, terribly ill in body and in mind. My nightmare experience had taken all the spirit out of me. I slept like one dead.

3

I awoke the next morning feeling ill and in great pain. My head was terribly swollen. My ears were in shreds—mere lumps of raw, bleeding flesh. My eyes must have been terrible to look at. They smarted very much. I had a funny sensation that they were going to drop out of their sockets. I tried to lie quietly and to compose my shattered nerves, for something told me that I was in for a lot more torture.

That same morning the detectives came to my cell. They asked me if I was ready to confess—else I would be taken to the woods again.

"You know what a terrible beating you got yesterday. How did it feel? Fine? Well, today we'll make it ten times as painful. Now be a good fellow and tell us what you have to say."

"I've told you everything I could tell you. I've nothing more to say," I answered firmly.

They then took me out into the jail yard for further questioning. One said to me:

"We have all the evidence on you that we want. We know definitely that you shot the girls. For this we are going to make you fry in the electric chair, just as we will those nine Scottsboro niggers. But if you will co-operate with us and tell us what you know about the other two niggers who did the shooting with you, we will make it easy for you."

To this I replied that I knew nothing about the shooting nor about accomplices and that there was no use their trying to extract any information from me because I had nothing to give them.

They next tried a new line of strategy. One of them, a shrewd look in his eyes, said to me with feigned friendliness:

"Well, Angelo, I don't see why you should want to shield those two niggers. You can bet your sweet life they didn't have any mercy on you yesterday. We took them out last night into the woods, the same as we did to you. And after we beat the hell out of them they opened up and squawked. They told us everything, Angelo, and it's no use of you pretending any further. They even told us where to find the gun with which you did the shooting. Here it is. Do you recognize it?"

With a sneer on his lips, he held up the gun before me. I shook my head in the negative. To all their other questions I refused to make answer.

At their wits' end they decided to lock me up again.

On the way to my cell we met with a Negro prisoner. He

carried a butcher knife in his hand. One of the detectives stopped him with the words:

"See this nigger here—won't you kill him for us if we ask you to?"

"Yassuh, boss, sure I'll kill him if you wants me to. Just say the word."

There was a look of insane glee in the Negro prisoner's eyes. I could see that he meant every word he said, and I broke into a cold sweat.

"Go ahead—cut his throat!" said the detective, grinning.

The Negro then started toward me, and while the detectives held my arms he gave me a terrific blow on the jaw. My teeth rattled. I was afraid that this time it was going to be the end. But one of the detectives intervened, saying:

"Leave this poor nigger alone, Bill. Spare him this time. Next time we'll let you make beef steak out of him, only you will have to fatten him up a bit. He's nothing but ribs now."

The Negro replied:

"Yassuh, boss, I'll kill him whenever you likes. Just tell me when."

They finally locked me up in my bare cell and left me to my own sad thoughts.

I grieved deeply to think that one of my own race, a victim of the same relentless persecution, should have taken part in the bestial torture inflicted on me by the bloodhounds of capitalist law and order. I could have wept for shame. To that extent had our white oppressors succeeded in degrading the weaker members of my people, so that the mark of Cain was on their heads in fratricidal cruelty.

4

At four o'clock that afternoon the turnkey unlocked my cell door and rudely dragged me with him to the pen where the prisoners received visitors. There, to my surprise, I saw the two friends who had been arrested with me. Immediately as I clapped eyes on them I saw that something was very wrong. They looked bitterly reproachful at me. They asked me:

"Why did you lie about our shooting those three white girls? We are terribly surprised at you, Angelo. We were your friends and trusted you, and look what you've done now! You've gone and betrayed us to those white butchers, so that now we'll have to die or be lynched for a crime we never committed."

Tears of deep grief came into my eyes at the thought that my friends should have harbored such wicked ideas about me. In a faltering voice I implored them not to judge me until I had explained everything.

I said to them: "Believe me, boys, I know how you feel. I know you think that I told the detectives that you shot the girls to save my own hide. But that's just another one of their old stupid tricks."

My friends laughed with relief. Not that my explanation in any way diminished their danger, but to decent men there is nothing so horrifying as the experience of being betrayed by one whom they have trusted. My comrades seemed to have had the same experience as I. The detectives assured them that I had confessed their guilt in the shooting. They suspected a trap and refused to speak. It was very comical and extremely touching the way we apologized to one another. The fact that we could ever have doubted each other was a source of genuine shame to us. We clasped hands silently. In that simple act we expressed to one another all the determination to fight on to the bitter end against our wily persecutors, united as one man.

5

They locked us up again in our cells. We awaited the uncertainty of the future with deep anxiety.

Sadly enough the events of the following days fully justified our fears. A reign of terror against all Negroes was begun by the city authorities at the instigation of the coal and steel magnates. The yellow press of Birmingham wished to make out of the shooting incident a sinister conspiracy by "bad" Negroes, corrupted by foreign Reds and Jews, to overthrow white rule of the South.

A threat hung over the Negro sections of the town like a pall. Negroes dared not show their faces on the streets. They hid in their houses, scared beyond words, their doors and windows tightly shut and barred against any possible attackers. Not only were the streets deserted by Negroes, but the houses gave the impression that no one lived in them. No Negro dared make a sound, for fear of attracting the attention of the white hoodlums, the vigilantes and the American Legionnaires who prowled through the streets like beasts of prey with shotguns and revolvers in their hands. Negro mothers sternly hushed their babies when they cried. The sinister word "lynch" was heard in tragic whispers on every side. Few Negroes slept during those eventful days and nights. They waited, waited with bated breath and constricted hearts for something terrible to happen. And it did happen, day after day, night after night. The news of these tragic happenings even penetrated to us through the thick prison walls. Our white turnkeys regarded us with a fat smile on their lips. My own turnkey, a muscular brute with a bullet-shaped head and a voice like a rip saw, took delight in taunting me through the bars whenever he passed by.

"I suppose you feel sorry for yourself for being in jail, you dumb, conceited nigger! Let me tell you it's your good luck that you're behind these bars. There won't be a nigger alive in Birmingham by the time the people in town get through with them."

My blood congealed in my veins, and flinging myself down in my corner, I gave vent to my despair. I raged at my helplessness. Outside, infuriated lynch mobs were massacring my people. I should have been outside, a free man, organizing resistance, but here was I, tucked away in a hole where I could only wring my hands. I recall those days of agony with the deepest shudderings. I remember that when the first news of lynchings in the town reached me I turned my face to the wall and wept. But later I got command of myself again. I said to myself in stern reproof: "Tears are not for Communists. They only weaken one. I must be strong and patiently await the opportunity to re-enter the battle for my class and people."

The lynch mobs rushed through the streets in the Negro sections of the towns like maniacs. They smashed all windows and even broke into houses on the slightest pretexts and dragged out the people who lived in them, either to beat them up, to drag them off to jail or to lynch them in a wild, murderous frenzy. The jails were choked with the hundreds of Negroes taken into custody. The coal and steel companies made a thorough job of it. They inspired the police to arrest every man that had been active in union work. If proof were needed that the orgy of lynching of Negroes was only a blind stimulated by the industrial robber barons to break up the labor unions, both black and white, it was to be found in the fact that all white labor organizers as well were seized, brutally beaten and flung into jail.

6

Beginning with August 3, the bloody reign of terror raged in Birmingham for a full month. Seventy Negroes of both sexes paid with their lives. Blood and more blood was demanded by the white butchers. No one in the South ever saw so much Negro blood flow. It seemed as if white Protestant churchgoers, who sang with piety "What a friend we have in Jesus" on every occasion, now tarred and feathered Negroes and roasted them alive over the scorching flames. And every moan and groan of the crucified Negro martyrs aroused in them neither human compassion nor shame. The lynchers went wild in a convulsion of bestiality. They howled with glee and, going insane, burst into a perfect frenzy of obscenity. Having worked themselves up into this state of excitement, they next clamored for the emasculation of their victims. Like high priests officiating at some unmentionable rite, the mob leaders, with flashing knives, flung themselves upon the tortured Negroes and with blood-curdling howls ripped out their bleeding genitals. These they carried off as souvenirs to display boastfully before their wives and children and friends. . . .

To the eternal shame of Christian America let it be said: These criminal exhibitions were held up before white children as lessons in white superiority, thus hardening their innocent young hearts with all the cruelties of the jungle pit, thus continuing in perpetuity the tradition of lynching and criminal bestiality. Thousands of white school children would stand spellbound watching the ghoulish proceedings and in their shrill trebles shouting their approval as their elders, finally, tiring of their work of mutilation, poured gasoline on the inert bodies and set fire to them. They blazed merrily, those poor tired men-children, no more able to moan their anguish to unheeding ears. They burnt and with them blazed in my own soul a terrible hatred of these lynchers. This hatred I know is going to be a torch to me for all the days of my life, never to relinquish my efforts until all lynchers are brought to justice and until the system that breeds such horrors is destroyed.

7

It so happened that several days after the shooting, two of the girls died from their wounds. The third, Nell Williams, received only flesh wounds and almost immediately was up and about. One afternoon, after having been locked up for several days, prison guards unlocked our cells and told us to follow them. As we entered the visitors' pen, we noticed two detectives talking to a woman. Her face and figure were indistinct as she was standing in the shadow of a steel-framed door. However, we did hear them say something to her. Apparently they were coaching her to say "yes." But it seems that this girl, whom we later discovered to be Nell Williams, had her mind made up on the subject; she shook her head in the negative.

Our mental relief was indescribable, for, to tell the truth, the public hysteria was such that we were prepared to get the electric chair. Yet we knew that we were not through with the messy business, for the lynchers were still there and our acquittal might so anger them that there was a likelihood that they would storm the jail and mete out "justice" to us in one-hundred-per-cent American style—a style draped in the stars and stripes and holding a Bible in its blood-stained hand.

As soon as the murder charge was dropped, the authorities put their wise heads together and frantically began looking for another charge against us. For brave-hearted people there is always a way wherever there is a will. So they finally cooked up a vagrancy charge against us.

8

The shooting drama of the three white girls had a very strange aftermath. I boil with rage every time I think of it, for it represents in my opinion the lowest degree of moral depravity of which the human animal is capable. In all history concerning persecuted and minority peoples there have always been individuals and even classes who, in order to curry favor with the powers that be, sink to the moral level of insects. They act as informers on their own people, as detestable lickspittles, and as social climbers suffering from the irresistible itch of being regarded, if not as the equals of the ruling class, certainly as superior and as a class apart from the rabble of their own race.

A few months after my release, the pillars of Negro society in Birmingham, the "upper crust" of successful doctors with big practices, of heaven-storming clergymen and of obsequious school teachers with a shine on their shoes, and of petty businessmen who puffed away at five-cent cigars and spoke with great excitement about high protective tariffs, of "we, the people," of liberty and of the merits of Hoover—well, these solid citizens got together one day and decided that once and for all they must disassociate themselves from their wretched racial brothers who were charged with such abominable crimes as shooting white girls. The symbolic act of this privileged group was to offer a reward of $3,000, jointly with the authorities, for the capture of the Negro shooter.

The speed with which they fell over themselves in admitting that the murderer was a Negro, although there was not the slightest evidence to prove it except the vague and confused contention of Nell Williams, only published abroad their pathetic spinelessness. In reality what did they expect to accomplish with the apprehension of the "Negro" murderer? Could it be anything else than to save their own wretched carcasses, their own cheap goods and little piles from the lynch mobs and looting white hoodlums? By helping to raise the hue and cry in the man-hunt, they hoped to divert from themselves the suspicion as well as the hostility of their white lords and masters. When the history of the Negro people will be written years later, after racial persecution and prejudice shall have been wiped off the face of the earth, these "Uncle Toms," these detractors of their people, shall receive the due reward which their infamy and betrayal have earned for them.

The announcement that there was going to be a reward of $3,000 let loose the filthiest orgy of greed among the people. The man-hunt was on in earnest now—a young fortune was to be gained. Was the murderer caught? Why, every Negro who had the misfortune of being tall, slim and brown was seized by the good citizens of Birmingham by the seat of his trousers and by the nape of his neck and dragged off in triumph to be placed in the welcoming hands of the authorities. What would not one do for $3,000? Even drag one's fellowman to the slaughter house!

Many Negroes in Birmingham can now recall with rising anger the price in bruises, in mauling and in mental anguish they were forced to pay for the "civic virtue" of the Negro Businessmen's League and of the Negro "respectables" when they offered the bait of money to informers with a love of gold.

As a climactic end to the tragedy came the arrest of Willie Peterson, a Negro World War veteran. He was "recognized" by Nell Williams as she was motoring down the street. She identified him with the utmost certainty, but all that she had to go by was the fact that his hat looked familiar. Poor Willie Peterson was exasperated by the nature of this identification. He argued that there must have been at least ten million Americans wearing his kind of head covering—a soft gray felt hat. But no one was influenced by this obviously logical statement.

No sooner had he been jailed when, with the permission of the authorities, he was visited by Dent Williams, Nell's brother. In the most cold-blooded manner, the latter shot the prisoner. Not only was the would-be assassin freed without trial for his murderous attempt, but he was played up by the press as a hero and protector of white womanly virtue.

The National Association for the Advancement of Colored People secured Mr. Adams, of a well-known firm of lawyers in Birmingham, to defend Peterson. In this case there was more than a grain of truth in the old saying: "O Lord, protect me from my friends, I can take care of my enemies myself."

Peterson was sentenced to die in the electric chair. The conviction created a furor not only among Negroes, but also among all decent and thinking white people. The most outrageous feature of the whole trial was the conclusive proof offered by the defendant that at the time of the shooting he occupied a bed in the Tuberculosis Ward of the city hospital, whose records corroborated this alibi.

One thing the police and the courts are always afraid of and that is public opinion. A perfect avalanche of protests rolled down on the trial judge and the Governor. Since Election Day was not far off and the latter stood in need of every vote he could get, he did a handsome thing and commuted Peterson's sentence to one even worse—life imprisonment.

Willie Peterson still rots behind bars in Wetumpka Prison Camp, Wetumpka, Alabama. His voice has been too weak to penetrate the thick prison walls to the outside world. It is high time than an outraged public opinion should take a hand in rescuing this helpless and inarticulate Negro from a fate worse than death. Elementary justice demands his immediate release from prison. Society must make adequate amends to this martyr for the five years of his wasted, tortured life.

If there ever was a man that the world forgot, it is Willie Peterson. He has long ago abandoned any hope of walking free in the light of the sun. Although I have been fortunate thus far in escaping the terrible fate that overtook him, I feel that as a man, as a worker and as a Negro, it is my highest duty not to relax my efforts until Willie Peterson is freed.

FIFTEEN

For weeks I walked about with my head swathed in bandages. My wounds were deep and they caused me excruciating pain. The police-lynchers had done a good job on me. Upon the order of my doctor I was forced into a long period of idleness. I almost made myself ill with impatience; so much important work still had to be done and there was I twiddling my thumbs behind the lines, so to speak. The feeling of relief which I experienced when I finally resumed my assignments as organizer for the Unemployment Council among Negro and white workers in Atlanta cannot adequately be described. I am of an active nature and have always led a busy life. Next to the fear of hanging, a state of prolonged idleness affords me the greatest pain.

2

The acute unemployment situation in the South in 1932 created the acid soil in which the "American Fascisti Order of the Black Shirts" blossomed out in all its exotic rankness. The "American Fascisti" grew luxuriantly in Tennessee, Alabama and Georgia. To Atlanta's eternal shame may it be recorded that it was one of the principal centers in the country for these whites. Fully twenty-one thousand white jobless joined the Order there. What made their joining so pathetic, beyond even the possibility of being regarded as contemptible, was the motive behind it. The cheap Fascist demagogues had seduced them into the organization with the tempting assurance that they would be given jobs once they became members. The human scavengers fattened upon the misery and despair of these men who moved heaven and earth to scrape together the large initiation fee and membership dues. The leaders even opened a plant where they manufactured the black shirts which their followers were obliged to buy from them at an exorbitant price.

The Fascist racketeers were no fools. They understood the psychology of their starving victims. Their appeal to them was irresistible. It went something like this:

"Run the niggers back to the country where they came from—Africa! They steal the jobs away from us white men because they work for lower wages. Our motto is therefore: *America for Americans!* And Americans don't mean niggers either! Old Glory waves over our white man's country and no real white man will work for nigger wages."

The Fascists drew to them two kinds of followers. There were the common hoodlums and social outcasts who found a profitable outlet in the Order for their criminal activities. There were also misguided white workers, the so-called poor white trash, the rejected, the poverty-stricken, who in their bitterness and unreflective rebellion, fell into the maw of the Fascist monster. To these my heart went out, for they were workers like myself and had suffered so bitterly at the hands of our common exploiters.

For months the Fascists terrorized the Negro population of Atlanta. Instance upon instance of mob violence against Negro workers who had jobs mounted swiftly into an orgy of hysteria. The whole Negro population of the city lived in constant fear of their lives. The hooded night riders now had an excellent opportunity to carry on their imbecilic mummery. They were "Knights" in regalia; they rode smartly on horseback and could delight themselves in delusions of grandeur. Like ghouls in a nightmare, they clattered through the streets in the dark, terrifying the Negro population with threats against life and limb and making babies cry with their blood-curdling yells.

Like the traditional knights of old, they too displayed matchless chivalry. They would swoop down on factories, railroad yards and hotels, and drag out all the Negro workers into the streets. Then the fun would begin. Bravely masked so that no one could recognize them, the "Knights" carried on their reign of terror over the whimpering Negro men and women.

One thing all lynch acts have in common: their unmentionable sexual degeneracy. It is indeed significant to note that every flogging, every beating and every lynching has as its point of emphasis the defilement or the mutilation of the sex organs of the victim! . . .

While the Fascists were carrying on their campaign of terror, the Unemployment Council and the Communist Party did not remain idle. They arranged educational meetings and issued leaflets by the thousands, warning the white workers of Atlanta that "they were being taken for a ride" by men who had no conscience, by common gangsters. Patiently they explained that the Negro workers were not the enemies of white workers, but that, on the contrary, both were being exploited, starved and abandoned by the same white oppressors. Because of our efforts at enlightenment, hundreds of workers were spared the degrading experience of becoming members of lynch mobs.

Things finally turned out as we Communists had warned, and our ranks became swollen with the disillusioned "Knights."

3

One of the most stirring experiences I had during my stay in Atlanta was my friendship with Jim, a white carpenter who at one time had been a member of the Black Shirts.* I met him in a very original way. That should not be any cause for surprise, for everything Jim did was done in an original way. He was honest and blunt and he had a happy knack of saying the right thing at the wrong time. Needless to say, he livened things up a bit.

One day, as I was paying a visit to the post office, I heard myself addressed in the following words:

"Say, buddy, can you give a fellow the price of a cup of coffee?"

I looked up and saw a timid little man. He was as lean as a bean pole. His face was emaciated; his skin was wrinkled like a dried apple. I noticed with surprise that he wore the black shirt of the Fascist Order. Misinterpreting my look of surprise as meaning that I did not believe that he was actually in need, he turned upon me his sad eyes, tearing with hunger, and in a tremulous voice said:

"Believe me, buddy, I'm hungry. I haven't eaten in days and my stomach feels like a lead pipe."

I, who knew so well what hunger and despair meant, would be the last person on earth to trifle with anyone down on his luck. But I felt that merely to fill this man's empty belly would not be enough. I wished to do something constructive for him and therefore I wanted first to understand him clearly. So I said to him without too much friendliness:

"I don't understand you. You can see that I am a Negro and I can also see that you're wearing a black shirt. Your kind hates and tortures my kind. What do you want of me?"

He was visibly taken aback and at a loss to answer. He finally muttered:

"I know. You're right, buddy—and yet, you're all wrong. You see how it is: If I'm wearing a black shirt, it's because it's

* I am disguising his true identity for obvious reasons.

the only shirt I've got. If you got a white shirt to spare, buddy, I'll be just as glad to wear it as this black one!"

It was now my turn to become embarrassed, and as I slipped him some money, he muttered hurriedly something about Fascists:

"They not only picked my pockets clean, but they stole my pants as well."

And he cursed out loud with a fervor that I respected and understood.

Before leaving me he told me that he had a large family, and what was one to do with a large family when one could not feed it? He said almost in a wail:

"No job—no money—no future—no nothing! Hell and damnation!"

A few days later I saw Jim again. He looked just as miserable and hungry as when I saw him last. He told me that he was still out of a job. I again offered him some money for food. But this time he refused point-blank. His face had actually turned scarlet. I was upset by his display of pride, for I well understood its origin. There is no pride so saddening as that of a starving worker.

To ease the embarrassment for both of us, I quickly changed the subject. I tried to do a little bit of missionary work on him. I told him all about the Unemployment Council and tried to prove to him how it was to his best interests that he become a member. He listened in grave silence and nodded his head in agreement. But it struck me that his agreement was not altogether wholehearted. He was accepting it with mental reservations. I sensed that there was something wrong somewhere. So I went exploring.

"What's the matter, Jim?" I asked. "What's troubling you, what's holding you back?"

Was it necessary for me to ask the question? I guessed the answer the minute I noticed his secret embarrassment.

But Jim was hardly the kind of man to leave a direct question unanswered. He said in his blunt and smiling way:

"See here, buddy, I think you're a swell fellow, even though you're a 'nigra.' So don't get me wrong when I say that God never intended white folks and 'nigras' to mix together and organize into one union and what the devil else you may think of."

I saw that arguing about God's racial intentions would do neither Jim nor me any good. So I left the divine plan of things behind us and turned to a subject that in my experience has always struck a sympathetic chord in every worker I ever spoke to. I said:

"Please tell me, Jim, when you had a job as a carpenter, did you get as much pay as a carpenter would in the North for the same kind and quality of work?"

"No."

"Did you ever try to figure out why?"

"No."

"Well, I'll tell you why. It's because the bosses have got us all split up down here. The Northern workers are not a bit better than we are and yet they get higher wages. And why is that? Because, Jim, they are united. They fight together. But we Southern workers are dumbbells. We remain divided. It does us no good, but it delights our bosses. It's easier to keep us down that way. Take, for instance, a strike down South. When the whites down tools, the bosses call in the Negroes to scab. When the Negroes strike the bosses call in the whites to scab. What are we doing? We are only cutting off each other's nose to spite each other's face. If you think there's sense in that you're a smarter man than I am.

"Did you ever try to figure out why the unions in the South are so weak? It's because the whites refuse to belong in the same union with Negroes. On the other hand, the Negroes don't trust the whites. Do you blame them? We are deprived of the most elementary human rights down in these parts. If we try to organize we are beaten up and thrown into jail on framed charges. If we hold our meetings, it is in secret and at the risk of our very lives. We Southern workers, both black and white, are like a house that is divided against itself; we are like an army marching out to engage the enemy, but on our way we get to fighting among ourselves and altogether forget the enemy. When we fight each other we grow weaker, and as we grow weaker, our enemy, the bosses, grows stronger. If you see any logic in continuing this condition, you're welcome to it."

I noticed that Jim was listening admiringly to my eloquence.

"You're damn smart for a 'nigra,' Angelo," he said to me.

I ignored the flattery and continued:

"I am not trying to show you that I am smart, Jim. I am talking to you seriously. Take this relief, now. The government authorities are passing the buck all the time. The Commissioners keep on telling you white folks that they cannot give any more relief than you are getting because they have to feed so many Negroes. Then they turn around and tell the Negroes that the grand old U.S.A. is a white man's country and that whites come first on relief. Hail Columbia! Now what is the upshot of all this? Both whites and Negroes feel they have a just cause to hate each other, and so while they are busy fighting each other, the government and the big bosses get away with the loot which they divert from relief. Now suppose all of us suckers, whether white unemployed or Negro unemployed, went down to the Commissioners and talked turkey to them:

" 'Look here, we are all starving. You have been making both ends of us fight against our middle: our stomachs. Now we have seen through your bluff and have decided to organize together into one big, powerful union. You cannot put us off now with lies and racial hatred with which you think you can cover up your real, shameful plot against the masses of the people. We'll make you listen to our demands!'

"Jim, don't you see how foolish it is to go into the fight with half an army when we could have a whole one? Don't you see that our bosses are bribing you into a state of helplessness with their wretched flattery, tricking you to believe that you are a big shot, a member of a superior race, a white man! How long can you continue being drunk on this popycock? You wish to march to battle strong, but how can you march if one of your two good feet, the foot that represents the Negro workers, is chained to the ground?"

Jim looked flabbergasted. All he could say was:

"Funny, I never saw it that way! Well, you've given me food for thought. I'll go home and think it over and if I come to see things your way, I'll come back and look you up."

I was therefore not at all surprised when one week later Jim approached me on the street. Externally I noticed that he had gone through an astonishing transformation. The timid, haunted look was no longer there. His feet no longer dragged. A curious nervous energy marked his movements. Why, he even smiled in a weak, apologetic way, an expression of jollity that he was not at all used to. I sensed something unusual was coming, so I stopped short and waited for him to open the conversation. He did not disappoint me. He went straight to the attack with the following words:

"*Mister* Herndon, I am calling a meeting for the unemployed in my house. If you care to come, I'll be very glad to see you."

When I heard the word "Mister," and noted the emphasis he placed on it, I understood fully what had happened inside of him. I was very happy for his sake because I knew that at last he was cured of that racial dry rot. I clasped his hand and shook it warmly and assured him that nothing would give me more pleasure than to come to his meeting.

When I came to the meeting I was pleasantly surprised to see that Jim had brought two other Negroes. It happens occasionally that when a decent white man finds a Negro whose manners and address are pleasing to him, he condescends to make an exception in his case and to treat him as an equal. Such a Negro usually is honored in the private conversations of white men with the inelegant description of "white nigger," something which in itself shows a deep racial prejudice. I must confess that I was ungenerous for a moment in believing that Jim had made an exception of me because he liked me personally. But when I saw the other two Negroes at the meeting, workers who certainly possessed no social graces of any kind to flatter a white man's interest, I recognized with pleasure that Jim was fully grown into a civilized man.

4

There was nothing unique in my experience with Jim. If I have taken the trouble to tell of the manner of his transformation from a Fascist to a class-conscious worker, it is only because he represents in type and experience a large mass of white American workers. During my stay in Atlanta as organizer for the Unemployment Council, I had many similar experiences with other white Jims. And I am somewhat vainglorious at the success I had in drawing them as active workers into the Council.

My friend Jim tried to make up for lost time. He was busy as a bee helping in the preparations for an open-air meeting of the Council. The meeting took place in a vacant lot where the neighborhood scalawags played their baseball games. More than three hundred Negro and white workers attended.

Before the meeting adjourned, a committee was elected to investigate the cases of those families which had been denied aid by the county and Federal relief agencies. There were thousands of such cases. It was a gigantic task that we had set ourselves. And as men whom bitter experience had taught to look at things soberly and realistically, we did not try to minimize the enormous difficulties we would have to face. Systematically and calmly we went about building Unemployment Council Committees, block by block, street by street and section by section. We held dozens of public meetings. Frequently all of us went without dinner to pay for the leaflets and other essential expenses. It is a miracle how with no visible funds at our command we would carry on such a lively and successful campaign. "Moscow gold!" charged our enemies. We who tightened our belts and made personal sacrifices of the most fantastic nature only smiled.

Why hide the fact? The officials of the county and Federal relief agencies did not like us a bit. We did nothing but embarrass them at every turn. And their tender governmental sensibilities could not endure the strain of our rough tactics. We harassed them at every opportunity and brazenly learned how to reject "no" for an answer. We had a partiality for the word "yes." And the authorities preferred the word "no." So we were deadlocked practically all the time.

Particularly offensive to the relief authorities was our handling of the Brandon case. We pressed the matter very vigorously and made ourselves a nuisance morning, noon and night. Mr. Brandon's story was as pathetic as any I've ever heard. It aroused wide sympathy among all those sufficiently human to be capable of sympathy.

Mr. Brandon was an elderly, sedate white worker who had given the best years of his life to increase the profits of the textile and railroad companies in Atlanta. He was always a model citizen. He never questioned the why and wherefore of things, minded his own business, went to church regularly, contributed to the Red Cross and the Community Chest and was a member in good standing of the Democratic Party. Mr. Brandon was not like many other workers who spent their pay before they even earned it on getting drunk on Saturday night and in card playing. He was scrupulously sober and respectable. Concern over his wife and his seven children, whom he dearly loved, made him a hard worker and a thrifty saver. Penny by penny he put his money by until he had several hundred dollars tucked safely away against a "rainy day."

That "rainy day" finally arrived. But it did not come the way he had expected. The bank in which he kept his hard-earned savings closed down. He now found himself old and decrepit, with no possibility of obtaining a job, for millions of other men, younger and stronger than he, were obliged to go without work. Unable to pay his rent, his landlord finally threw his few sticks of furniture out into the street. He had no friends and he was too proud to ask for charity. So he and his family dragged their belongings on a borrowed wheelbarrow into the woods just outside of the city. When members of the Unemployment Council found him he was living in a hole which he and his children had dug in the side of a hill. He had covered the inside with boards and got his water from a rain barrel.

I volunteered to go with a delegation of Negro and white workers to intercede for him. The dispensers of public charity received us with hostility. The supervisor said to me:

"What are you butting in for? Are you related to Mr. Brandon?"

"Certainly!" I answered with conviction. "He's my class brother."

Jim now lost his temper. He spoke with bitterness:

"It's all right for you, mister, to be so high and mighty. Your belly is full. You have a fat job, for which we citizens pay. But not everybody is as fortunate as you. Hungry people have as much right to live as you who live off the fat of the land. One would think that a man like Mr. Brandon, who has lived a useful life, would now in his old age be treated with some concern by you whose job it is to look after him. Just go and take a look at the way he lives—like an animal in a hole in the ground, only unlike an animal he can no longer fight to keep alive. He's too old and tired and sick."

The face of the supervisor became flushed with anger. In a loud voice, feeling secure because of the presence of a squad of hastily summoned policemen, he said:

"I'm not interested to listen to your speeches, Mister Bolshevik. We are perfectly capable of taking care of the business of this office without your assistance. You better mind your own business and don't come nosing in on other people's affairs."

All the while he spoke, excitable Jim was vainly trying to calm himself. I could see that the thing nearest his heart at the moment was the desire to punch the supervisor in the nose. I understood his feelings. But I pulled at Jim's sleeve.

"Let me answer him," I whispered.

And addressing the relief official, I said in a determined voice:

"You say it's none of our business. Well, whether you like it or not, it *is* our business. No human being is going to die like a dog while we are around, just because heartless officials like you handle the people's funds. Rest assured, mister, this matter is so much our business that if you will refuse to help Mr. Brandon immediately, we promise you on our word as workers and citizens that, within one hour's time, we'll hold a demonstration in front of the Governor's mansion and we'll plaster your name on every placard we can get."

My words had the desired effect. I saw that the supervisor had broken into a cold sweat. The prospect of being so flatteringly advertised by us before the whole city did not appeal to him very much. In fact, the thought of it made him a changed man. It was quite astonishing. From a snarling, contemptuous bully, he now had turned into a polite, sugary gentleman. He offered us cigarettes. . . .

"Calm yourselves, calm yourselves, boys, I am afraid you have misunderstood me! Please be reasonable! Please try to understand my position. Is it my fault that Washington doesn't send me any money? Complain to them and not to me. They've got the power. I haven't. Believe me, my heart bleeds for all the poor unfortunates in the city. But what am I to do? I am not a mint."

We could clearly see that he was stalling and trying to pass the buck. We were determined not to let him get away with it. And so I said to him:

"We don't care where you get the money from. My fellow-workers here on the delegation are agreed that if you don't immediately come to the aid of Mr. Brandon, we'll demonstrate before the Governor's mansion."

"All right, all right," muttered the relief supervisor wearily. "You win."

In our presence he called in a relief investigator and ordered her to move Mr. Brandon and his family into a house and to supply them with food regularly.

Our delegation left the supervisor's office in high spirits. Jim seemed overawed by our extraordinary success. He said to me in the incredulous voice of a man who had just witnessed a miracle:

"Do you know what, Angelo, nothing succeeds like success."

"You mean nothing succeeds like organization," I answered.

5

When the news of the Brandon victory circulated through the city, hundreds of letters from workers poured into the office of the Unemployment Council, requesting information on how to organize block committees. About a month later, another incident occurred which further added to the prestige of the Council.

On a certain day a Negro worker and his family were evicted from their home. As they had no place to go, they sat down on their household goods and abandoned themselves to their grief. Suddenly a car drove up and stopped near by. A drunken white man and woman got out and began tinkering with the motor. They fumed and cursed and despite all their efforts could not get the car started. The evicted Negro worker, who was an obliging fellow, volunteered his help. As he busied himself over the motor, the white owner of the car continued his cursing out loud. At that moment two police officers passed by, and, hearing the blasphemy, stopped and arrested the Negro worker for using "abusive language in the presence of a white woman."

The Negro worker protested his innocence. The white man kept chivalrous silence and his drunken woman companion complained out loud about those "filthy-mouthed niggers." Obviously, she wished to protect her male companion.

After the police had mauled up the poor Negro worker, they locked him up in jail. Later they came back and performed a similar service for his wife. They beat her up black and blue and also locked her up. The two were later found guilty of using blasphemous language, and as they could not pay their fine of twenty dollars, they received a twenty-day sentence.

When I told Jim about the incident, he grew hot under the collar. Righteous indignation turned the former lamb into a roaring lion. He looked ready to storm the city hall single-handed. But I calmed him down and assured him that an organized effort would be more effective than any individual act. So Jim immediately went to work and formed a shock brigade of volunteer movers to carry the furniture of the evicted Negro worker back into his house. As they were doing this, the landlord came by. He was threatening and overbearing and promised the committee on his honor as a white gentleman that he would see them, the "poor, white trash" and the "dirty niggers" hang by the neck by the time he got through with them.

He proceeded to padlock the house. And as he began to walk away, he turned without warning on Jim and, throwing all of his heavy weight into his arm, punched him in the jaw, felling him to the ground. For a man of Jim's spindly architecture, the drubbing he gave the landlord after he got to his feet again was truly astonishing. The landlord had to be treated by a doctor on the spot after the skirmish.

When later I saw Jim, I congratulated him heartily upon his victory.

"Oh, that was nawthing," he drawled modestly. "It wasn't my strength, but the anger in me that knocked that blankety blank landlord cold."

6

That same day Jim headed a delegation of white workers to the mayor of Atlanta. But His Honor refused to be seen. Instead, his secretary preached them a sermon on the dignity of the white race.

"You ought to be ashamed of yourselves," she rebuked them sternly. (So Jim reported to me later.) "How can you be interested in niggers and call yourselves white men and women?"

Jim who was the spokesman for the delegation answered her:

"Now, when you want to flatter us you call us white men, but behind our backs, what do you call us? 'Poor white trash,' no? Well, we poor white trash have learned that being white does not make us any different from the Negro worker. We are no more the dumbbells that we were. We have learned our lesson from bitter experience. Today we are organizing both Negro and white workers, and although you may not like our company, you and the mayor are going to see a lot of us from now on."

A few days later Jim came to me with a beaming face and told me breathlessly that by the mayor's order, the two framed Negro workers had been released from jail.

"Nothing succeeds like success, does it, Jim?" I asked, banteringly.

Jim thumbed his nose at me, playfully.

"You mean nothing succeeds like organization!"

7

About this time the World War veterans were preparing for their historic Bonus Expeditionary Force march on Washington. Kenneth Murrel, a notorious Red-baiter, who was Commander of the Atlanta American Legion, took charge of the local contingent. He issued an order that no veterans belonging to the "Communistic Unemployment Council" would be allowed to march to the capital. However, the veterans in our organization were no mollycoddles. They appealed to the rank and file of the American Legion not to fall into the hysteria of Red-baiting that their Commander was whipping up.

The Atlanta B.E.F. called a meeting at the state capital one night. The Negro-hating Murrel saw to it that no Negro veterans were invited. As he could not possibly overlook the Negro veterans, he and other officials of the Legion had called for a special Negro veterans' meeting the following Sunday.

That Sunday night I was one of the most interested spectators at the Negro meeting. Kenneth Murrel presided. He gave us the typical demagogic applesauce about how much concern he had for the Negro veteran. As the first speaker, he introduced a certain suave gentleman without mentioning his name, but referring to him merely as "a member of the State Legislature." This "statesman" immediately launched into a tirade against Communistic and subversive elements that were trying to stir up trouble among the classes with the avowed aim of overthrowing the United States government. He warned the assembled veterans that they must not allow the paid agents of Moscow to talk them into seditious acts against their government.

I noticed with gratification that the audience remained silent and hostile to these warnings. There was something unpleasant and slimy about the "legislator's" heart-warming concern "for the law-abiding poor Negroes."

It would have taken very little encouragement for the audience to have given him the classic razzberry.

After he had ended speaking, I went up to him and, with an ingenuous air, said:

"You're right, Mr. Speaker, about those Communists. They are just a bunch of foreigners who want to set up their Soviet dictatorship here. But as long as there are men like you, that will never happen."

He beamed at me benignly and said:

"You've said a mouthful, boy. The Jew Reds have been trying to cause us trouble down here by stirring up members of your race against white people all on account of that damn Scottsboro rape. Now, look here, you're an intelligent boy, admit that those nine niggers raped them white girls. Do you think they would have been arrested for nothing, now do you?"

"Right you are, mister," I agreed hypocritically. "By the way, I did not catch your name when the chairman introduced you. Won't you be so good as to tell it to me so that I can tell other Negroes about the inspiring speech you made here tonight?"

The speaker was touched.

"Sure, sure, you bet I will. My name is James Barksdale."

"Thank you, Mr. Barksdale."

I made a careful investigation the following day and discovered, not to my surprise, that the benign Mr. Barksdale, who loved the Negro people so touchingly, was no "member of the State Legislature." What he really was—I laugh with amusement when I think of it—a Kleagle of the KKK!

8

The following day the Communist Party of Atlanta issued ten thousand leaflets bearing the title: "Who are the Reds and what do they stand for?" Needless to say, this leaflet was an exposé of the "legislator" Barksdale. We distributed these leaflets to the War veterans. They succeeded in tearing the blinders from the eyes of many. The best gauge of their success was the intensive campaign which the *Atlanta Georgian*, the Hearst yellow sheet, and other local newspapers, suddenly unleashed against the Communists. They quoted from the leaflet very freely, in fact so freely, that there was not a word of similarity between their quotations and our own original statements. This did not surprise us. The most degraded journalistic prostitute of the world was capable of the most revolting perversions of truth that it was possible to imagine.

The *Atlanta Georgian* was not the kind of newspaper to do things by halves. Before long the effects of its howling the Red scare from the rooftops got the police all warmed up. They began to stir up muddy waters in order that they might be able to fish. They went in search of all those suspected of Red activity. And Red activity to the police meant anything from reading the Declaration of Independence in public to eating candy manufactured in the Soviet Union. The latter statement might appear ridiculous to the reader, but a certain lady of unimpeachable patriotism once confided to me in a dread whisper that she believed her neighbor, Mrs. X, must be one of those Communist Reds because when she visited her she was offered some taffy wrapped in little red papers on which were printed the words "Made in the U.S.S.R." What made the story amusing to me was the fact that I knew Mrs. X was a Seventh-Day Adventist and she just happened to like Russian taffy.

Here at this point, I am very unhappy to say, is the proper place to assure the reader that if ever there was a man who innocently got into trouble with the police as frequently and as easily as I, I have still to meet him. Fortunately, I am not superstitious and so I cannot regard my almost daily habit of getting arrested as the fulfillment of some predestined course.

What should happen at this time but that I blunder into an accident. I was riding with a Jewish grocer in a car which the Unemployment Council had hired to trail the Atlanta contingent of the B.E.F. on its way to Washington. As we were crossing a certain square, an impatient motorist who tried to beat the traffic lights beat into our car instead and shattered his windshield. When our automobilist Paul Revere caught sight of the Jewish grocer, he thought it would be a fine opportunity to collect some easy money. Despite the fact that it was he who caused the accident, he decided to frame us. Perhaps it was because he had friends in the police department. As for the police, they were not too particular when it came to pinning down manufactured evidence against a "Jew" and a "nigger."

However, when the police discovered that the "nigger" was Angelo Herndon, they sent scurrying all their trained bloodhounds to apprehend me. I got wind of it in time and made myself scarce. It may sound laughable, but I was obliged to hide for more than two months on account of this absurd incident.

My education with regard to capitalist justice was already now well on in its post-graduate state. Knowing the temper of the police and the judges and their special attitude toward me, I had not the slightest doubt that they were capable of presenting against me a case of a serious nature.

Unable to lay their hands on me, the police began to imitate the tactics of the Spanish Inquisition. They arrested a Negro worker who was a very dear friend of mine. Once in every twenty-four hours they took him out of his cell for an "examination." The examining officer was a rubber hose.

"Talk, nigger—you know damn well where Angelo Herndon is."

My friend would rather die than tell them. So each time they questioned him they beat him to unrecognizability.

I was very much shaken when I heard how my friend was being tortured. My feeling of distress was so keen that I fell ill. The need of rescuing him from the danger in which he found himself forced me out of my despair. I began to use my wits and fell upon a stratagem. After all, wasn't I almost a detective once? I went into a telephone booth in a corner drug store and called the police station. I asked for the chief. The voice on the other end of the wire told me that he was sorry that the chief was not in, but perhaps he could help me. To this I replied with all the vocal authority I could muster:

"Maybe you can, captain. Now listen carefully, and get it straight. I am the superintendent of the Atlanta Plow Works. I understand you've locked up a nigger of mine by the name of Felton Wimbley."

"Yes, sir, boss, we have."

"Well, captain, he's my nigger and a good one too. Let me warn you that I am not going to stand for any monkey business. If you don't let him out of the coop by six o'clock this evening, I am coming down to the police station and give you wise guys all the hell you want."

My words had an astonishing effect upon the police official. He sounded all maple-syrup.

"Yes, sir, boss, we are terribly sorry to have given you trouble. I'll see what I can do about it right away."

"All right, don't forget," I muttered angrily into the receiver, and hung up.

That evening I went to the house where my friend Felton lived. What was my astonishment to see him sitting at the dinner table shoveling food down with great scoops. Poor boy, they had starved him all the time he was in jail. My joy upon seeing him and my pride over the success of my "white man's" trick vanished when I looked at his bruised and swollen face and body. The savages had almost killed him!

SIXTEEN

The presidential campaign of 1932 was just getting under way. The Communist Party had chosen William Z. Foster and James W. Ford as its national standard-bearers. That summer we were kept feverishly busy in Atlanta setting up numerous Foster and Ford for President Clubs in both Negro and white neighborhoods. I suppose it will come to many as a shock, but we had to carry on our work secretly. As for our rights as citizens, so far as the local authorities were concerned, the Constitution be damned! Who would have the temerity to stop them? Appeal to the United States Supreme Court? That costs thousands of dollars, and, besides, the Supreme Court is not inclined to interfere in the sovereignty of "states' rights." So the Southern industrialists and bankers rule without hindrance.

The designation of Ford for the Vice-Presidency created a great sensation. This was the first time in American history that any political party had selected a Negro to run for such high office, although there are more than fifteen million Negroes in America. The reaction of superior Nordics generally was that of amusement and disgust. Southern papers commented upon the choice with savage irony. They characterized it as "vulgar," and a "gross effrontery," and but the logical consequence of the agitation carried on by Jews and Russians that Negroes were the equals of whites. Did one need further proof that Moscow was invading America? Those damn Communists, editorial writers urged, ought either be deported to the country where they came from or better yet be made examples of with tar and feathers!

Different was the reaction of the Negro workers of Atlanta. They felt proud to see a Negro sharing honors with a white man—the highest honors a political party could bestow. While it is true that the lying press had succeeded in universally whipping up prejudice and hatred against Communists, these had penetrated in the Negro only skin deep. The Negro was sorely oppressed and he was made aware of it every moment of his life. So when the Communists came along and opened up their wounds and pointed out to them the reasons why they were oppressed and who their oppressors were, they thawed and broke down all their defenses against them.

The 1932 platform of the Communist Party was so simple and brief that even the most illiterate man could remember and understand it. There were only six planks and these were:

(1) Unemployment and Social Insurance to be paid at the expense of the state and employers.

(2) Against Hoover's wage-cutting policy.

(3) Emergency relief for the poor farmers without restriction by the government and banks; exemption of poor farmers from taxes and from forced collection of rents or debts.

(4) Equal rights for Negroes and self-determination for the Black Belt.

(5) Against capitalist terror; against all forms of suppression of the political rights of the workers.

(6) Against imperialist war; for the defense of the Chinese people and of the Soviet Union.

The Foster and Ford Clubs in Atlanta buzzed like bee hives despite the necessity of working underground. The color line passed unnoticed among our workers. Negro and white stood shoulder to shoulder, laboring together to reach our common goal. Of course we had no illusions about the outcome of our campaign. In the main, Communist sympathizers and adherents come from the working class and the poor tenant farmers. The state authorities found a cunning method to disqualify our voters. Negro and white poor alike were confronted by an unscalable obstacle: the high poll tax. We knew we would be deprived of many thousands of Communist votes in Atlanta alone by this un-American conspiracy against the rights of universal suffrage. But that did not diminish the energy of our campaigning. For Communists do not work for a day. We build an indestructible edifice, stone by stone and story by story, for all time and for all men—high poll tax or no high poll tax.

2

Absorbed as we were in the business of the campaign we did not allow ourselves to neglect our work among the unemployed. By June of that year the relief situation in Atlanta had reached the low water mark. The relief officials with farcical intent were giving the unemployed a free carousel ride. White unemployed recipients of relief were given less than sixty cents a week for each individual in the family. It goes without saying that Negroes got the leavings—and there was mighty little of that. As for those Negroes who got nothing, stars fall in Georgia even as they do in Alabama, and so they had the privilege of growing rapturous about the beautiful Southern nights, with fever-ridden eyes and bellies swollen with hunger.

As if this were not enough, the city and county authorities decided to drop twenty-three thousand families from the relief rolls. In consequence, those who had been driven by starvation from the farms were to be rounded up and shipped back again. This decision caused wild excitement among the unemployed. They read in it a sentence of death.

However, what still remained was the moral consolation of going down fighting.

The relief officials heard the low mutterings of a gathering storm, but pretended that they did not hear. The heart of Pharaoh was hard as stone, and his sense of authority was smug and over-confident. Just the same, the ruler's of our lives were to meet with a surprise or two from us before long.

In explanation of their decision to drop twenty-three thousand families from the relief rolls, the city and county authorities declared that their treasuries were empty. They tried to blame it all on Washington, as usual preferring to pass the buck rather than to face realities. Then adding insult to injury, they made a pious grimace. What unemployment? The New Deal had done away with it already. Where? How? the unemployed asked in astonishment. The officials scorned to answer. However, in order that the myth of the democratic right to petition might be sustained, the Fulton County Commissioners made a grand gesture. They invited all those who were in actual need of relief to present their grievances in person. We accepted the invitation with little faith in obtaining any satisfaction from it.

The Unemployment Council lost no time and issued a call for a city-wide emergency conference. All organizations of unemployed, regardless of their political tie-up, and all individuals abandoned to starvation by a government supposed to protect them, were invited to participate. The conference vibrated with militancy and bitterness against the high-handed and callous acts of the County Commissioners. It drew up a list of demands and one fine day, to the great amusement of the relief authorities, submitted them for their perusal. "Amusement" is a mild word to describe their reaction. Of all unmitigated nerve! We had the cheek to demand of them the following:

(1) The release of all workers arrested and framed up on charges of vagrancy.* For the repeal of the vagrancy law.

(2) That each unemployed worker with a family should get $4. weekly, no matter how small the family is. But in the case of a large family, the amount should be enough to provide for the whole family, e.g., if there are twelve in a family, the amount should be $12. per week, etc.

(3) There should not be any form of discrimination in the distribution of this relief, against Negro workers, mainly, and other workers who do not have families, etc.

(4) Half of the above amount to be paid in the form of cash and the other half in scrip, e.g., if a family were given $6, half of this amount should be paid in cash and the other half in scrip.

(5) That the city and county begin immediately to make arrangements to provide 1½ tons of coal for all unemployed workers for the winter, beginning with September first, and ending the latter part of April.

(6) That the city and county officials and their government provide shoes, clothing, free meals and carfare to schools for the children of the unemployed workers of Atlanta.

We ordered printed ten thousand leaflets † calling for a demonstration at the court house. Because of the possible dangers that might be encountered during the day, we were obliged to work secretly, distributing them from house to house under cover of darkness. I could not sleep all night and

* Unemployed workers were being arrested by the hundreds and sent back to the farms. There were special police assigned to arrest everyone who did not have any "visible means of support."

† For text of this leaflet see Appendix One, p. 335.

waited impatiently for daybreak. All sorts of fears robbed me of my rest. Frankly, I was worried whether the demonstration would prove a success. If the workers failed to come out in large numbers all our strenuous efforts in the past would be made negative. Workers generally would be discouraged from joining us and the relief authorities would refuse to have any dealings with us.

Early that morning before anybody stirred, I made my way to the court house. It was partly from anxiety and partly to collect my thoughts, for lack of sleep had made me groggy and restless. To my amazement and joy when nine o'clock arrived, which was just one hour before the meeting was scheduled to open, workers, both black and white, and small tradesmen began pouring into the square. At ten o'clock about one thousand workers, of whom more than half were white, formed ranks, and marching shoulder to shoulder, oblivious of color difference, filed into the court-house building.

What a tragic lot of men and women these were! It was a great wonder that they had any strength left to protest. Listless, emaciated, with dragging feet and hollow eyes from which the light had been extinguished, they nevertheless seemed determined to do the last thing that their slowly expiring humanity dictated. What added pathos to the scene was the sight of many mothers walking into the building with their whimpering babies in their arms.

To one who has always lived up North a meeting attended by one thousand black and white workers would be regarded in a matter of fact way. Such things happen daily by the hundreds in Northern cities. But in the South such a spectacle caused alarm and consternation. It meant that the end of the world was at hand. This meeting in front of the court house was unprecedented in Atlanta. Never had such a huge gathering of black and white workers taken place in all the South. This was truly an historic occasion and the news reporters in the town went running around the court house with their eyes literally popping out of their heads.

But for all progressive workers this was a field day. It was a demonstration of the Southern worker's power. Like a giant that had been lying asleep for a long time, he now began to stir.

Despite the fervent hopes of the police and the yellow press, the demonstration was a model of order and peace. I have never seen a better-behaved audience even in the refined middle-class circles of Boston. In vain the police tried to provoke us, but we maintained an iron discipline. No one fell into the trap so deliberately laid for us by our enemies. It goes without saying that the meeting was a huge success. Nothing else was talked about the next few days in Atlanta and in other cities in the South with as much interest and excitement.

Our efforts succeeded beyond our wildest hopes. The following day the relief authorities announced that they had appropriated $6,000 for additional relief. Furthermore, the order about dropping the twenty-three thousand families from the relief rolls was rescinded. . . .

The reaction of Atlanta's unemployed to all this was most eloquently expressed in the following exclamation of a very old Negro worker who in his boyhood had been a slave in Georgia:

"Hot damn! Who would have thought it!"

SEVENTEEN

Little do men suspect the future consequences of even their most innocent actions. One day after the courthouse demonstration, I went to the post office for my mail. It was a beautiful, starry July night.

As I entered the post office, tranquil with the evening's peace and gentleness, I was rudely shaken out of my mood by an invisible assailant. I felt myself grabbed from behind by two powerful hands. When I was whirled round I looked into the sneering face of a police officer. He nudged me viciously in the ribs with his elbow and without a word clapped a pair of steel cuffs on my wrists.

"Why are you arresting me?" I challenged him.

"Solicitor Boykins wants to see you, sonny boy, about those threatening and scurrilous letters that you have been passing around."

I surmised he meant the leaflets which we issued for the demonstration.

I was then taken to the city jail. By this time I had already developed a sixth sense. The hunted animal has premonitions when danger threatens. Somehow I had the certainty that something serious was afoot. Repeatedly I pressed the detective to tell me what the charges against me were. He answered me, and I knew that he was lying, that until the Solicitor returned to the city I would merely be held as a dangerous suspect.

Then the gruelling commenced. I already knew most of their questions by heart. I anticipated them even before they were uttered.

"Now out with it and confess! We know that you are not smart enough to be the head of this Red outfit in town. No nigger is. It must be some slick white guy, a Yankee from up North, who has been doing all this plotting and stirring up of trouble among the workers in this town."

I listened to my inquisitor and made no answer. Facing me, glowered a pot-bellied beefy detective. He amused himself swinging idly in his swivel chair and chewing vigorously at the end of a cigar. He too felt obliged to put in his two cents, and, cocking a baleful eye at me, he said rather irrelevantly:

"I used to belong to a labor union myself. And, boy, it's a swell idea—a swell idea! But you god-damn dirty Reds try to get by the law, and you are always hiding like rats in a sewer. You ain't no good, you rascal, you! If you meant any good would you be dodging around like that and make us sweat looking for you?"

But another detective who was of a more practical mind than his colleague had a concrete suggestion to make:

"What's the use of jawing with this bastard? Let's take him upstairs and give him the works, I suppose he thinks he's in the hands of the New York police now. Well, let's show him!"

They did.

They led me up a flight of dark stairs into a little dark room. At first I could distinguish no object, but as my eyes became accustomed to the darkness I began to discern objects. If my situation were not so serious I would have burst out laughing, for it seemed that the detectives had a very childish understanding of the spooky. They had never out-grown their bogey-man conception of horror. What they wished to scare me with was, believe it or not, a heap of grimacing skulls and a collection of coffins!

Then suddenly I held my breath. An astounding thing happened. One of the detectives turned on an electric switch in the dark and through the slits in the skulls, where eyes, nostrils and mouth were supposed to be, a fiendish blood-red illumination shone out against the blackness in the room. At this point I lost all my self-control and doubled up with laughter. The performance was excruciatingly funny. I said aloud:

"I suppose you frightened little boys wish to scare me, the Communist bogey man with your own bogey men whom you have lit up like Japanese lanterns. Well, you can't scare me because I am *the* one and *only* bogey man."

"Shut your damn trap," shouted a detective.

Someone gave me a terrific kick in the shin. I realized now how unwise of me it was to banter with such blackguards. The joke cost me dearly. I went limping about for more than a week.

Having failed in their plan to frighten me, the master minds resorted to an even more stupid and vicious trick. They commanded me to seat myself in a steel chair which stood in the center of the room. One of the detectives connected some wires to it and, turning to me, said:

"We have brought many niggers in here and you can bet that those who refused to talk never left here alive. I see you don't believe it. All right, then look at them heads over there. They grin, eh? They give you a nice sniggly feeling, eh? I just wonder how you would look with a nice red electric bulb in your eye sockets?"

With these words he grabbed hold of me by the throat, and, putting his face close to mine, bawled:

"Talk, nigger! If you won't talk we'll electrocute the hell out of you."

To say that I was not frightened would hardly be the truth. Those legal criminals were capable of any act of violence and I really had an agonized feeling that I was not going to leave that room alive. But as I did not intend to sell myself cheaply, I said to them:

"Since you have made up your minds to kill me, you might as well shoot me because I'm not going to sit in that chair."

I may have said other things, but I really do not recall, for at that moment one of the detectives struck me on my forehead between the eyes with a flash light. As I sank to the floor, half fainting, I heard him say to the others:

"Take the damn nigger downstairs. He's as crazy as your Uncle Joe."

2

Where would the authorities put a "dangerous Red" like myself? Naturally, in the death house, where murderers waiting for sentence resigned themselves to their end. I know of more cheerful places.

My entrance into the cell was the signal for general pandemonium. There was every indication that my arrival had been expected. And so the "boys" with touching hospitality prepared to give me a rousing reception. Did I say "rousing"? They raised such a furious din with their maniacal howling, yelling and shrieking that they could have roused the dead. I was so astonished that I remained rooted to the spot. They did not look to me like human beings; they behaved like wild beasts, and I recoiled from them with revulsion.

"Bring him here!" some of the prisoners shrilled in chorus.

I looked at them in fascinated horror. About sixty or seventy of them of all ages and descriptions stood lined up against the wall. In their hands ready for instantaneous action they held sticks, empty bottles and pieces of iron pipe. My blood congealed when I saw a mere child, who looked no more than twelve years, start toward me brandishing a stick and yelling in his shrill treble:

"Fresh meat! You son-of-a-bitch! What do you mean by breaking into jail on us?"

Then it suddenly dawned on me that the role I was now involuntarily playing was that of defendant in a "kangaroo court," that extraordinary prisoners' institution which carries on mock trials, issues sentences and carries them through with a lot of rude horse-play and even violence on the new prisoners.

The "judge" of the kangaroo court, a lean drowsy-looking young fellow of about twenty-five, called me over with an imperious gesture. As I stood before him he regarded me intently and in contemptuous silence. Then he spoke with almost mournful reproach:

"So you are the ——, the tough guy who goes around killing people! Well, you ain't goin' to go around here killing any of us because . . ." Here the judge waved a threatening finger under my nose. ". . . because we're all killers here. You know what you are—you little S.O.B.? You are only a rank amateur as a killer. We are professionals. Get me? So come down off your riding horse, boy, because we're running the show here."

After much weighty deliberation within himself the judge yawned and began reading to me the rules of the "house" from a dirty piece of paper:

"Got any money? No? Well, you'll have to pay with two hundred and fifty lashes on your naked ——"

With great politeness I then requested a chance to explain why I had been arrested. One of the prisoners interrupted me rudely and said:

"You don't have to explain. The detectives told us all about how you go around killing people for the fun of it."

The judge looked annoyed, and, turning savagely upon the individual who had just spoken, barked:

"Who's running this court, you or I? Stop interfering, will you?"

Looking at me he burst out laughing and said to the others:

"All right, let's give him a chance to explain. I am curious to hear what kind of a lie he's goin' to tell."

I began to talk. I spoke words that ran along this order:

"Fellows: I have never seen any of you before, nor have you seen me before. That does not matter. By the very color of our skin we are brothers. The detectives have told you that I am guilty of killing a lot of people. They thought that since they could not get away with beating me that you would do it after you had heard a lot of lies about the charges against me. I am not here for murder. I am here for standing up for my rights and for the rights of the Negro people. I am one of the Reds. No doubt you have heard about them. About a week ago one thousand Negro and white workers marched on the court house and made the county authorities appropriate $6,000 for relief . . . You read about it in the newspapers, didn't you? Well, I'm the one that helped to organize it. That's why they have me here, for demanding bread for starving people.

"As for you, you too are victims of the same system of cruelty and oppression. Crime may have brought you here, but if we had a decent government that would be concerned with its workers, then you and hundreds of others like you would not be in jail today. Believe me, I didn't come here to run your business. If anything, I would like to help you, for we are all in the same leaky boat."

As I was talking I was intently scrutinizing the faces of my fellow-prisoners. I was greatly relieved to see their expression of sullen contempt and cruelty gradually being transformed into one of neutral indifference. Certainly one could not expect brotherly love from that hard-boiled, murderous crew. It was enough of a victory for me that they dropped their sticks, bottles and iron pipes.

One short fellow, who kept staring at me in an idle sort of

fashion, sidled up to me with a look of envy in his one good eye, and said to me:

"Gee, you're lucky! You're a government man, ain't you? They won't keep you here long. This hotel is reserved specially for high-tone guys like us."

I told him much to his disappointment that I was not important enough to be a government man. My alleged offense was of another kind.

"Then how in hell do you expect to get out," asked the little man, "unless you use a can-opener?"

I assured him to his bewilderment that only the united efforts of the Negro and white workers could force the authorities to release me.

The little man made a funny face and, pointing at his forehead, made a circular motion with his index finger.

"That guy is nuts!" he gasped, and turned away from me with amusement.

I realized that I was now the most flattered person in the cell. I was the center of all attention. I was, so to speak, a symbol to them of the outside world. In the drab humdrum of their prison life a new face, a new story, had the stimulating quality of a new experience, in fact of *news*. The prisoners gathered round me and plied me with questions. They spoke at once and I broke into perspiration, for they pressed me so hard for answers. I found momentary relief in the sudden interruption by the kangaroo judge, who drawled in his drowsy, sarcastic voice:

"Why don't you leave this guy alone? He ain't done no wrong! Because of this it is the court's decision that he don't have to pay a fine."

3

I could not fall asleep that night. My mind was feverish. My thoughts were like runaway horses. I tried to rein them in vain. All my senses became fully aware of my surroundings. Everything in me ached painfully. While I was awake and holding my own against the verbal attack of my fellow-prisoners, I found some distraction from the hideous surroundings. But no sooner did I stretch out my weary limbs upon the unyielding concrete floor with only one filthy blanket between me and the cold damp, than I listened painfully to every sound and became conscious of every smell.

The men slept like the very dead. What a change had come over them! During the daytime they were perpetually quarreling, fighting furiously over every trifle, making murderous attacks on one another just so as to distract themselves from their insufferable confinement. But now they lay curled up, looking so helpless and so forlorn! The first thought that came to my mind was: "They are only children!" Some were snoring in all sorts of keys and falsettos. Others were groaning or muttering incoherently in their sleep. One gaunt prisoner was fighting some imaginary enemy. His face was twisted with fear, and broken curses escaped his trembling lips. He was bathed in perspiration and he was constantly gnashing his teeth. A great pity welled up in me. If I could only soothe these men in their sorrow! If I could only make them whole again and let them start new lives and bring them into a world far more designed for men than for machines—how gladly I would sacrifice my life for them! What a vicious society it was to degrade men that way!

There was no toilet in the cell—there was no water to drink—there was only one mattress to sleep on. The lice and the bedbugs crawled over our naked bodies and left a trail of blood wherever, in self-defense, we struck out at them. What

I found most unendurable of all was the noxious stench of human excrement. It turned my stomach, and in the middle of the night I got up to vomit. My nerves were shattered. In my rage against the savagery of our superior white "civilization" I could find nothing but impotent tears to relieve me.

4

For eleven days I was held incommunicado in the jail, without any specific charges against me. Every effort that I made to induce the warden to allow me some communication with the outside world failed. I began to develop an attitude of fatalism toward my imprisonment. It looked as if I were being buried alive.

When I was about ready to surrender all hope, an opportunity suddenly turned up from an unexpected quarter. One of the prisoners who was being released consented to smuggle out for me a letter to the International Labor Defense. My friends responded with lightning speed. The I.L.D. attorney of Atlanta sued out a habeas corpus writ for my release. Judge Virlyn B. Moore of the Fulton County Superior Court denied the writ. He did order, however, that if an indictment were not drawn up against me by the following day, I was to be released from custody.

My release was the last thing on earth the local authorities wanted. So they got busy and cooked up an indictment. In their haste they did a fantastic thing, something which later contributed to their discomfiture. They indicted me on July 22, 1932, for attempting to incite to insurrection on July 16. Inasmuch as I had already been in jail for almost three weeks, will the reader please figure out how that could have been possible?

The indictment read in part:

THE GRAND JURORS selected, chosen and sworn for the county of Fulton, to wit: . . . in the name and behalf of the citizens of Georgia, charge and accuse ANGELO HERNDON with the offense of:—ATTEMPTING TO INCITE INSURRECTION for that said accused, in the County of Fulton and the State of Georgia, on the 16th day of July, 1932, with force and arms, did make an attempt to incite insurrection and did make and attempt to induce others to join in combined resistance to the lawful authority of the State of Georgia, with intent to the denial of the lawful authority of the State of Georgia and with intent to defeat and overthrow the lawful authority of the State of Georgia by open force and by violent means and by unlawful acts, said attempt to incite insurrection intended by accused to be acomplished by acts of violence, said attempt to incite insurrection being made by accused in the following manner, to wit:

(1) Accused did call and did attend public assemblies and mass meetings in the homes of various persons whose names are to the Grand Jurors unknown and did make speeches to various persons to the Grand Jurors unknown, the purpose of said meetings and the purpose of said speeches being to organize, to establish and to set up a group and combination of persons white and colored, under the name and style of the Communist Party of America, for the purpose of uniting, combining and conspiring to incite riots, to embarrass and impede the orderly processes of the courts and for the purpose of offering and making combined opposition and resistance to the lawful authority of the State of Georgia and for the purpose of overthrowing and defeating by force and violence the lawfully constituted authority of the State of Georgia, all which said meetings held in various places and on various occasions which are to the Grand Jurors unknown.

> (2) Accused did by speech and persuasion, solicit and did attempt to persuade and solicit persons whose names are to the Grand Jurors unknown to combine with, to join and to confederate with and to become members of the Communist Party and the Young Communist League and to become members, agents and parties to and of the Communist Party of America, to the intent and purpose of creating, offering, establishing and waging war against the lawful constituted authority of the State of Georgia for the purpose of overthrowing the lawfully constituted authority of the State of Georgia by acts of violence and by revolution and establishing in the place of said lawfully constituted authority of the State of Georgia a new government know as United Soviets Soviet Russia, sometimes called and known as the "Dictatorship of the Propertyless People." *

And what was the law upon which the indictment was based? It was the anti-slave insurrection law of 1861 which the State Legislature of Georgia had passed to crush all slave rebellions. One flattering thing may be said about courts, particularly about Southern courts: they are never at a loss to find a law with which to bait its working-class victims. Some states have even gone to the trouble of digging out of their antiquarian legal chests some moldy seventeenth-century laws with which to smash the labor movement. Only a person with a diseased imagination or one who had ulterior motives in distorting the meaning of the anti-insurrection law of 1861 could see in it a legal or a practical application to my "crime." What evidence they brought to uphold the indictment and how they obtained this evidence I first discovered later in the course of the trial. That in itself showed to what outrageous lengths my

* For full text of the indictment see Appendix Two, p. 337.

accusers went. The statute under which I was indicted originally read as follows:

> If any person be in any way instrumental in bringing, introducing or circulating within the state any printed or written paper, pamphlet or circular for the purpose of exciting insurrection, revolt, conspiracy or resistance on the part of slaves, Negroes or free persons of color in this state, he shall be guilty of high misdemeanor which is punishable by death.

Having had no occasion to use it except in the case of a Negro minister who shot at a jail but was later released, the law was revised in 1871 so as to apply to both Negro and white alike and to include all incitement to insurrection. It read:

> Any attempt, by persuasion or otherwise, to induce others to join in any combined resistance to the lawful authority of the State shall constitute an attempt to incite insurrection. Any person convicted of the offense of insurrection shall be punished with death; or if the jury recommend mercy, confinement in the penitentiary for not less than five years nor more than twenty years. Insurrection shall consist in any combined resistance to the lawful authority of the State, with intent to the denial thereof, when the same is manifested, or intended to be manifested, by acts of violence.

The prostituted press of Atlanta and all the upholders of law and order in the South gloated over my downfall. They were now going "to teach those black — their place."

There lay a superb irony in the state's choice of the man who was to prosecute me. He was Assistant Solicitor General, Colonel and Reverend John H. Hudson. In his august person he represented the majesty of the law, the might of the National Guard and the sanctity of the Methodist Church. Generally regarded as a pillar of society and a dauntless champion of Southern chivalry, no better person could have been chosen to win public confidence. People said with the greatest solemnity and much shaking of the head: if John H. Hudson directs the prosecution, dollars to doughnuts that nigger's guilty!

All good citizens rejoiced over the triumph of society over the criminal, while I grew bitter and despondent with the perfidy of it all. I could far easier endure the vile stenches of my prison cell and the murderous atmosphere of the death house than the stench of smug and well-rotted respectability outside the prison walls—the respectability of those who condemned me before they even heard me.

5

On the same day that application for a writ of habeas corpus was denied I was transferred from the city jail to Fulton Tower to await trial.

The latter institution is an old dilapidated jail. It looks like those sweat tanks in which prisoners were tortured during the eighteenth century. The building has five floors, and on each floor there are four tiers. Two cell blocks are on each floor and there are eighteen cells to a block.

Normally, only four prisoners occupied a cell. But during the summertime when the warden did a thriving business, what with innocent people being sentenced from one to five years for vagrancy and drunkenness, six to eight people were crowded like sardines into a single cell. Where didn't they sleep? Wherever the law of gravity permitted—on the bunks, under the bunks and on the floor.

The month of July, 1932, was a memorable one for me. It had exceptionally scorching weather. I was locked up in a cell with seven other prisoners. It was as hot as in an oven. We literally had to sleep one on top of the other. Such intimacy bred not only contempt and excessive discomfort, but it did not take much for the men to be at each other's throats. Three of the prisoners were confessed murderers—two for robbery, one for the non-support of his common-law wife, and the seventh for violating the prohibition law.

This last one, although his crime was the least serious, was the most obnoxious one in the group. We tried not to hurt his feelings by showing our disgust openly, but we recoiled instinctively whenever he came near us. The man was in the last stages of syphilis. Every time I ate I went through untold agonies. We were obliged to eat out of the same plates and drink out of the same cups with the diseased man. He showed a callous disregard for the rest of us. He paced up and down the cell, spitting his foul saliva on the floor and against the walls. Our efforts to dodge him became quite an indoor sport. I could almost have sworn that he was gleeful over our panic. It gave him a feeling of power over us.

But the prisoner who aroused the greatest compassion in me was Mr. Wilson, the man who was jailed for non-support. He was 65 years old and his stooped shoulders and his attitude of utter dejection made me feel very sorry for him. He told me his story without hesitation; he was overjoyed at the opportunity of unburdening himself to a sympathetic human being.

He had fought in the Spanish-American War, in which he was badly wounded. Because he was practically disabled the government granted him a small monthly pension. Everything would have been relatively well for him had he not met with a designing woman who insinuated herself into his life. She assured him that he was too helpless to care for himself and that henceforth she would look after his health. Overjoyed, he made her his common-law wife. But no sooner were they living together when the woman demanded that he sign over to her his pension. He recognized that he had fallen into the clutches of an unscrupulous woman, so he refused to comply with her wish. She lost no time in having him arrested for non-support. And so now poor Mr. Wilson had already spent eight months in jail, pondering in seclusion the strange ways of the world.

"Did I ever do anyone any harm?" he asked me almost tearfully. "I gave my life and my health for my country—I was always a good citizen—I voted the straight Democratic ticket every time and always minded my own business. Why in hell do they do that to me? That's what I'd like to know."

Despite all my efforts to explain to him the real social and economic causes for his plight he persisted in his wish to regard it as a unique case of personal injustice.

"They done me wrong!" he wailed.

I recognized without anger that this victim of a topsy-turvy society was too old and fixed in his ideas to learn anything new. He was like a lifeless puppet. Outer forces pulled the strings and he danced to their mad music.

A few days after my first conversation with him he was taken ill. Prior to that he had made several complaints to the turnkey. He wished to see the doctor, he said. The turnkey only glared at him, but did nothing about it. Now the old man was so ill that he could not sit up. So the turnkey called the doctor. The latter, an unpleasant and irritable man, came and looked him over. We all stood round watching him. He made a wry face and said to Mr. Wilson:

"Stick your tongue out, nigger."

Mr. Wilson obediently stuck his tongue out.

"M-m-m-h!" muttered the doctor. "Nothing's wrong with you. You are healthier than I am. What you need is a pick and shovel and a good kick in the ——."

For three days the old man lay on his cot, moaning. He kept it up all day and all night. He could not fall asleep. We were all sorry for him, so we showed no irritation. Even the murderers kept quiet and said nothing. Only the syphilitic grew violently abusive. He kept up a running barrage of obscenity until one of the murderers could stand it no longer, and, turning savagely on him, shouted:

"Look here, Mr. Syph, if you don't pipe down the judge will at last have a reason for hanging me!"

The diseased man subsided.

One thing I have always marveled at—the extraordinary capacity that human beings have for adjusting themselves to every circumstance, no matter how difficult. There was something ghastly about our situation. The old man lay moaning on his bed. Maybe he was dying! Did it stop us from our routine of living? Not a bit! The men quarreled, laughed at each other's smelly jokes and fought like wildcats. I watched the goings on with dismay. I sent a nameless curse winging at the enemies of mankind and at the way they degrade human beings so that they sink lower than the wild beasts.

6

On the third night of Wilson's illness the seven of us sat about in idleness. I was lost in my own dark thoughts. But the others were playing poker, except Wilson, who lay in his corner, moaning in a stifled undertone. No one paid any attention to him. Absorbed in their cards, the men shouted and quarreled with one another. Suddenly I awoke to the realization that above the rude cries of the men I could no longer hear the insinuating gasp of the sick man. I looked closely at him and I had a strange feeling that he was no longer breathing. I bent my face to his and convinced myself that he lay absolutely still. I cried out. The men raised their heads irritably from their game. But the spectacle of death overawed them. They became subdued and silent. I was almost sure that they grew despondent and morose, thinking of their own fate.

For twenty hours the corpse remained in our cell. I protested its presence to the chief jailer, but he angrily told me to keep my mouth shut. I lay awake all night. Even the three murderers could not fall asleep. The body had begun to decompose and its stench was unendurable.

The days that followed seemed endless and leaden. I was cooped up like a wild beast in a cage, with a heavy steel chain securely gripping both my legs. As I was not allowed any exercise, I developed violent headaches. My contact with the outside world was of the very barest. I was not allowed to receive any visitors. The only reading material permitted me was the elevating Salvation Army *War Cry*. Reading it made me laugh. What I really stood in need of was not the salvation of my soul, but elementary justice.

7

Unless one has had the doubtful benefit of a stay in prison, it is hardly possible to grasp fully the viciousness of life there. Men who even once had a spark of humanity have it soon extinguished in the degrading atmosphere. An indefinable air of something slimy, monstrous and unnatural hangs over the entire prison. There is no room in it for any fine feelings, for love of men or of nature.

What were the men to do with themselves in their state of perpetual idleness? They were not given any work. The livelong day was wasted in card playing, buffoonery, quarreling and fist fights. It was but natural that under such unhealthy circumstances the prisoners' sexual instincts and practices should have become diseased. Many tried to while away the unending hours with lecherous day-dreaming. Always the principal topic of conversation was about sex, but sex in its most degraded and revolting aspects. Never in my life did I hear such obscenity! I could only regard it as the ravings of imbeciles and not men. The prisoners lived through in their imagination all the pleasures of sexual intercourse. They competed with each other boasting of their sexual experiences, a wretched compensation for their unnatural life in confinement.

The walls of the cells bore pencilled illustrations of the most obvious sex symbols, rudely drawn but unmistakable in their meaning. Everywhere one turned, one read the classic four-letter words and the most infantile smutty jingles.

It is noteworthy at this point to remark that these relatively harmless pastimes were indulged in mostly by the better elements among the prisoners. The others, hardened in crime and degenerated in their tastes and habits, looked for a more concrete outlet for their sexual appetites. They preyed upon all the young boys, some of whom were mere children!

Every day at nine o'clock the cells were opened by the turnkeys, and the men circulated freely in the entire prison block for the rest of the day. They had access to all the cells and thus could come in close contact with one another. This made it possible for the prisoners with homosexual inclinations to go prowling around for their private pleasures. However, these pleasures could not be very private in a place like a prison. They were practiced so that everyone knew about them. "Love making" was carried on in full sight of everybody. (Frequently I had to turn my eyes away in disgust and pity.)

The principal victims of these sexual orgies were mere children of twelve or thirteen years, boys who had been convicted of petty thievery. The prisoners had a curious name for them. They called them "Old Ladies." The arrival of a new boy became the signal for big-game hunting among all the perverts in the cell block. They fought like vultures among themselves, attacking each other with sharpened spoons until they bled like pigs. The other prisoners made bets on them as if they were prize fighters. Everyone was keen to know who was going to capture a particular "Old Lady." Usually the strongest and the most brutal of the prisoners succeeded in bagging his prey. What heartrending prey it was! The boys were like frightened little swallows. They fled from cell to cell, hoping against hope for a miraculous deliverance. But the hunters were hot on their trail. They cornered them at last and then would begin a free-for-all scramble, the horror of which will not escape me as long as I live. The "Old Lady" of twelve would tremble and weep and argue and plead. The men laughed. It always ended the same way—with the victor vaingloriously carrying off his prize into a dark corner of some cell. . . .

Once I became so indignant over the rape of a little boy that I was ready to throw myself bodily upon his seducer, but one of the prisoners seized hold of me and dragged me away, whispering in my ear:

"What's the matter—have you gone bugs? Don't you know that the rule in all prisons is—no interference? If you'll try to interfere you'll surely be killed."

The decent men among us grew sick at heart and turned their eyes away. As for the guards—they were old hands at it. They behaved in a callous manner. These incidents afforded them endless amusement.

Of course there were quite a number of "Old Ladies" who already were veterans at the game. They usually were second offenders who, during their previous imprisonment, had been initiated into homosexual practices. These behaved like the lowest street walkers. They always drove a sharp bargain, selling themselves to the highest bidder. They were given money and gifts. The men who "kept" them bought them girl's clothing and forced them to wear it at every opportunity. "Gal-Boy" parties were frequently given. A number of prisoners and their "Old Ladies" would come all dolled up for the occasion. The little boys wore girl's pink bloomers. This caused a lot of horse-play among the prisoners who stood outside watching through the cell bars.

I recall one incident with considerable pain. In the dragnet which the police had drawn around the Negro belt in Atlanta, during the campaign instigated by the Black Shirts against all Negroes who held jobs, was a gray-haired old fellow. The charge under which he was convicted was—procuring. I was absolutely convinced of the old man's innocence. He was a mild-mannered and serious individual who angrily disapproved of the bestiality among some of the men. One day when he heard the piteous outcry of a little boy who was being raped, he lost all self-control and began to grapple with the child's seducer. Old and feeble as he was he dared attack a powerful middle-aged brute. The outcome was a foregone conclusion. The latter knocked out his few remaining teeth, broke his nose and threw him against the steel bars of the cell with such force that it cut deep gashes into his head. For weeks the old man lay in the hospital. Subsequently, when he was released, he tried to have a number of the homosexual prisoners indicted by the Grand Jury. As an indictment would have meant laying the sores open of the entire prison system, the corrupt politicians saw to it that the charge never reached the Grand Jury.

8

One night a new prisoner was brought in, or, to speak more precisely, he was dragged in. His entrance created a sensation among us. Being taken to prison was the end rather than the beginning of his troubles. The police had beaten him up. They had bashed his head in; it was full of gaping wounds. His whole body was smeared with blood. The prisoners came trotting up, knowing that their evening's entertainment had arrived. The kangaroo judge sidled up to him and looked him over critically. Then he pulled out of his pocket the dirty piece of paper containing the rules of the kangaroo court and read them to him. The same rigmarole that I had experienced when I first came to prison was repeated. As the new arrival had no money to engage a lawyer for his defense, the judge, to the delight of the other prisoners, got ready to give him two hundred and fifty lashes on his bare buttocks.

I saw that the man was on the verge of collapse, so I stepped forward and offered to defend him free of charge. The judge looked at me contemptuously.

"You come from out of town—don't yer?" he drawled in his nasal way. "You don't practice law in this state—do yer? So yer ain't got no legal right to defend the prisoner in this here court."

To this I replied with an exaggerated respect to the court that it was true what His Honor had said about my not being legally entitled to plead the case of the prisoner, but I pointed out that inasmuch as he looked so ill, having been beaten up by our common enemy, the police, I wished to appeal to the court's magnanimity to overlook technicalities and to appoint me as attorney for the defendant.

The judge scratched his head and very reluctantly gave his consent.

I demanded a jury trial for my client. Twelve men were sworn in. Throughout the trial the prosecutor, a pompous-looking individual, referred to them as "representative citizens of the community." They certainly were representative of the "community"—in callousness and bestiality.

I opened my defense with a plea that the spirit of humanity and not the technicalities of the law should guide the jury in its deliberations in order that justice might be done.

At this point the judge pounded his gavel, cutting short my eloquence, and without rhyme or reason cited me for contempt of court and fined me one dollar.

Upon my paying the fine, the judge said:

"Where does the attorney for the defense think he is anyway—in a Sunday-school? From now on you must confine yourself to the facts in the case and lay off jawing about humanity and all that bosh—will yer?"

I continued with my defense. It became evident from the conduct of the judge that my client was not going to escape the two hundred and fifty lashes. But I actually did succeed in winning his acquittal on a legal technicality. The prosecutor had blundered, in that he made his final summary to the jury before even presenting the evidence in the case. I thereupon moved for a directed verdict in favor of the defendant because his guilt was not supposed to be taken as a foregone conclusion, for, according to law, a man is innocent until he is proven guilty.

The judge finally ruled in my favor and acquitted the prisoner. This made the prosecutor and his friends mad, so they impeached him for showing partiality. Not satisfying themselves with this they seized the unresisting acquitted man and began beating him in the face with brass knuckles until he fell in an inert heap to the floor. Hearing the commotion, the turnkeys came running up and dragged the unconscious man out of our cell block.

He never came back again. Later we were told that he had died of the beating. What the police had begun, the kangaroo court had obligingly finished.

EIGHTEEN

FOR THREE MONTHS I ROTTED in the degenerate atmosphere of the jail. There were times when I was afraid for my sanity. The vileness of our life seemed to pour into my veins and robbed me of all peace. I had little appetite left for living in such a wretched world. What sustained me and still sustains me is the moral duty of acting in the light of my Communist convictions.

Although my imprisonment in Fulton Tower was utterly without legal justification, the state was not ready to try my case. Guilty or innocent they were determined to keep me there until they would be able to go through with some farce of a trial. A farce it had to be because they did not have an iota of evidence against me. They waited for something to happen—hardly for a miracle, but to hatch some contemptible plot against me.

Let not this difficulty be underestimated: it was harder for me to obtain competent counsel on account of the prejudice against me as a Negro and a Red, than for me to become President of the United States. Of course, money could buy lawyers even in the South, but what kind of lawyers—unscrupulous and mercenary blood-suckers, battening on human misery!

The distinguished criminal lawyer, H. A. Allen of Atlanta, orated with great effect as soon as he took over the case:

"I am a Southern Republican gentleman and as such I cannot help but do everything I can."

However, there was a hitch in his devotion to justice, for he concluded:

"I don't think it is the proper thing to raise the question of the exclusion of Negroes from jury service."

This obvious piece of racial contempt and prejudice indicated to us beyond doubt that he was the wrong man to defend me.

However, it was hardly necessary for us to dismiss him, for after a while he himself declined to go on with the case. He also refused to return the considerable retainer he received from us. . . .

This left us high and dry, with our case suspended perilously in mid-air. But then an unusual thing happened.

Two young men visited me in jail and introduced themselves as Ben Davis, Jr. and John H. Geer. They were Negro attorneys in Atlanta and with great earnestness offered to defend me without remuneration. It was unmistakable that they were sincere and motivated by a selfless desire to protect a persecuted member of their race. They believed that I was being given a raw deal, which was more than they could stomach. Were they Communists or perhaps sympathetic to the movement of the workers? I asked hesitantly. Not in the least! They merely saw in my case a denial of the most elementary rights guaranteed to the citizens of the United States.

Immediately after they left me they sued out a writ of habeas corpus attacking the validity of the indictment which had been drawn up against me. The indictment, they charged, was too vague and insufficient to convict a cat. They challenged the legality of excluding Negroes systematically from jury service. Therefore, they demanded that I be released.

The machinery of my case ran perfectly. There was never a hitch in it. The judge denied the writ and I was ordered back to Fulton Tower to await trial. My case became a classic joke in legal circles. There were seven judges in the Superior Court of Fulton County, and each one of them was afraid to try me. So they played football with me and tossed me gingerly about from one to another like a deadly bomb from Moscow.

2

If my systematic education was neglected I had learned something even more valuable in the world of crass realities: I believe I had a sober and practical understanding of the ways of men. One of the most valuable lessons I derived from my trade-union experience was knowledge of the power of an enlightened public opinion. From early morning until I went to bed I sat in my cell, writing endless letters and articles to influential persons and to newspapers. As can well be imagined, it was not a personal plea for assistance. I regarded my plight merely as a symbol of the struggle of the Negro people for freedom. An example of the kind of appeal I wrote is the letter I addressed to the Negro newspaper, *The Liberator*, some time in October, 1932:

> Fulton Tower,
> Atlanta, Ga.
>
> Dear Comrades and Friends:
>
> Having been able to hear of the recent raids of Negro and white workers' homes, headed by the Rev. Assistant Solicitor General Hudson and the so-called Red Squad, I have been upset to know that this fanatical Fascist spokesman for the Southern ruling class is trying to use the Red Squad in order to make you accept the vicious starvation program of the slave-holding lords. United with him in this are the local yellow sheets of the slave drivers. They have printed base and dirty lies about the Reds with the express purpose of misleading you from the real true facts. Or, in other words, to make you believe that you are not being oppressed and starved, when you know better. Such stupid falsehoods as printed in *The Constitution* of Octo-

ber 3, which stated that "Communists are imbeciles, people who are insane or partly insane and those who are down and out," and then with the contradictory statement that "Some are intellectuals and millionaires," have not the least possible bit of authenticity. However, we shall grant them this, that there are over sixteen million workers out of employment throughout America—people who are not "down and out" but who are caught in the decaying grip of the gone-mad capitalist system. Well and good, gentlemen, if you want to call these people "imbeciles," "down and out," etc., they shall in the not very far distant future let you know what potential qualities such a number of "outcasts" possess. But we do not need a microscope to find out the real meaning of such insidious lies. We know that aside from their general outrages, etc., that the state of Georgia is trying to justify the means by which it so savagely convicted me. And we know at the same time that the preposterous sentence perpetrated upon me is not directed against me as a person, but against the whole working class. They have given the legal sanction to increase the starvation measures against the workers and Fascist lynch violence that is daily being practiced on the doubly exploited Negro people. But now how dare you, starving Negro and white workers, even mention the fact that your already miserable and intolerable lot is daily growing worse? Oh, yes, the state of Georgia "has a law for such people with teeth in it," and, "we are determined to use those teeth." In short, if you ask for bread and a decent living for your family, the state of Georgia has its chair with electric currents that will still your very life and "rid itself of Communism." What sheer nonsense! The workers will not let their human rights, which other civilized communities enjoy, be taken away from them by such ruling-class tricks. It is absolutely inconceivable to anyone who has made a close study of history and who has an insight into the forces of history to imagine that the ruling-class clique will be able to patch up its rotten system through sheer lies. Their days are already numbered! They can tell lies and keep Negroes from jury service. They can call me "darkey" and "nigger" and make that be law—but through the course of history they shall be introduced to a new law without its mountains of legal phraseology and corruption. Today they persecute Tom Mooney, Warren K. Billings, Ann Burlak, me and many more. But we shall hold fast and shall not perish! And, surely, we here in Atlanta will not smile at the bitterness of a depraved Southern ruling class.

ANGELO HERNDON

3

The response to this letter, as well as to my other appeals, was more than gratifying. A perfect avalanche of letters and telegrams from every part of the country rolled down upon me. White and Negro workers of Atlanta sent me money and baskets of fruit almost every day. It was most touching to receive such testimonials of regard and even affection from people whom I had never met. Therein lies the unifying power of an ideal. It draws together even perfect strangers within one indestructible bond.

The jailers were both amazed and mystified by my popularity. One day, while bringing me a mass of letters and telegrams, one of them looked at me quizzically, yet with respect and even a little awe.

"Say, nigger," he asked me confidentially, "tell me, who are you anyway? Are you the King of Abyssinia or something?"

"I ain't sayin' I ain't, and I ain't sayin' I is," I answered unsmilingly. "But anyway I expect you to do me all the royal honors."

My jailer laughed almost civilly. Obviously he was impressed. The other jailers too were impressed, if not cowed, by the mass protests of thousands of people from the outside. How they would have liked to beat me up! But now they did not dare do me any harm. The outside was now watching alertly what was happening to me. Just the same, they did indulge themselves in one petty meanness. They deliberately crushed all fruits, cakes and candies sent to me by my invisible friends, and with an ill-concealed sneer laid them before me absolutely uneatable.

The prosecutor, the Reverend Hudson, demanded high bail for me "so that damn Red will come back for trial." The judge was obliging and fixed it at $25,000. It stands to reason that I could never raise such a fortune. In default of this I was kept in that hell hole of a prison many months more. Repeatedly my attorneys, Davis and Geer, argued with the court for a reduction in bail. The judge finally agreed on $2,500.

On December 24, 1932, the day before Christmas, Messrs. Yates and Milton, Negro druggists in Atlanta, bailed me out of prison.

As I left the jail the guards sarcastically called after me:

"A merry Christmas and a happy New Year."

I made no answer.

Once again I breathed the brisk wintry air as a free man. For six interminable months my body had been tortured and my spirit had been crucified by capitalist law and order in an effort to break me. If anything, the spirit of rebellion was more aflame in me now than ever before. The power of an idea is undying. It gives one wings. As I walked hurriedly through the streets of Atlanta to rejoin my friends, I became lighthearted and I smiled—yes, smiled most friendly into the face of every passer-by. It was wonderful to be free again, but it was far more wonderful to feel my brotherly kinship with all the world.

NINETEEN

My release on bail created two main bodies of opinion in the South. One, represented by the lynch officials, rent the air with their denunciations of giving "niggers" legal protection. Their slogan was: Hang him and damn him! The other group was more "cultured," more refined, set on preserving the tradition of Southern gentility. They upheld the notion that the "law should take its course." If I was to be hanged they would have it done with the sanction of Section 56 of the Penal Code of the State of Georgia. They too were determined that no "impudent" or "uppity" nigger should get away with insulting the white upper class of Georgia. Yes, they were going to make an example of me for all those "damn Reds" and Yankee "nigger lovers"!

The day on which my trial opened, January 16, 1933, proved a Roman holiday for Atlanta's best "citizens" and "Social Registerites." My case was unique. It promised to give them a real "thrill." They were intrigued by the novelty of a "dirty little nigger" trying to overthrow their autocratic power. They crowded the court room, devoured by curiosity to see how this monstrosity looked.

A feeling of revulsion came over me as I looked into their faces. I read in them: No mercy, no compassion. At the moment I was not only an entertainer in a legal burlesque show to divert them from their boredom, but, even more, I became the outlet for all their hatred, all their fear of the rising power of a working class becoming fully aware of its rights and its ability to enforce the granting of those rights.

On the other hand, I was not at all devoid of consolation. Besides the "respectables" who hoped for a death sentence, the court room was also packed with Negro and white workers. I looked into their grave faces searchingly. I was not turned away. They were my class brothers and they were visibly afraid that my fate had already been sealed by the court.

2

Promptly at 9:30 that morning Judge Lee B. Wyatt called the court to order.

The clerk mumbled:

"The State of Georgia vs. Angelo Herndon. Are you here?"

Oh, was I there!

The judge, without even looking at me, repeated the sacred formula:

"How do you plead, guilty or not guilty?"

"Not guilty, Your Honor."

The "respectables" snickered and laughed out loud.

The prosecutor then rose very solemnly and began in a pious voice:

"Your Honor, ladies and gentlemen, and may it please the court. I will attempt here on the basis of the indictment to prove that the defendant, Angelo Herndon, is guilty of attempting to overthrow the lawfully and constituted authority of the State of Georgia."

This was the first time I had come face to face with Mr. Hudson. I tried to size him up mentally. Watching him, I became gloomy. I read in his eyes the sentence of death that he was going to ask for me. He was a lanky, tall man, partially bald and with deep sunken eyes that were sharp as gimlets. He had a curious way of talking—stretching out his long arms like the blades of a windmill and casting them about as if he were ready to fly off like an angel. But there was nothing angelic about the man in any other way. He was one to stand in fear of, for he seemed to possess the unscrupulous courage and the determination of a man-hunter. His cynicism and contempt for me were undisguised.

My Negro attorney, Mr. Davis, moved to have the case dismissed on the grounds that the anti-insurrection law under which I was indicted was unconstitutional, that the indictment was too vague and that Negroes were systematically excluded from jury service.

The judge glowered at the Negro attorney who dared challenge white justice. But young Mr. Davis could not be put out of face by any display of white superiority. Unafraid and with the dignity of a man who knows his worth, he fought both judge and prosecutor with great energy. I was fortunate in having him for my lawyer. There was a sympathetic communication between us throughout the course of the trial which sustained our spirits in the general hostility against us.

The judge asked for evidence to prove the last allegation. Mr. Davis then requested Oscar Palmour, the Jury Commissioner, to testify. Mr. Palmour deposed:

"I do testify that the reason I haven't selected any Negroes' names as a Grand Juror or Grand Jurors is because of the fact that there isn't a single one, in my opinion, that comes up to the requirements, except those professional men excused by law. I am familiar with the law by which we select them—'the most upright men serve as Grand Jurors.' We can tell whether a man is a black taxpayer or white taxpayer . . . As to how the Jury Commissioners dispose of the tickets with Negroes' names on them, we will suppose: 'It is a Negro taxpayer, John Jones.' Somebody will say 'one list.' Probably he knows something about it. If nobody suggests 'a double list,' he isn't starred and therefore couldn't go on the Grand Jury list. Since I have been a member of the Jury Commission, as to whether

I can remember any time which a Negro has been selected as a Grand Juror in this county, the fact is 'I haven't paid any attention at all'— The actual fact is 'I didn't know until somebody called my attention to it, that there were no Negroes in the Grand Jury box. We have about 4,000 names in the Grand Jury box. About a third of the population are Negroes.' "

This lame and hopelessly confused account of the witness did make one thing clear: The Jury Commissioner had a distaste for Negroes on the jury.

My lawyer then called a college-trained Negro, R. L. Craddock, to the witness stand. Mr. Davis asked him:

"Have you ever been called for jury service by the Federal Court of this district?"

As if struck by lightning the Reverend Hudson leaped to his feet and shouted his objection to the question. He said it was irrelevant and immaterial.

Judge Wyatt agreed with him. Both he and the prosecutor showed a great partiality for those magic words: irrelevant and immaterial. Whatever evidence seemed to favor my defense was immediately dismissed with those two wonderful words.

Mr. Davis put in a spirited denunciation of the anti-insurrection law and of the flimsy evidence that had been brought against me. Judge Wyatt listened with impatience and irritation. When Mr. Davis got through speaking, the judge sarcastically asked him:

"Are you through?"

Then he recited the good old formula:

"I overrule all three of the motions as being irrelevant and immaterial to this particular case."

He then ordered the trial to proceed.

The business of choosing a jury was a very disheartening one. My lawyers exhausted all the defense's peremptory challenges, so that they were finally obliged to accept every man backed by the prosecution, with but a feeble show of resistance. The whole procedure was a farce. The prosecutor grinningly asked each one in a sing-song voice,

"Have you any prejudice or bias resting on your mind against the prisoner at the bar?"

"Why, of course not!"

And the broad-minded gentleman would then take his seat in the jury box, his face wreathed in snickers.

My lawyers looked at me and I looked at them, and all three of us knew what the outcome was going to be. Only we were not going to resign ourselves, but put up a good fight.

The jury having been sworn, the Reverend Hudson called Mr. F. B. Watson, the policeman who had arrested me, to the witness stand. He was asked to identify every piece of literature that he had taken from my room without even the legal pretense of a search warrant.

The Reverend Hudson held up a copy of the *Daily Worker* in a melodramatic manner, as if it were a stick of lighted dynamite.

"Can you identify this as being in the possession of the defendant?" he asked the witness.

"Yes, I got it from that nigger's room," answered the latter, pointing at me.

Mr. Davis jumped to his feet and vigorously protested against the use of the word "nigger" because it would prejudice the jury against his client.

A slightly mocking smile lurked in the corners of Judge Wyatt's mouth as he overruled the objection.

Mr. Davis was beside himself with rage at the court's decision. He did not dare look in my direction, out of fear that I would read in his face what he most feared for me.

Piece by piece the witness was made to identify all the reading matter found in my room. Ripley's *Believe It Or Not* series never illustrated more hair-raising monstrosities than the exhibits placed in evidence against me by the prosecutor to back up his charge that I had incited to insurrection. In a literal sense, the lion and the lamb were here lying down together—the pamphlets: *The Communist Position on the Negro Question*, and *Communism and Christianism*, by the Rt. Rev. William Montgomery Brown—competed in revolutionary bloodthirstiness with copies of the New York *Times*, the *Wall Street Journal*, and the *Red Book Magazine!* The latter was thrown in for good measure because of the word "Red" in it.

I did not know whether the occasion called for crying or laughing; the thing appeared simply too weird! I glanced rapidly at Mr. Davis and I felt sorry for him. He looked so stunned! We did not expect this. But what were we to do? We just had to make a strong effort to expose their humbug.

3

The prosecutor began reading aloud from Bishop Brown's pamphlet. When he came to the passage "Banish the gods from the skies and the capitalists from the earth and make the world safe for industrial Communism," he began to choke. I recognized his fine acting. It was clear as daylight that he was trying to whip himself into a magnificent frenzy of righteousness. He grew red in the face and bellowed like a bull until he became winded, so that his voice could hardly be heard above a whisper. The spectacle he made of himself was perfectly revolting! Whirling his arms about like a dancing dervish, he pleaded with the jury:

"Gentlemen, is any more damning evidence needed to prove that the defendant, Angelo Herndon, sitting over there with the red tie on, is guilty of trying to overthrow the State Government of Georgia by distributing and circulating this ungodly literature written by the damnable unfrocked bishop?"

Up to this point the Reverend Hudson spoke with the grave piety of a church man. But suddenly the colonel in him got the better of the Holy Ghost. He began to rattle off his words in the sharp manner of a sizzling machine-gun:

"The defendant claims to be interested in the unemployed, but that is just a disguise. He is only trying to stir up the races, to foment and create trouble that will bring about an industrial revolution so he and his Communist friends can set up a godless dictatorship in this country based on the style of the Bolsheviki dictatorship in Soviet Russia. The Communists know that they cannot overthrow the American form of government by open propaganda. So they have tried to sneak into our schools and churches, to get control of the press so they can disseminate their insidious propaganda to poison the minds of the people against their elected representatives. They publish, own and dictate the policy of the newspapers and magazines that I have just offered into the record as evidence. Look at the red covering of this magazine, *Red Book*. Is not that proof enough?"

The prosecutor handed the literature to the members of the jury. They solemnly passed it from one to another, slightly embarrassed. It was evident that it was all Chinese to them. They did not know what to make of it. Yet they seemed ready to rely on the authority and good judgment of such a great gentleman as the Assistant Solicitor General! Surely he knew what it was all about, and that was sufficient for them.

The audience, however, acted in quite another manner. It followed the thundering argument of the prosecutor with amusement. And when he pointed to the cover on the *Red Book Magazine*, the laughter became general and open. Even I could not resist the temptation of a chuckle. The scene was too comical for words.

After the luncheon recess, the prosecutor resumed his attack. This time he switched his role to that of prosecutor. He spoke with the severe voice of the hunter who never fails to bag his prey. Surely, he admitted, there was nothing wrong in organizing a demonstration of the unemployed. Why, of course the people have the perfect right to petition the government against wrongs done to them. But did I, or did I not, admit that I was a member of the Communist Party? Was it not true that Communist literature was found in my possession? All this was sufficient to send me to the electric chair. As an officer of the law it was his solemn duty to see that this was done. As for all other Reds who might plan to invade the sacred boundaries of the State of Georgia, he issued the warning: "As fast as the Communists come here, we shall indict them and I shall demand the death penalty in every case."

The issue, concluded the prosecutor, was not between the State of Georgia and its unemployed citizens, but Communism vs. the State.

"This is not only a trial of Angelo Herndon, but of Lenin, Stalin, Trotsky and Kerensky, and every white person who believes that black and white should unite for the purpose of setting up a nigger Soviet Republic in the Black Belt."

This last argument proved the most telling blow against me. The judge shook his head vigorously in approval and the jury like one man expressed their solidarity with both the judge and the prosecutor by the look of triumph they flashed at me.

My defense attorney, Mr. Davis, knew that he was fighting a losing battle. But he nevertheless jumped to the attack. He argued that it was wholly unconstitutional and unjust for a person to be arrested and placed on trial for his life for a crime that is foreign and neither here nor there. What did I have to do with Lenin, Stalin, Trotsky and Kerensky? he asked.

"Irrelevant and immaterial," decided Judge Wyatt.

As evidence that every member of the Communist Party must submit to its discipline and to that of the Communist International, obliging him to engage in plots and conspiracies against the United States government and to assassinate its officials, the prosecutor read the following statement by Lenin:

"We are the party of the working class. Consequently, nearly the whole of that class (in time of war and civil war, the whole of that class) should work under the guidance of our Party, should create the closest contacts with our Party. He who weakens, no matter how little, the iron discipline of the Party of the proletariat (especially during the period of dictatorship), effectively helps the bourgeoisie against the proletariat. The Party, as the training school for working-class leaders, is the only organization competent, in virtue of its experience and authority, to centralize the leadership of the proletarian struggle, and thus transform all non-Party working-class organizations into accessory organs and connecting belts linking up the Party with the working class as a whole."

As he orated he jumped around the jury box like one possessed. He waved papers and magazines in the air and screamed like a man gone out of his senses. Torrents of perspiration poured from his face and body. I sat watching him spellbound. This was one of the worst vaudeville shows I had ever seen, and yet the most interesting to me, for this particular vaudeville show happened to hold my life in the balance. The Reverend Hudson made the impression of a ham actor upon me. He ran the gamut of all emotional expression, and there is nothing Southerners love so much as a good theatrical show. They thrilled to every blessed word of his. He warned them of me as if I were Satan himself:

"Some may think that there is no serious immediate danger to be expected from the work that the defendant was engaged in before the law stretched out its hand and brought him before the bar of justice, but I ask you gentlemen of the jury, must the State of Georgia sit idly by while he, Angelo Herndon, is organizing his army to march into the state to murder, kill and assassinate all white people, take away their property and set up a nigger kingdom?"

No sooner had he said these words when an elderly, gray-bearded Negro worker, who later told me that he had been a chattel slave in Georgia, chimed in from a bench in the rear of the court room, where he was sitting, with the following words:

"Horse feathers! He only asked for bread for the unemployed and got it—that's all."

The court room rocked with laughter. This made Judge Wyatt furious. He banged with his gavel and warned that if there was any further demonstration he would have the whole court room cleared.

A telegraph messenger boy came in and laid a batch of telegrams before the Reverend Hudson. When he read them he flushed angrily and looked at me with narrowing eyes. Then he handed them to the judge. I surmised that they were messages of protest from liberal workers' organizations, demanding my unconditional release, for when the judge read them he exclaimed loud enough for everyone in the court room to hear:

"Sons of bitches!"

4

That evening proved to be one of the happiest in my life. When the court adjourned until the following day, Negro and white workers rushed up to me and my attorneys and warmly shook hands with us. One old Negro patriarch, gnarled like an oak tree, said to me in a quavering voice as he laid his withered old hand in mine:

"I lived in Georgia when Negroes were still slaves. I never dreamed of the day when I would see a black man stand up in a white man's court and fight like you people have been fighting here today. You sure did get that judge riled up all right.

I could see his face turning red. Son, I feel as if a new day is coming for the Negro. We have waited for it long enough."

Nothing in my whole life moved me more than what this old man said to me, for through him spoke all the tribulations and the dreams of redemption of the Negro people.

5

My defense suffered many setbacks on the second day of the trial. The judge saw fit to overrule every motion or objection that my defense counsel raised. Mr. Davis moved for a *prima facie* case in my favor because the state had admitted that there were no names of Negroes in the Grand Jury box from which the Grand Jury that indicted me was drawn, and because the state did not think it necessary to offer any evidence that Negroes were not excluded from the jury.

Curtly Judge Wyatt overruled the motion.

Mr. Davis then called Professor Mercer G. Evans to the witness stand. He wished to qualify him as an expert on Communism. Professor Evans recited his pedigree:

"I am a teacher at Emory University, in the Department of Economics. I have the Bachelor of Science (B.S.) degree from Emory University, and the Master of Arts (A.M.) and Doctor of Laws (LL.D.) degrees from the University of Chicago. I have been a teacher of economics at Emory University for nine years. I have read widely in the field of theoretical economics, including a good deal of Anarchistic and sociological or Communist literature, which is, of course, of an economic nature. Some of the magazines that have carried my articles of an economic nature are: *The Annals of the American Academy of Social and Political Science*, *The American Federationist*. I have read the books stated in this indictment."

During the state's cross-examination of Professor Evans and over the objection of defense counsel, the court allowed him to testify as follows:

"I am acquainted with what is known as the Communist of Soviet Russia or the Soviet Union, of the present form of government in the nation of Russia, that it is a government which succeeded the Kerensky government, which succeeded the former Czarist government; that was brought about by a revolution, putting out the Czar and the assassination of the Czar and his family came later, not necessarily as the result of a revolution. As to the Russian Revolution, history so regards it, that there was a revolution. The Czarist government overthrown, the Kerensky government took charge, and after about six months another revolution of bloodless character in which the present regime succeeded the Kerensky government. I wouldn't attempt to dispute that as an historical fact."

The Reverend Hudson then interjected:

"Have you ever been to Russia, Doctor?"

"Yes, I have been to Russia. I was over there this summer. I spent about two weeks in Russia, I think."

The second expert for the defense, Professor T. J. Corley, also of Emory University, next took the witness stand. The Reverend Hudson asked him:

"Doctor, are you familiar with the Communist platform in the 1932 election?"

Professor Corley replied: "Yes, parts of it."

"Do you agree with the full platform?"

Mr. Davis objected to this question as irrelevant. Judge Wyatt overruled him and Professor Corley was obliged to answer:

"Most of it."

The prosecutor continued:

"Did you know that the platform demands the right of self-determination for the niggers in the Black Belt?"

"Yes."

"Would you want a nigger to marry your daughter?"

Mr. Davis jumped to his feet:

"Your Honor, I object," he said.

"Objection overruled," snapped back the judge.

"Excuse me, Your Honor," said the Prosecutor, as he resumed his questioning of the witness, "I will re-frame the question: Do you understand the Communist position on the Negro question to mean the right of a colored boy to marry your daughter, if you have one?"

Mr. Davis was on his feet again.

"Your Honor," he remonstrated, "we object to the question on the ground that it is irrelevant and immaterial and call for a conclusion of the witness."

Tiresomely as well as tirelessly Judge Wyatt droned:

"I overrule the objection."

Professor Corley then answered the question put to him:

"That is against the laws of the State of Georgia."

To this the Prosecutor answered with the following question:

"Did you know that there are twenty states in the United States where the two races (white and Negro) can intermarry or mix?"

"I do not know how many states there are in the union where they have that right," answered Professor Corley. "I only know that a Negro doesn't happen to have the right to marry my daughter under the laws of this state."

Judge Wyatt now interrupted in a manner which appeared to me, to my counsel and to the court audience as rather "irrelevant and immaterial:"

"If Emory University is guilty of anything, we will try them; I think even if Emory University had actually attempted to incite riot, it wouldn't be material in this case; it is a question of what this defendant has done. If the defendant attempted to overthrow the government he is an anarchist. The defense has failed to qualify the professors as experts on the question of economics. I, therefore, overrule the motion as experts on the ground that Communism has nothing to do with economics. Of course, I don't deny that the defendant might not be an economical man."

The spectators doubled up with laughter and the judge again brought his gavel down with a bang. He ranted:

"I am not going to have any demonstrations in this court room. A man is on trial for his life, and I am going to see that justice is done. The next one I catch demonstrating, I am going to have the bailiff bring you up here, and I will send you where you can't demonstrate."

What did the hypothetical question of a white woman marrying a Negro, put to Professors Corley and Evans by the Prosecutor, have to do with my attempt to incite insurrection in the incomparable State of Georgia? Was I mad or were they mad? It was all gibberish to me. I just could not make head or tail of it. Nor could anybody else, for that matter.

6

The Reverend Hudson finally called his star witness for examination. He was E. A. Stephens, one of the assistant prosecutors. It was he who was supposed to have "investigated" me and obtained a "confession."

Confession? What confession? Had I ever confessed?

Mr. Stephens testified:

"I called on the chief of police to have that box * watched and the man who got the mail out of there taken in charge and questioned; the same day, Officer Watson or Mr. W. B. Martin, I don't recollect which, brought this darkey, Angelo Herndon, to the solicitor's office, and I talked to him in the Grand Jury room."

When Mr. Davis objected to the use of the word "darkey"

* My mail box in the post office.

on the ground that it was an insulting and prejudicial name, Judge Wyatt drawled:

"I don't know whether it is or not; but suppose you refer to him as the defendant."

Thereupon my counsel moved for a directed verdict in my favor on the ground that it was impossible for me to receive a fair trial because of the race prejudice exhibited throughout the trial by the court, the prosecutors and the state's witnesses.

Judge Wyatt looked surprised. Apparently he had never heard of a directed verdict issued on such grounds and he overruled the motion.

Mr. Davis knew that I did not have a ghost of a chance for acquittal. If he made so many exceptions, it was with an appeal to the higher courts in mind.

7

At last I was called to testify. I was very calm and collected. I felt that the worst that my legal inquisitors could do to me they had already done. Any statement I could make to the jury seemed superfluous, as it was altogether obvious that the jurymen had already made up their minds to render a verdict of guilty against me. Taking this into consideration, I decided not to mince my words and speak what I thought. At least I could let people know what kind of justice was being given me and for what reasons.

I did not address myself to the judge nor, for that matter, to the prosecutors nor to the jurors who were deciding my fate. Far beyond them I saw a vision of millions of white and Negro workers, oppressed and hungry, listening to every word I was saying. It was they who were going to be my jury. By them I wished to be judged. I knew that my case was a challenge to them and to their right to organize into labor unions and to live in peace and security. In their name I accepted this challenge and spoke, not as if I were in a court room, but as if I were addressing my fellow-workers at one of our educational meetings.*

There was great silence as I spoke. Men and women sat pale and tense. I looked at them and they looked at me, and I felt that we were fused together by the deepest bonds of sympathy. A warm glow shot through my body and I tingled with the joy of it. The hard cruel faces of the state's instruments of class injustice receded from me. The walls of the court house seemed to melt away and I walked the earth erect and free. I thought of the rugged beauty and greatness of heart of the American people. It was to them that I was now speaking. Yet what I was saying could not be in the nature of a defense. Quite the contrary. It was a scathing indictment of the system. It was also a plea to the workers to rise and change the world. My words sprang from the heart and I directed them to the heart and the conscience of my fellowmen.

8

To disprove the charges that I had made in my address to the jury that I had been persecuted and mistreated in Fulton Tower, the state brought forward Chief Jailer Bob Holland to testify.† He lied like a Trojan. His childish chatter amused the court audience very much. He was a little shamefaced and angry when Mr. Davis in his cross-examination exposed the contradictions of his denials. He did not dare look in my direction because he knew he was lying.

Very remarkable is the fact that the two principal witnesses against me were the Assistant Prosecutor and the Chief Jailer, as if my "crime of insurrection" was committed after my arrest!

The defense finally rested.

* For complete text of this address see Appendix Three, p. 342.
† For text of Mr. Holland's testimony see Appendix Four, p. 349.

The following day, January 18, 1933, Mr. Davis made his summary before the jury.* It was clear that he was under a great mental and emotional strain. He knew the jury that he was appealing to, but this knowledge did not prevent him from fighting as gamely and as long as it was possible. Although he was the son of a wealthy Negro politician, a National Republican Committeeman, and had been educated at Harvard, he felt that all that separated us were merely surface differences; that in reality he and I and millions of disenfranchised and exploited Negroes shared the same rotten fate. I looked at him and I felt wretched for his sake. He was tense and his voice shook. It was one of the most moving adddresses I have ever heard. He spoke with the dignity of a man belonging to a despised race and who has the courage to assert his manhood in the face of his people's oppressors. The audience of black and white workers thrilled to his words.

9

The Reverend Hudson followed with his final summary for the state. He looked like the avenging angel. The court room was filled with the thunder of his eloquence. He went through the most incredible antics. This was the final curtain, and he was going to perform his level best. For this purpose the role of man of God would suit him best. So he fell on his knees before the jury box, just as if he were before a church altar and, with tears in his eyes, pleaded in the holy name of God that such a fiend as I should be electrocuted and wiped off the face of the earth. Folding his hands piously he outstretched them to the gentlemen of the jury, beseeching hoarsely:

"Gentlemen of the jury: You have heard the defendant lay down his defy to the State of Georgia. He is a confirmed revo-

* For text of Mr. Davis' address see Appendix Five, p. 351.

lutionist, with an unbreakable soul. But we accept his challenge. Gentlemen, when you go into the box, I expect you to arrive at a verdict that will automatically send this damnable anarchistic Bolsheviki to his death by electrocution, and God will be satisfied that justice has been done and the daughters of the state officials can walk the streets safely. Stamp this thing out now with a conviction."

As I listened to him, it struck me with full force that he had made a sensational impression with his speech upon both judge and jury. It became very clear to me why that was so. He spoke their language. He interlarded his lynch frenzy with goodly sprinklings from Holy Writ. Blood and piety, these are the two principal ingredients of boasted Southern civilization. Murder is perfumed with the altar incense of religion to hide its rotten stench.

When the Reverend Hudson had concluded, the judge gave his instructions to the jury. He said:

"You are the sole judges of all the facts, and the court can express no opinion, and does express no opinion as to what has or has not been proven; it is for you to determine whether or not any of these things that I have charged you upon have been proven."

10

At eight o'clock that night the jury sent word that it had reached a verdict. When they filed into the jury box the silence in the court room became painful. Now, by nature I am an optimist. One might say it is a strange sort of optimism. It largely consists of a realistic expectation of the worst that can possibly happen. The optimism part of it is that in expecting the worst there is no longer any room for suspense. Therefore, there is no more cause for anxiety or inner conflict. For this reason I imagine that I was the jolliest person in the court room that day, with the possible exception of that man of God, the Reverend Hudson, who knew what was coming.

"Gentlemen," said the Clerk of the Court, "have you arrived at a verdict, and if you have will you please read it to the court?"

Judge Wyatt ordered all doors locked, and, glaring at the court audience, he warned:

"While the verdict is being read there must not be any demonstrating to indicate your approval or disapproval of the verdict. The jurors have arrived at a verdict and no one knows whether it is in favor or against the defendant."

The foreman of the jury then rose and read from a little piece of paper:

"We, the jury, find the defendant, Angelo Herndon, guilty as charged, but recommend that mercy be shown and fix his sentence at from eighteen to twenty years."

At this a great commotion rose in the court room. Men and women of both races and belonging to all classes sprang to their feet and raised a clamor of protest. Some pounded on the benches and others cried out. In the general hubbub it was not clear what they were saying except that they were registering general disapproval of the verdict.

A bright newspaper reporter leaned over and asked me:

"How do you feel, Angelo; are you scared?"

As if he cared a lot whether I was or not! But it might make good reading copy.

"No," I answered. "I am feeling fine. This verdict is the surprise of my life. I expected the electric chair, but these fine gentlemen of the jury have made me a Christmas present. They have recommended mercy, and so I am getting away with only twenty years on the chain gang. Am I not lucky?"

The newspaper man looked bewildered at me. He could not make up his mind whether I was crazy or just a simpleton. Maybe, he will find out some day. Who knows?

Judge Wyatt called me to the bar. He was almost fatherly to me now. So much "mercy" had softened his heart toward me. He could well afford it now. The show was all over except for the applause. And he was sure to get the lion's share of it from the newspapers and all good citizens. Almost benignly he smiled at me as he said:

"Angelo, the jury has found you guilty of attempting to incite to insurrection and fixed the sentence. I think they are justified in doing so. Have you anything to say before I pass sentence upon you?"

"Yes, Your Honor," I answered, "I have this to say:

"You may do what you will with Angelo Herndon. You may indict him. You may put him in jail. But there will come other thousands of Angelo Herndons. If you really want to do anything about the case, you must go out and indict the social system. But this you will not do, for your role is to defend the system under which the toiling masses are robbed and oppressed. You may succeed in killing one, two, even a score of working-class organizers. But you cannot kill the working class."

Judge Wyatt then passed sentence upon me:

"Whereupon, it is ordered and adjudged by the court that the defendant, Angelo Herndon be taken from the bar of this court to the jail of Fulton County, and be there safely kept until a sufficient guard is sent for him from the Georgia Penitentiary, and be then delivered to, and be by said guard taken to said penitentiary, or to such other place as the Governor may direct, where he, the said Angelo Herndon, be confined at hard labor for the full term of not less than eighteen (18) years, and not more than twenty (20) years, to be computed as provided in the Act approved August 27, 1931."

Again a commotion was raised in the audience. The judge pounded his gavel, but the noise would not subside. One Negro woman cried out in a ringing voice:

"It's a damn shame! If they ever get him on that chain gang, they will sure kill him!"

A policeman clapped handcuffs on me and led me out through the rear entrance of the court to a waiting automobile. Outside a large crowd of Negro and white spectators crowded around us to bid me good-bye. Men and women shouted encouragement to me. Their cries were indistinct. I could not make out what they were saying. But their eyes were more eloquent than words could be. With earnest, tense faces they clenched their fists in farewell salute.

My class brothers! I knew they would never forget me and would fight tirelessly for my freedom.

Tranquilly, in a gravely reflective mood, I followed my jailer as he led me back into Fulton Tower.

It was a clear mild night although in mid-winter. The only things that looked fresh and green were the magnolia trees stirring in the wind at the entrance of the jail. I looked at them long and yearningly with a last caress of the eyes as the heavy prison gates swung close behind me.

Would I ever see those wonderful magnolia trees again? I wondered! . . .

TWENTY

As soon as the verdict became known, all the newspapers in the South began to raise a hue and cry after me. Like the bloodhounds that they were they yelped their hatred of me, trying to whip up a lynch frenzy. In screaming headlines they gloated over my conviction. I knew it was not me alone whom they wished to crucify; it was the entire downtrodden Negro people they aimed to strike at through me, so that we might all continue as slaves in Egypt.

The Mississippi Meridian Star, in its issue of February 4, 1933, motivated by benevolent concern for the Negro people, held me up as a threat and as a warning, how not to be and what not to follow:

> "Halt!
>
> "Angelo Herndon, nineteen-year-old Cincinnati Negro, comes down to Dixie on a crusade. It seems that the sole purpose of his jaunt below the Mason and Dixon line is to promulgate the many 'blessings' and advantages of Communism.
>
> "But Georgia's Judge Lee Wyatt, after a jury had found the Negro guilty under an old law passed during the troublesome days of reconstruction that followed the war between the states, passes sentence of eighteen to twenty years against the youthful Negro and he will now have plenty of time to ruminate upon the blessings of freedom if he had it. The South needs none of his kind. The better

class of the Negro race knows that Communism has nothing to offer, save chaos and destruction.

"We white people of the South, having lived in close touch with the Negro race for years and years, are well aware of the fact that Communism is deadly 'intoxication' that leads to trouble, not only for Negroes who listen to its tempting lies, but for law and order as well. Under the old Georgia law by which Herndon was tried and convicted, the death penalty is possible, but the jury, as well as the judge feels that a command to 'halt'—brought by an eighteen to twenty year prison sentence—will effectively curb the culprit's 'teachings.' "

That Southern white newspapers should rejoice over my misfortune I could readily understand. But what pained me more than anything else was the conduct of the lickspittle, cowardly Negro newspapers. They too wished to yelp with the white bloodhounds, partly out of fear for themselves, partly to curry favor with their white masters. Oh, no, they were not "dirty niggers" like me, they were "good darkies!" The Negro *Pittsburgh Courier* thus delivered itself editorially in its issue of February 4th:

> "If Herndon dies, the responsibility for his death will rest not only upon the planter-manufacturer dictatorship of Georgia, but upon the Communist Party, which persists in callously sending these youngsters down to certain imprisonment and death. His imprisonment and the jailing of others in Georgia and adjoining states is not only a disgrace to American civilization, but a severe indictment of the Communist Party policy, which persistently ignores realities while chasing Marxist will-o'-the-wisps."

I have always found that one kind word has usually compensated me for all the torrents of abuse poured upon me. Here and there a white Southern voice was raised in indignant protest against the frame-up which brought about my conviction. It is true that it was a lonely voice crying in the wilderness, but it heartened me.

The editor of the *Macon Telegraph* expressed his horror in the January 20th issue of this paper. The title of his editorial was: *Shameful Verdict.* It read:

> "Undoubtedly there was about it the element of 'teaching a Negro a lesson,' as the attorneys for Herndon charged. A statute that was sixty-two years old was raked out of the dusty law books as the basis for a grand-jury indictment. The law itself represented the thinking of other days and conditions of other days.
>
> "After all, those who stupidly use our courts for such purposes ought to keep in mind that the ultimate purpose of Communism is to provide enough food and clothing and shelter for oppressed people and that the danger of overthrow, if there is any danger, is not from outside propaganda, but from fathers who look into faces of pinched and hungry children and mothers who are not able to protect their children against the most intense of all suffering, the suffering from cold.
>
> "The *Telegraph* hopes that the Supreme Court of this state will substitute common sense for the Bourbonism of the jury that tried Herndon."

But not all Negro newspapers had an Uncle Tom attitude nor repeated parrot-like "Yassa, boss" all the time. The *St. Louis Argus*, for instance, carried an editorial in its issue of January 27th, captioned: "Nineteen Years for What?" It read:

> "The cause which Herndon represented is eternal and those who are to deal with it cannot hope to stop its progress by imprisoning a few leaders. The same drama was staged in the days of slavery. The Negro slave spoke about his condition in a low breath. The abolitionist who spoke

out against slavery endangered his life. Prison and death stared those in the face who would dare to speak out against slavery. 'John Brown's body lies amolding in the clay,' but his truths are marching on. The protest of Herndon has resounded the world over. No doubt it has been heard in every language in the civilized world. The significance of his statement and the righteousness of the cause he represented have been heard by everybody except the people of Georgia, particularly the prosecutor, the judge and that class which is still asleep to the onward march of civilization."

Almost overnight my case had become a battlefield for the reactionaries against the liberals of the South.

2

One night, about a month after I had been returned to Fulton Tower, I was suddenly visited by the Chief Jailer and about fifty deputies. It was not exactly a social call they were making. It literally was an invasion. They swooped down upon me like an attacking army, tore the newspaper which I was then reading out of my hands and threw me against the bars of my cell.

"So you thought you were going to make a quiet getaway?" raged the Chief Jailer. "You know, Angelo, you might have asked permission first and I surely would have obliged you."

I was dumbfounded, although I guessed that they were up to no good. The deputies rushed about searching for hacksaws, so they said. I told them that nobody was trying to get out and that it was foolish of them to search for something I did not possess. At this, one of the deputies walked up to me and said:

"Shut up, you black —."

A white prisoner, who in order to curry favor with the jailers had joined in the search, now made a startling discovery.

He picked up several pieces of iron and held them up triumphantly. He volunteered the expert judgment that these had been freshly broken. One of my cellmates indignantly asked him how he knew. A deputy standing near by struck him with a broomhandle.

"Who asked you, you dirty nigger?" he shouted.

Hastily I placed myself between the deputy and my defender. I assured the former that, although I recognized that it was his duty to look for hacksaws as long and whenever he pleased, we certainly were not going to stand for any rough treatment. The deputy turned savagely on my cellmate and rasped into his face:

"Nigger, if you will ever talk to a white man like you did tonight, I'm going clean home and get my shotgun and blow your God-damn brains out."

Enraged because they could not find any hacksaws, some of the deputies suggested that all prisoners in my cell should get a good shellacking. Others wanted to put double shackles on us and padlock us in solitary. We finally were locked up in a filthy hole, where it seemed that not even a wild beast could have survived for long. Puddles of stinking water and heaps of excrement made the cell unendurable. I felt that if it had not been morally my duty to fortify the spirits of my fellow-prisoners I would have longed for death.

3

Late that night, as I lay on my bunk, feeling very drowsy but unable to sleep because of the distressing thoughts of the day that came crowding in, I became so tense that I had to bite my lips to keep from screaming. Suddenly I heard the shuffling of many feet and the sound of voices speaking in undertones. I was all alertness, for I knew that it could not be the prisoners who were raising the commotion. I strained my ears to hear what was being said and my blood almost congealed when I caught the words: "He's in the last cell." It was about me then that they were talking and so I understood that I was about to receive another visit from my tormentors. As they approached nearer I heard one voice raised above the rest:

"Oh, what the hell is the use of bothering with that darkey? It really doesn't matter whether he has hacksaws or not. Let's take him out and string him up to a tree and be done with it."

Hearing these words, a shudder ran through me. My eyes fell on the broom in the corner of my cell. Unreasoningly, my instinct for self-preservation sent me flying to it. I was not going to submit to lynching with folded arms. I would defend myself and the dignity of my manhood to the bitter end. So I seized hold of the broom and bearing down upon it with the whole weight of my body I snapped off the handle. Then holding it behind me I placed myself against the wall in my cell.

I heard the metallic click of a lever; the jailer was opening my cell. He shouted at me in a drunken voice:

"Come on there, God-damn you, and get out of here!"

I did not budge.

"Hurry up and get the hell out of here so we can find that hacksaw you have hidden away."

This last statement reassured me somewhat. Perhaps they were not going to lynch me after all, I hoped. Concealing the broom stick behind my back, I edged out of the cell, for if I had left it behind they would surely have discovered it. Then it would have been all over with me.

Disappointed in not finding what they were looking for, my jailers continued their search in the other cells. But their chagrin was so great that they tried to take it out on a certain other prisoner. For some reason that I have never been able to find out they pounced upon him and began beating him mercilessly. His shrieks rang out mournfully through all the prison blocks. I stood clutching at the bars of my cell, heartsick and borne down by a sense of guilt, for it was because of me that they had found a pretext to beat him. Every blow they dealt this unknown prisoner they struck at me.

Poor unknown prisoner, a stranger to me yet a brother in sorrow, forgive me, whoever and wherever you are! . . .

4

The week that followed seemed as if it would never end. The hours were leaden and I whiled them away with trying to recall passages out of the writings of Marx and Lenin. I went over them in my mind in order to understand their meaning more fully. It was a comfort to know that, regardless of what other men might do to me, my mind was free and like a bird could fly out of its iron cage and soar beyond the meanness and the bestiality that surrounded me. A year before, a certain white lady had told me that the founder of her faith, Abdul Baha, had said:

"After fifty years of imprisonment in a horrible Turkish dungeon I can truthfully say that there is no prison except that of the darkened mind."

My jailers fed me on stale bread and foul water. They ruined my digestion, but I kept my spirit cheerful despite my depressing circumstances. Now I find it hard to believe but I actually sang the livelong day. My jailers looked puzzled at me. They could not quite understand the cause for such jubilation on my part. I have no doubt they thought me crazy. Once even an amusing thing happened. As I began to sing the stirring first lines of the Internationale,

Arise ye prisoners of starvation,
Arise ye wretched of the earth!

one of my jailers was under the impression that I was calling on the prisoners to mutiny. Scared out of his wits, he ran to report the incident to the Chief Jailer. Henceforth, I was warned against singing the Internationale.

One day a white prisoner planted himself before me and with an embarrassed grin said to me:

"I don't mind telling you that I do like that Internationale song of yours and I think its sentiments are right. Also I don't mind telling you that I think you are a mighty fine fellow and that I believe in your innocence. I have even composed a song in your honor and if you don't object I will sing it to you now."

To my amused surprise he began to drone his song with a nasal intonation to the tune of "There's a Rainbow 'Round My Shoulder":

There's a chain gang down in Georgia
Where the judge is sending me.
It sure will hurt
To sling the dirt
Till I come free.
There's a chain gang down in Georgia,
That's where they are keeping me.
It makes me sick
To swing a pick,
It's misery!
Halleluiah! How I hate this job!
And this dirty, rotten lynching mob!
How I long to get a chance to get away!
There's a chain gang down in Georgia
That will soon be missing me,
For by my soul
A "bush parole"
Will pardon me.

II

There's a chain gang down in Georgia
Where they work the men to death.
They are so rough
It's mighty tough
To catch your breath.
There's a chain gang down in Georgia
Where they keep the men in chains.
The keepers there
Are never fair,
They have no brains.
Halleluiah! How I hate this job!
And this dirty, rotten, lynching mob!
How I long to get a chance to get away!
There's a chain gang down in Georgia
That will soon be hunting me.
You can bet your roll
A "bush parole"
Will set me free.

5

My lawyers of the International Labor Defense filed a motion for a new trial. Pending the appeal, application for bail was made, but it was promptly denied. The hearing took place before none other than Judge Wyatt, the gentleman who had condemned me. His new role seemed to amuse him very much. He denied my motion with relish and made no attempt to conceal it. My lawyers then appealed from Judge Wyatt's decision to the State Supreme Court. Whether we would fare any better there was problematical. Most of Georgia's judicial luminaries are cut out of the same piece, reactionaries to the core and willing servants to the economic ruling class.

The outlook for me looked dark indeed. I did not try to delude myself with any false hopes. What added to my anxiety was the heavy depression which descended upon me because of my confinement in the Death House. It was sufficient to have broken down a much tougher and stronger-willed person than I.

There could have been no more ideal stage setting for a melodrama. My cell was about 8 by 12 feet, but exceptionally high. It was always cast in shadow. There were no lights inside. Outside of the cell a little bulb cast its dim illumination into the cage. A cement wall rose outside our bars, emphasizing the darkness. I had never understood before what it meant to be buried alive. Now I knew. It gave me a curdly feeling, as if I had been swallowed up into the bowels of the earth where no light of the sun could reach me, where only the ghostly voices and movements of my three fellow-prisoners and the jailers made it possible for me to realize that I still belonged among the living.

My fellow-prisoners and I burned candles all the time. These we bought at an exorbitant price from the jailers. Candle light proved very insufficient. It only accentuated the shadows the more. It made me feel that I was living in a perpetual night, which would never come to an end and from which there was no escape.

On the floor just above my cell was the laundry. There the prisoners washed their clothes once a week. Although it took only one day to do the washing, the laundry was being operated night and day. This, I discovered, was done deliberately, in order to create an unendurable nerve tension in us. How we hated the whirring motors as they ceaselessly throbbed! The noise, insinuating and persistent, almost like a mocking human voice, drove me and the other three prisoners frantic. We stuffed our ears with pieces of cloth but we could not keep out the sound. It continued to purr in a steady unhurried manner, as if it had decided to last through all eternity. It was as if it were running a race with us in endurance.

Our jailers were very inventive. They had imagination. They were never at a loss to discover ways to torment us. Their cruelty was raw. It hurt like an open wound. They allowed the water from the laundry to trickle down into our cells. Overhead, the sewage pipes had rotted and fallen away so that excrement and urine dribbled down upon us. It defiled our beds. It outraged our decency. It made us send unmentionable curses against those unfeeling people who were the cause of it. We wrote letter after letter to Chief Jailer Bob Holland demanding that our tortures cease. He never as much as acknowledged receipt of our protests.

6

In all the twenty-three years of my life, I have gone through a great deal, I have seen much human misery, and even more wretchedness and cruelty. All these experiences have moved me one way or another—but always deeply, with a shattering impact. Yet I am ready to say that nothing has left such a blighting impression on my heart and mind as my contact with three of my cellmates in the Death House. Their story and their fate will pursue me like a nightmare as long as I live. If there was much horror in it, it was also brightened in relief by a beauty of spirit and tenderness which has given the tragedy of their lives a moral dignity and a touching sweetness.

These three cellmates were Richard Morris, Mose White and Richard Simms. Richard Morris was the youngest. He was only fifteen and full of promise. I have rarely met a mentally more alert young mind. He had an unquenchable thirst for learning, and in our conversations he expressed eagerness to do worth-while things in the world. Ah, if only he could be free and back in town, what wouldn't he do to acquire an education! Best of all, he would have wanted to be a scientist, to make great discoveries with which to enrich mankind. Whenever he spoke of his dreams a light would shine in him, but it would soon be extinguished when he recalled the stern reality. He had a little sensitive face and when the hopelessness of his situation was made apparent to him, his dark sad eyes grew even darker and sadder with an unfathomable sorrow. He would hang his head and walk off by himself into a corner to brood.

Richard Simms, the second Negro boy, was a year older. He was always saying his prayers. The atmosphere of the Bible class still clung to him. Refined and of quiet ways, he kept to himself a lot. What he was thinking of, I do not know. But I have a suspicion that it was of God and of the joys awaiting His saints and His martyrs. Once he told me bashfully that if life were only different for him he would want to be a preacher and a saver of souls. Quietly, in a soft, almost childish treble, he would sing hymns on Sundays and smile gently upon us all. We also responded warmly to his friendly attitude.

Mose White, the oldest of the three, was seventeen years old. Curiously, although he was the oldest of the three, he was the most childish of them all, childish not in any offensive sense, for it was the joy of living which palpitated in his every limb. He was always laughing, always full of good spirits, playing inoffensive pranks upon us all. His good humor was contagious. When he laughed we laughed with him so that our little scientist was distracted from his brooding of frustration and our preacher quite forgot to say his prayers. Mose was very confidential. But he shouted his very confidences, so to speak, from the very housetops. From morning to night he kept on boasting of his prowess as a sprinter. He could run faster than Metcalfe, he bragged. He said it with such conviction we almost believed him. What he wanted to be was champion sprinter of the world. There was no selfishness in Mose. He gave us all confidential tips on how to start in a race, on developing a good wind and how to end up victoriously at the tape.

I watched the three boys at their games. They were mere children. It struck me suddenly with amazement that I was not much more than a child myself. I grew sad at the thought that I could not be as carefree as they. I could not play with them. The struggle for survival and for a new world had saddened me so that I could no longer play.

In my eagerness to tell of my three fellow-prisoners I have forgotten to mention the fact that they were dangerous criminals whose crimes had brought them to the Death House with me. Every time I looked at them there was a constriction around my heart, for they had been condemned to die and were only waiting for the Law's final reckoning with them.

It seems that the three boys were walking one night down the streets of Atlanta with an older brother of Mose. It was a hot night so they stopped by in a confectionery store to get ice-cream cones. When Mose White's brother was paying for the ice cream, the proprietor gave him short change. When the young Negro asked for the correct change, the proprietor became abusive. The former stood his ground. Whereupon, a policeman off duty, who was sitting in the rear of the store, drew his service revolver and started firing. A bullet struck Mose's brother near the heart. As he fell to the floor, he managed to draw a revolver from his hip pocket. With his last ounce of strength he fired back at the policeman, shooting him in the chest. Both were taken to the hospital where they died after several hours. But Richard Morris, Mose White and Richard Simms were arrested as accomplices in the shooting and were sentenced to die in the electric chair.

Their lawyers took the case on appeal to the State Supreme Court. There was no doubt in the boys' minds what the outcome would be. With the baffling hopefulness of the young and the unworldly they were convinced that the Supreme Court would acquit them. It was all very simple, a little too simple perhaps. To my caution not to be too optimistic, Mose broke into a loud and ringing laugh. His eyes danced with amusement.

"Oh, Angelo," he said, "you make me laugh! I ask you, did we commit a crime?"

"No."

Mose looked triumphant.

"Well, you silly child, if we didn't commit the crime, why should they electrocute us?"

He thought he crushed me with the question.

What could I answer to that?

Almost wearily I told him that he and the other two boys must not forget for one moment who they were.

"You are Negroes and no Negro can expect justice from the white lynch courts."

Richard Simms lost patience with me. He said:

"You always see things in a dark way, Angelo. White folks are not as bad as you are making them out to be."

I tried to reason with him, told him that he ought to look the facts in the face. What was the use of fooling himself?

To this the clever little fellow had a ready answer. Sure, even should the State Supreme Court uphold their conviction, Governor Talmadge would pardon them.

How did he know that?

How! Why hadn't I read how Governor Talmadge granted fifty pardons, more than fifty commutations to life imprisonment and seventy-four paroles to men convicted for murder?

I argued with him gently. Was all this kindness shown to any but white prisoners? Did he ever hear of any Negro sentenced to die who had escaped the electric chair at Milledgeville?

But the boys' faith in Governor Talmadge, "Our Gene," was as indestructible as the Rock of Ages.

"He's the best Governor we ever had," said little Richard defiantly, "and he will play square with us."

A great pity welled up in me. Little lambs led to the slaughter!

The three boys had never heard anything about the labor movement. They simply could not grasp my assertion that both Negro and white workers were together organizing to improve their conditions. They thought I was joking with them and bantered me about it.

Said the little preacher Richard Morris to me:

"Do you think you are as good as a white man, Angelo?"

"Why not?"

"No wonder they sent you to jail!" teased Mose.

I knew that, although they had a genuine liking for me, they were puzzled about me. They could not make out what the devil I was, whether fowl, bird, fish or red herring!

One day Richard Morris came up to me and in his grave, churchly manner asked me pointblank:

"Did you murder a man, Angelo?"

"No."

"Did you rape a woman?"

"No."

"Did you rob or something?"

"No."

Almost overawed, he asked:

"Then what the hell are you doing here?"

Even after I had gone through a lengthy explanation, he still looked puzzled. With the most serious face imaginable, he said to me:

"For all I may know, Angelo, you may be a Moses or some kind of a Deliverer that God has sent to rescue His children from the hands of the Egyptians."

The solemn air with which he said this amused me very much, but out of regard for his feelings I kept a straight face.

In the eyes of Richard Morris my elevated role as God's messenger hardly tallied with my insensitivity to the prison chaplain. Whenever the latter came around to help usher some poor devil to the electric chair with the cold comfort of some pious twaddle, I stubbornly chose to remain in my cell. The man with his hypocritical drooling about sin and repentance annoyed me greatly. Whenever he passed by me I ostentatiously looked the other way. My frank aversion for him made him hate me. Had he been a sincere believer he would have consigned me to perpetual hell-fire. But as I was ready to swear that he did not believe he used the less divine method of egging the jailers on me.

Sometimes the boys would beg me to come and listen to him as he gushed with sanctity.

"Oh, come along, Angelo!" coaxed Richard Simms. "It will sure do your soul good."

"Please don't bother about my soul," I answered. "The good Lord Himself will take care of that without the chaplain's assistance."

"You ain't against prayer, are you, Angelo?"

To this I replied with a familiar saying:

Prayers are all right in a prayer meeting
But they are not worth a damn in a bear meeting.

"What's a bear meeting?" asked Mose.

"You are in one now."

The boys laughed good-naturedly, but declared me a tough one.

7

One Sunday afternoon the chaplain, accompanied by the Chief Jailer, entered our cell block. The latter called us together to listen to the reverend's preaching. This time, out of sheer curiosity and boredom, I went to hear him. Putting on the gentle-forgiving look of Christ the Saviour he asked us one by one what we were in jail for. But when my turn came he glared at me and quickly passed me up. I must confess I felt no hurt at the slight. However, I had brought some paper and pencil along with me and I copied his sermon word for word. How full of tenderness and concern he was for us! An apostolic gentleness hovered about him like a white dove of peace. He spoke in this fashion:

"I did not come here, fellows, to find out what section of the law you violated, or what crime you committed, whether murder or rape. I came here to teach you the word of God so that your souls might be saved, even though your bodies may burn in the electric chair. But, boys, you have a soul to save for the Lord. For twenty years I too was a criminal, a sinner and a drunkard, but thank God I have been saved and sent to teach His word. It's true, boys, you might be mistreated here on this side of man's world because of your race. But in sight of God there is no difference of race or color. He accepts all into His kingdom. You are my brothers and I am your brother. I would accept you in my house and let you sit down and eat at my table, because in the sight of the Lord we are brothers and there is no difference. Isaiah said, 'Come now, and let us reason together.' We have had a difference, but don't let us be enemies. Let us come closer and reason together. Confess your sins to Him, and, boys, you don't have to wait until you get out of jail. This little jail doesn't amount to anything in comparison with the great Judgment Day of God. Forget about the jail and remember you have to live for the Lord, for He can shake this jail down.

"You take the Hunkies, Dagoes and Jews who blaspheme the Lord and never pray that their sinful souls might be saved. As wicked as they are when they come to this country they always save money to send back to their parents in their native lands. That shows that they have got something to live for, even though it may be the Devil. And, boys, you have something to live for too. The Lord wants your souls to be clean and sinless. Let not your hearts be troubled! Give God your hearts and the Devil your sins! Amen."

As I listened to him my anger began to mount. Perhaps it was wrong of me, but I felt that I could not keep quiet any longer. To remain silent on such an occasion as this would be equal to a betrayal of the truth. Barely had he finished when I raised my voice:

"What do you know about God? And what do we know about sin? Here are three children, as innocent and as upright as only children can be. What have you done out of your Christian compassion to save them from their terrible unjust fate?"

My words startled the chaplain. He trembled as I took a menacing attitude toward him. The other prisoners looked on unbelievingly.

"None of your uppity talk, nigger!" snapped the man of God at me.

I laughed:

"I thought I heard you say a moment ago something about your being our brother and we being your brothers, and that you would let us sit down to eat at your table because in the sight of the Lord there is no difference between us?"

The chaplain's voice rose almost to a scream:

"I'll tell Mr. Holland what a godless nigger he has in this jail."

At this I lost all patience. I ran into my cell and fetched some water in a cup and sprinkling it after the retreating clergyman I cried out:

"I will speak to you in your own language, Mr. Preacher: 'Oh, ye Scribes and hypocrites . . .' "

But at this point the guards came up and pushed me into my cell.

My three little friends looked at me with pained expressions.

Why had I acted so rudely with the chaplain? After all, he was a man of God and I should have respected his cloth. Patiently I explained to them that the clergyman had insulted us as Negroes and as human beings, violating everything men hold decent.

I was touched to see at least a glimmer of understanding in their eyes. They had never seen it that way before, they assured me. I did not at all feel like a criminal for having robbed them of their trusting innocence. The world as I revealed it to them was a sorry affair, to be sure, but I did point out to them the way leading to a new and better society. For the perfumed deception I had taken from them I tried to substitute something that was vital and true and full of promise.

8

Ever since that day the three boys and I became fast friends. All the food and money we received from the outside we shared equally. I felt truly like their elder brother and I have never loved anybody more than I did them. I was also happy and fortunate in that my sentiments for them were reciprocated fully. Now as I look back upon those harrowing days I feel consoled somewhat that my brief association with them had proved of some benefit to them in their last hours. Sympathy and love is all that the unfortunate who share a common sorrow can give to each other. I have tasted unhappiness and misfortune as probably few men of my acquaintance have, but I have been happier than the most happy and fortunate of them because I have learned the simple wisdom of distracting my own unhappiness by the effort of dispelling the unhappiness of my fellow-beings.

Hardly anyone ever came to visit me in jail and yet I doubt whether there was one prisoner who felt more secure with his invisible human connections than I. But I found endless pleasure in identifying myself, as if I myself was their blood-relation, with the families of the boys. Their mothers, brothers and sisters visited them regularly every Tuesday. I looked forward to their coming with the same eagerness as the boys. I was particularly fond of Mrs. White, the elderly gray-haired mother of Mose. She was a very charming and good-natured soul and whenever she came she seemed to bring with her into the dark foulness of our prison life a whiff of the fresh, intoxicating air from the free world outside. She was good enough to do my laundry for me and she would take no money for it.

"My son," said she, "you are my son's friend and as unfortunate as he and so I want you to be my son, too."

Whenever she brought candy or cake for Mose, she was sure to keep me in mind as well. She was better informed about worldly matters than her athletic-minded son. One day she looked long and unbelievingly at me and said:

"So you are Angelo Herndon! I can hardly believe my own eyes to think that you are the one, that same one, who told the white judge and the white jury that they could do with you what they pleased, but that they could not stop you ever from fighting for your people and that if they were to sentence you to death thousands of other Angelo Herndons would come to take your place. We ain't never had one do that before."

"There have been others, Mother White, only our white masters have seen to it that you never heard about them."

"At any rate, as a Negro mother, I am proud of you and your own dear mother must be mighty proud of you! God be with you, son."

9

One day my jailer with a smile of derision on his face handed me a copy of the *Daily Worker*. I was thrilled to my innermost being. I knew all along that my friends in the movement had not forgotten me and that my entombment in Fulton Tower was not going to be passed in silence by them. The *Daily Worker* which they had sent me came like a message of glad tidings. In its own impersonal way it was the most direct message possible from the movement. When the jailer left me and I could read it in the privacy of my own two eyes, I felt myself overcome by deep emotion and had to turn my face away when the boys came up to make inquiry what my excitement was about.

We all sat down to read the *Daily Worker*. We read every precious word of it, including the ads. We discussed in great detail every article and every piece of labor news. I told them about the Soviet Union. The little preacher's eyes grew large with the surpassing wonder of it. They thought it sure must be a paradise for workers. Mose, however, seemed to have something on his mind. Somewhere in his appreciation of the Socialist state there seemed to be a flaw. With a great deal of hesitation, finally, he let the cat out of the bag:

"Are there sprinters in the Soviet Union?"

I was a little taken aback by this question. But when I assured him that there were sprinters in the Soviet Union and good ones at that, he beamed happily.

"Suits me fine, Angelo."

I told them about the Communist Party of America and explained to them in detail what its aims were and the nature of the struggle it was carrying on. They seemed very much taken with the idea. For days and days they walked about in half a trance asking numerous questions of me and discussing heatedly all the fine points in my answers. When my friends managed to get through to me the two volumes of Marx's *Capital* and M. J. Olgin's pamphlet *Why Communism?*, their excitement reached the fever point. It may sound laughable to some but I have never seen a more heroic example of man's indomitable urge to understanding and truth than the sight of these boys with knitted brows and strained expressions reading with difficulty the highly involved work by the founder of modern Socialism. The surprising element in this was that they were barely literate. Most of what they read went over their heads, as I must admit a good deal went over mine too, but they must have gone over the book at least ten times. They shot so many questions at me and shoved me into so many tight corners that I burst into a sweat. In their hero-worshipping eyes I took on the stature of a "professor."

"Gee, Angelo, you certainly are smart—you know everything!" exploded Richard Simms with enthusiasm.

This sounded so comical that I burst out laughing. He looked hurt.

Toward the end of our acquaintance, the boys wanted to know what likelihood there was for the workers to achieve power in America.

"A very great likelihood," I answered.

"How soon?" asked the little preacher impatiently, for he seemed filled with an evangelical zeal.

"That will largely depend on what you boys will do when you get out of jail and what thousands of others like you will do in the struggle for the liberation of the working class."

10

There was nothing that the boys loved more than to sing their beautiful Negro spirituals. They harmonized very effectively. Their singing was the greatest pleasure that I derived from prison. It made me think of my childhood, when the world, for all its tragedy, still seemed garbed in wonder and beauty for me. They had fresh sweet voices and when they sang the prison bars disappeared, the laundry motor overhead was silenced, the walls of the prison melted away in a sea of beauty. As long as I will live there will ring in my ears the melancholy wail of their voices blending in the tear-laden strains of the spiritual, "When I'm in Trouble":

When I'm in trouble
Walk with me,
Walk with Moses
Walk with me, Lord!
I know my Lord will
Walk with me.
When I am dying
Walk with me!
If I could just touch the hem of His garment
I know my Lord will
Walk with me.

When the boys sang, all sounds of quarreling and dissension ceased among the prisoners in the entire jail. They became grave and thoughtful. They listened raptly. The music drew them away from the sordidness of their lives and even if only for a moment, through the miraculous intervention of music and sincere words, beauty, in ways unbeknown to them, entered their spirits.

The prisoners showed their gratitude and appreciation in many touching ways. They showered the boys with cigarettes, letters of encouragement and even money. There was something incongruous and fabulous in hearing such ethereal singing in a vile place like the prison. This strangeness was strikingly emphasized to us by the clang and bang of chains and steel doors as an accompaniment to their singing.

Those who have never been entombed in a prison can never know the uplifting comfort that lies in a mere trifle like a song. . . .

11

While the boys, under my encouragement, were rapt in their beautiful dream of a better world and the part they proposed to play in it when they would be free again, invisible hands sealed their destiny with a rubber stamp. One day their lawyers came to see them in jail and with deliberately hard faces told them that the Supreme Court of Georgia had ruled adversely on their appeal. The lower court, the opinion stated, "did not show cause for error in its findings. The judgment thereof is hereby sustained."

"You have three more weeks to live," said the lawyers as they made their departure.

That night the boys did not sleep. I too lay awake, helpless to still the agony in their young breasts. They cried and moaned all night long like little children. It sounded so piteous that I thought I was going insane.

I tried to speak words of comfort to them, but they stuck in my throat. What could I possibly say to them? They were beyond the comfort of words.

The prison guards alone seemed to derive pleasure from the boys' troubles. I heard one of them say to several others:

"You boys won't fail to be at the grand exhibition when those three little niggers who shot that white police officer will be burned in the chair. It will sure be a great sight."

After a few days the boys regained control of themselves. They laughed and joked again, but their mirth rang false. It was the bravery of indomitable youth. It was plain as day that they were hiding behind their smiling faces the knowledge of the certainty of death. Their lawyers, unfeeling greedy vultures, came around every once in a while to tell them not to worry. Sure, everything was going to be all right! In the meantime, they squeezed every nickel they could out of the boys' unhappy parents.

They had told the boys that they would ask the Governor for clemency. The children clung to this hope like drowning persons in mid-ocean to a spar. Wait and see, "Our Gene" would show his usual humanity and passion for justice, they assured me vehemently. But I saw that they themselves had a secret doubt about it.

At last the lawyers came hurrying to the prison to inform them of the results of the clemency hearing. The three boys and I stood scanning intently the faces of the lawyers, in order to penetrate their expression. The lawyers finally spoke.

"I see no reason," stated Governor Talmadge, "for interfering with the decision of the lower court."

As the lawyers turned away, little Richard Simms broke into sobs. The other two wept with him. My eyes too were not dry.

12

It was on an early Tuesday morning that the jailers came to take the boys to their death. All night long the four of us kept vigil in separate cells. Conversation was hardly possible under these circumstances. Hardly a word passed between us. The condemned boys seemed to have receded from each other's consciousness. Each one now lived in a world apart, agonizing silently like Jesus in the garden of Gethsemane the night of the betrayal. They wept silently, revealing their anguish occasionally by an involuntary moan. The little preacher seemed to be most affected. He prayed all night in an undertone, uttering his words with a passionate intensity, as if trying to stave off the terrible end that awaited him by constructing walls of prayer about him. Most of the night I stood at the bars of my cage straining my eyes to see my friends and to give them proof that I was with them.

The executioners were insistent. They could not wait. The Chief Jailer ordered the boys to get ready. Mutely, with dragging feet the boys took their Bibles, prayer and song books and put them away in a little Boston bag belonging to Richard Morris. Tears were streaming from their eyes. And in their broken state they seemed to have achieved a deep goodness and a beauty.

I felt the need of saying something, of comforting, of lending them the necessary bit of pathetic strength with which to enter the great shadow. But I was tongue-tied, paralyzed in every limb, trembling violently and feeling as if my knees were about to cave in.

When they got ready, they fell in line, one behind the other. First came Mose. He seemed the bravest of the three. He smiled weakly, but it was a twisted smile, almost ghastly, for he was yellow as with jaundice. After him came Richard Morris. He looked like a child who had been beaten by his mother because of some naughty prank he had been playing. He sniffled and as he had no handkerchief he looked very woebegone, trying ineffectually to wipe his nose with his bare hand. Last came Richard Simms. He was weeping and appeared more terrified and unhappy than his companions. He looked about him like a frightened bird, frantically searching with his eyes for some invisible Deliverer to come to his aid.

I would have come to his aid, if I only could. But I too was only a bird in the selfsame cage. I too stood in need of rescue. Only there was no one to rescue them or me. I seized hold of the bars and dug my hands into them until the palms became bruised. I gave vent to all the despair I was capable of. But I finally had to get control of myself. In another moment the boys would be passing my way and I must not be found wanting by them.

When Mose White came alongside my cell, he stopped and said:

"Good-bye, Angelo, I wish you all the luck in the world. There doesn't seem to be any for us."

Then came Richard Morris. He extended a trembling hand to me, which I grasped hard. With eyes swimming with tears, he said to me in a broken voice:

"Good-bye, Angelo, you have been a good friend to me—you believed in my innocence and God will reward you for it. We surely will meet in Paradise some day, for you too are innocent."

Wrenching his hand out of mine suddenly, he shuffled off, weeping.

Richard Simms came last. He held the little bag with the holy books.

"Please give these books to our parents," he begged me in a moaning voice. "We will have no more use for them. We three want you to remember us, Angelo. Please take my gold Elgin watch. Richard Morris wishes you to have his hair brush, and Mose White wants you to wear his belt. You have been the only person good to us in a long, long time, and I hope you will never forget us."

Impatiently the guard pushed the boys forward, saying:

"We are late, hurry!"

TWENTY-ONE

THE MONTHS LENGTHENED INTO YEARS; the seasons came and went, and I began to lose all sense of time. Prisoners kept on coming, and departing prisoners heard the doors of the prison close behind them. Each new arrival told horrible and shameful stories of the chain gang for which I was headed. It was a dying by degrees, a slow nightmarish death that awaited me.

Conditions in the prison were indescribable. The food was rotten and inadequate. I retched every time I took it into my mouth. Because of that I almost starved myself to death. For weeks I went without food. I began to lose weight rapidly. I looked like a skeleton. My feebleness became so excessive that I found difficulty not only in standing up, but even in sitting down. I lay on my cot most of the time, thinking, thinking, thinking of the things natural to my wretched state. I became morbid and I began to curse the world and everything in it. I vomited incessantly and I felt a sharp gnawing in my intestines. My eyes began to fail me. I had to wear large horn-rimmed glasses. Reading became very difficult for me because I was obliged to do it by candle light.

When I felt that all my strength was leaving me and that life was getting to be insupportable I wrote a letter to the International Labor Defense informing it of my wretchedness. Without loss of time this workers' defense organization addressed the following sharp letter of protest to the Georgia authorities—to Governor Talmadge, to Warden Holland, to the State Prison Commissioner, and to the Chief Justice of the Georgia Supreme Court:

"Sir:

"Information recently reaching our office indicates that there is a deliberate plan to torture Angelo Herndon to death in the prison at Fulton Tower.

"For the two years that Herndon has been imprisoned in your infamous hell hole, he has been subjected to the most barbaric cruelties. Your jailers have made him the victim of unimaginable horrors. Without comfort of any kind, suffering with cold, darkness and damp, he has been kept in the Death House, where he has been forced to witness the steady parade of those whom you have doomed to die in the electric chair. For good measure you have seen fit to place him in solitary confinement on frequent occasions. Vermin, rats, the constant dribbling of water and excrement in his cell and poisonous food have been his daily lot. As a result of this his health is thoroughly undermined and today his friends throughout the whole world fear for his life.

"It has been reported to us that he can no longer eat your vile food and he is compelled to do so only because of gnawing hunger. In addition, he is losing the sight of his eyes, which is directly caused by these bestial conditions.

"Your purpose is clear. We charge you with the attempted murder of Angelo Herndon. You have sought first to break the spirit of a militant fighter, one who has stood for a united struggle against unemployment and unbearable conditions imposed by a decaying capitalist system. But you cannot do this. The spirit of Angelo Herndon is unconquerable. Deathly sick, he is still able to hold his head high and defy his torturers.

"Failing in this, you seek to kill him, but here too you must fail. The working class will not allow it. Angelo

Herndon does not stand alone. The principles for which he has fought and suffered are embraced by millions who, in this hour of need, will respond to the fight for his full and complete freedom.

"The International Labor Defense is calling upon the working class of the United States to rally to the support of Angelo Herndon and to bring an immediate end to your abominable system of torture of this working-class leader innocent of any crime.

"We demand the immediate, unconditional release of Angelo Herndon!

"We demand immediate action on the appeal from his conviction, which has been pending since October, 1933!

"Pending this we demand that Angelo Herndon immediately be transferred to a hospital, where he will receive the best medical treatment, proper food and the care he needs! The I.L.D. pledges untiring efforts to mobilize the entire working class for a mass militant struggle to enforce these demands.

"Yours very truly,

"WILLIAM L. PATTERSON
"National Secretary
"International Labor Defense."

2

Shortly after this letter was sent to the Georgia authorities I received an unexpected call from the Chief Jailer. He said to me with fatherly concern:

"Angelo, is it true that you don't get any medicine from the doctor?"

"Yes, it is true," I answered. "And what good would it do me to see him? I know what he would tell me—the same as he tells other prisoners when they report to him as sick: 'Nothing's wrong with you, boy.' "

Mr. Holland looked scandalized. Dear, dear, this is the first he had ever heard of such a thing! He sure would look into that matter personally, dad-blame it! He assured me that he was going to see the doctor first thing in the morning. He also told me that whenever I wanted anything I could come to him directly and if it was only within reason he would see to it that I got what I wanted.

I had told Mr. Holland that my stomach was the seat of my illness. What was my amazement when an hour after he had called a prison guard brought some medicine to me. I looked at the bottle of medicine with dread and loathing. What a farce! What inhumanity! What ignorance! Or was it deliberate callousness and mockery? The doctor had not even examined me, had not diagnosed my illness and here they were already feeding me medicine! Apparently they had only one kind of medicine for all stomach trouble, whether it was cancer, gallstones or a plain bellyache. I raged and sent the medicine back with the guard. Why, even a horse or a dog was treated with more concern, I shouted after the retreating turnkey.

"Don't be so uppity and choosy, nigger!" he shot back at me.

A little while later I received another unexpected call. It was from the prison "engineer." I never could learn what he "engineered" at. His name was Big Bill Turner. Apparently, I conjectured, his task was to weigh me, for he put me on a scale, saying:

"I just want to see how much you weigh, Angelo."

He critically sized me up in my nudeness:

"Mh-mh, looks as if you have been putting on a lot of weight these days."

I saw he was taking me for a ride. The scales indicated I was twenty-one pounds underweight. I seemed just a bundle of skin and bones.

There was no use arguing with this "specialist." So I said nothing.

The "engineer" was only a herald preceding two more distinguished gentlemen. Two doctors, one Negro and the other white, came up to examine me. The Negro doctor gave me a thorough examination. He shook his head. My condition was very serious, he said. The white doctor, on the other hand, behaved in a very hostile manner. He too, like the jailer, must have thought me "uppity," for when he was through with his examination he transfixed me with his cold blue eyes and said:

"Why don't you use your head? Where do you think you are? You don't expect to get the same treatment in jail as you would outside, do you? My advice to you is to behave yourself and stop bothering us."

The unpleasantness of this medical experience was completely wiped out by an unexpected incident. A highly intelligent white woman doctor from Chicago, who at the time was on a visit to Atlanta where she had been brought up, became greatly interested in my case. She had the courage of her convictions, and her good heart overcame her fears of the possible consequences of her step. She brought pressure to bear upon the Warden that she be allowed to visit me at the prison in order to examine me.

I was very much taken aback when, several days after the prison doctors had looked me over, I received a visit from this very pretty and charming woman. She was genteel and soft-spoken and looked as if she came from the upper middle class. She addressed me in a very warm and sympathetic manner. My case had interested her at the very outset, she said, because it was evident to her that I was being outrageously treated by the sordid industrial interests of the South.

"Does my talking to you this way surprise you?" she asked with a smile. "I have learned a great deal about exploitation, brutality and corruption in the South ever since I left it, for then I had occasion to look back and revaluate it objectively."

The Warden and the jailers could not believe their own eyes. The sight of this attractive Southern white woman doctor visiting an inconsequential "sassy nigger" fairly bowled them over. Furthermore, they had never before seen a woman doctor, and they were filled with amazement as they looked at her. It was immoral enough in their eyes for a woman doctor to examine any man, but for a white woman doctor born in the South to examine a *coon*—that was the last straw! One of them later told me with a look that was half envy and half hatred:

"Tell me, is she your sweetheart, Angelo? A fine-looking gal, hot-jiggity-jig!"

At her request I was removed from my cell and taken to the hospital ward. The event proved something of a sensation. Not only Chief Jailer Holland, but all prison guards off duty hurried in to watch the performance. Did I say "performance"? It was a circus! My doctor was visibly annoyed. She was finally obliged to say to them rather tartly:

"It's very good of you to lend me your company, but I don't think I need an army to watch me. A couple of you will do mighty fine. I don't intend to do anything shocking. All I wish to examine is the patient's chest."

Like small-town yokels they snickered and sniggled and looked a bit abashed, but they made no move to leave the room. Maybe this lady doctor was a smart un? Maybe she would fool them and there would be a "regular show," after all? . . .

While examining me with the stethoscope, the doctor bent over and whispered to me in an undertone:

"The blackguards! I understand perfectly what you have got to stand from them. I am so sorry!"

"What's that?" rudely interrupted Holland. "What are you whispering there, you two?"

"Oh, nothing important!" replied the doctor, with open contempt.

Her diagnosis was exactly the same as that of the Negro doctor.

She ordered that I be immediately put to bed in a hospital. Mr. Holland promised faithfully to do so.

A year later I discovered that she had brought a lot of medicine to the jail for me. But the prison officials threw my medicine into the garbage can. . . .

3

A few days later I was led to the Grady Hospital under heavy guard. They X-rayed my chest and stomach, but the pictures were so poor that they gave no indication of my actual condition. Whether these misty pictures were the result of incompetence or deliberate, I was not able to learn.

A sympathetic young woman employed in the hospital and who had been present at the examination telephoned my lawyer, Mr. Davis, and informed him that the hospital had issued an incorrect report when they stated that nothing was wrong with me. She said that the doctors had privately admitted that my lungs were in a very bad condition.

Mr. Davis immediately released a statement to the press in which he castigated the hospital and prison authorities for their callousness. As a result of this statement, a committee of liberals was organized by John Howard Lawson, the playwright, to go as a delegation to Governor Talmadge in Atlanta to protest my treatment. The other members on the delegation were: Williams Rollins, Jr., the novelist; Miss Winifred Chappell, executive secretary of the Methodist Federation of Social Service; Martin Russak, editor of the *Textile Workers' Voice;* Herbert Abrons, a Yale student, and William

Server, the Southern field representative of the American Civil Liberties Union. When the delegation arrived in Atlanta it was joined by my attorney, Mr. Davis, and by the late Reverend J. A. Martin, Negro editor of the periodical issued by the Negro Methodist Sunday Schools of America.

The members of this delegation first called on the Reverend Hudson. With loud abuse he ordered them out of his office, bawling at them: "Communists! Anarchists! Reds!" Lashed into a real fury by his conduct, the committee next called on Governor Talmadge and protested against the outrageous treatment they had received at the hands of the Assistant Solicitor General. They demanded protection against the mob violence which lynch editorials in the local press had been whipping up in preparation of their arrival.

Governor Talmadge was all blandness and honey. Oh, they had nothing to fear! Not a thing was going to happen to them! He offered to give the delegation a National-Guard escort to Fulton Tower. His offer was turned down. Adjutant-General Camp of the National Guard, who was present, expressed to the delegation his utter disgust with me. He said I "was pretending to be sick in order to get in the hospital." Worse yet, I was "uppity." Would the delegation please advise me to be more respectful to whites in the future?

When the Reverend Martin protested the General's contemptuous description of me, he was insulted in a very rude manner by Governor Talmadge. But the Reverend Martin was not the sort of Negro to be cowed by white bullying. He answered him, as I later discovered in a press report, in this wise:

"There is not a single Negro in the United States who doesn't know that Herndon is innocent. He is being persecuted in your infamous jail for no other reason than because he is a Negro. If something isn't done about the matter, I, for one, can say that in the next election I will vote Communist and so will many other Negroes."

Governor Talmadge was very angry. With offensive insinuation he replied to the clergyman:

"I know a nigger who is an educated man. He graduated from college. But with all his education he is just as humble as any backward farmer in South Georgia. I love that nigger."

The Reverend Martin was so angered by this insult that he replied to the Governor with a good deal of indignation. This so angered a National Guardsman present that he threatened him with his fixed bayonet, demanding that he apologize to "His Excellency." The Reverend Martin was the last man in the world to apologize to an aggressor. He defiantly stood his ground, but with the bayonet pointed murderously at his middle he was obliged to withdraw from the room.

4

A guard came to me one day and called me out of my cell, saying:

"Come on into the main lobby and talk to some people who are there."

When I came into the lobby I saw a number of men seated on chairs against the wall. I knew immediately that it was a delegation of friends that I was facing, for Mr. Davis and the Reverend Martin were sitting with them. About ten feet from where the delegation sat I was placed into a chair. A guard who stood behind me ordered me to talk.

I certainly needed no urging to do so. I never talked so volubly nor with such great attention to detail as I did then. I knew what was in my jailers' minds. They figured that I would be too cowed to say anything in criticism of them for fear of reprisal later on. But I called their bluff. I told the delegation without restraint of the treatment I was receiving in the Death House, of the leaking sewer pipe, of the rotten food that ruined my digestion and now had resulted in illness.

When the guard heard me speak in this vein he ran off to

call the "engineer." The latter hastened in and indignantly denied that human excrement had been dribbling into my cell. For proof he would be happy to show the delegation that there was no leak. To his mind the prisoner was only telling tall tales, so help him God!

To this I answered that the "engineer" was quite right when he said that there was no leak, but if the delegation had come just the day before they would have seen the leak with their own eyes.

"He fixed the leak all in your honor, ladies and gentlemen," I explained, as he glared daggers at me.

Blocked at this point he tried to divert the conversation into another channel.

"What did you have for dinner today?" he asked hopefully.

"I don't know. I didn't eat any of it!"

The "engineer" now seemed to have lost his tongue completely. He left the questioning to the delegation.

I complained that all the books, pamphlets, newspapers and periodicals that had been sent to me by my invisible friends and organizations had been confiscated by the Reverend Hudson. He had made it clear that he wished to use all this reading matter as future evidence against me. In fact, he was planning another indictment.

When members of the delegation later asked Mr. Holland whether he would allow them to give me some books, he answered:

"No prisoners are permitted to have a large quantity of books and papers because they might make a fire and heat the bars in order to bend them."

But when he saw that the response of the delegation to his explanation was only surprise and amusement, he went on to say that he had put a ban on radical and insurrectionary literature because I was a propagandist. He charged that I gave my books and pamphlets to the other prisoners, thereby causing radical ideas to spread in the jail. But as the delegation was determined to make a test case of the matter, they told Mr. Holland that they wished to leave with me a copy of Anthony Bimba's *History of the American Working Class.* They demanded a definite answer on the spot. Mr. Holland reluctantly promised that I would be given the book.

A few minutes after the delegation had left the jail, a guard with a broad grin on his face brought me the book, saying:

"Here, Angelo, take this book and read the devil out of it. It sure is good to have friends. Sometimes they are worth more to you than a million dollars."

I nodded my head fervently. Never had I agreed on anything more wholeheartedly.

5

Worse than the taunts and the threats of the jailers, worse than the tortures they inflicted upon me, worse than the horrible conditions under which I lived, was the way time dragged and dragged for me. Every minute became an eternity of suffering. I had to fight this enemy with all the strength of my mind, with all the energy of my will. What a long succession of months they were! Month after month, I counted them wearily—first six, then twelve, then seventeen, eighteen, twenty, twenty-six! Would they never end? I would lie groaning on my filthy hard bunk, and to save myself from going mad I painstakingly studied the weird patterns of mud and discoloration on the walls and ceilings. I learned to know every line and crack. Day in and day out, I watched the shadows of the jail bars shorten and lengthen on the floor—shorten and lengthen. Would this never end?

A distant sympathizer of mine, a white banker, to help me while away the time had given me a book. Its title was: *Love on Top of the Hill.* It was one of the most absurd and trivial books I have ever read in my life. But no one will ever know with what love and eagerness I devoured it from cover to cover. Not once but twenty times did I read it! And for what reason? To help kill time, my enemy. For that matter, I would have found even a telephone directory exciting reading.

What a crazy yarn that novel spun! It was the story of an American who had a friend in London. He was a pugilist and won many bouts. Times grew hard and his friend cabled him to come to London. When he arrived in London a pretty blonde awaited him at the pier. She explained to him that his friend was out of town on very important business and he had asked her to take his American friend in tow. So she took him to a house in the country where men gambled, drank whisky and caroused with naughty beautiful women every night. After several days of this exciting life, he fell madly in love with the blonde girl. She finally got him interested in the gaming tables. One night, at the suggestion of the head of the establishment, she gave him a drugged drink. All this time, because he was so smart, he had been the winner. But after having taken the drink with the dope in it, he began to lose fast. This made him mad, so he started to curse. He suddenly discovered that the man he had been playing with had been stealing cards from the deck.

By this time the drug had taken full effect. He became possessed of the strength of a giant. First he knocked the card sharper unconscious; then he played mud pies with all the men. But the owner of the dive, the sole remaining male, stole up behind him and knocked him over the head with a bottle of gin. Our American pugilist crumpled in a heap on the floor and was left for dead.

A few minutes later when everybody had left the house, he suddenly came to and began to fight like an ox with his imaginary foes, for he was still semi-conscious. He smashed chairs, tables and bric-a-brac. The drug was making him do wonders. Heaven knows what further damage he might have done had he not submitted to a brain operation, after which he forgave his blonde seducer, and, as a reward for all she had done for him, he married her.

When I read the book for the first time I had violent nightmares. I dreamed that I had been drugged and that I was cracking up all eternity with my fists. My excitement had been mounting in my dream, so I woke up with a cry. Instead of feeling like a conquering hero, as I really should have, I was almost frightened to death. For the life of me I could not recall where I was. The place no longer looked like a jail. To make certain that I was not dreaming, I struck a match and began to feel the walls. They were cold and dank, the same as ever. Suddenly I became aware of a brilliant silvery shimmer. I could not understand what it was or where it came from. I began to tremble with excitement. For I had seen that light before, illuminating the dream castles of the princesses in the fairy tales I had read with such breathless excitement when I went to grade school.

I called to my cellmates who were still awake and asked them if they could make out where the beautiful light came from. They laughed uproariously. They asked me if I was drunk. However, I was only prison drunk, sleep drunk and misery drunk. The light I had been seeing was only the light of the moon. It was shining down into my cell through an aperture where the steel lining in the wall had rusted and fallen away. For more than two years I had not seen it. And now that I saw it, I stood petrified, with my face against it, and with my eyes closed, letting the beams play on my eyelids.

TWENTY-TWO

SEEMINGLY, EVERYTHING WAS QUIET; nothing stirred in the little hideous world in which I was condemned to live. Yet momentous things were afoot. For the working class of the country suddenly perceived in me a symbol of its embattled aspirations. Feverishly it now worked night and day for my freedom. Not all the time did I have a clear conception of what was going on, for I practically lived in a hermetically sealed universe. Only occasionally a far voice would reach me, setting my heart aquiver and my blood coursing madly through my veins. The working class was fighting for me! Far from being alone I now felt warmly and intimately associated with hundreds of thousands of invisible well-wishers and friends. It was a terrifying but beautiful feeling!

Sometimes the guard would bring me a newspaper that some distant comrade had sent me. It usually came in tatters and so dirty that only muddied feet trampling deliberately on it could have produced such startling results. For good measure, perhaps to make my reading more pleasurable, my jailers would pour on it a bottle of ink before giving it to me.

I would lay the tattered newspaper on the floor of my cell and with infinite patience piece it together again. To hold it together I pressed pieces of moist soap on the edges. Sometimes it took me several days to complete such an operation. But I did not mind. For all I cared it could have taken me weeks and even months. What value did time have in my circumstances? My preoccupation with my newspapers even came as a blessing in disguise; it kept my mind and my hands busy and preserved me against a nervous breakdown. The tattered newspaper assumed a symbolic aspect for me. Even as my jailers had torn it into bits in their rage and hatred of me so was the working class being mutilated and assaulted.

2

Several months after my troubles in jail had been aired publicly the Warden was forced to grant me my rights as a prisoner. It was then that I got a first clear indication of the great interest my case was arousing. A perfect avalanche of communications descended upon me. Letters came from workers, intellectuals, middle-class people and even highly placed individuals, expressing sympathy and encouragement, and offering to help in the fight for my freedom. Not only were they from every part of the United States, but from practically every foreign country in the world, especially from the workers and peasants in the Soviet Union.

My Negro and white comrades in Atlanta worked tirelessly to expose the viciousness of my treatment and to enlist the support of workers everywhere. Probably the most touching of all expressions of sympathy for me came from Belle West, a sixteen-year-old white girl in Atlanta. She dedicated a poem to me. It was first published in the Negro *Liberator* and later was reprinted in a leaflet. Whatever its poetic merits, it unquestionably was aflame with youthful ardor and eloquence.

Listen, white bosses—lynchers!
I'm white, too!
I'm sixteen.
You love to call me
"The flower of Southern womanhood!"
And breed hate in my heart

With sneaking lies of
"Nigger rape."
But I laugh in your face,
And stretch my hand
To a black boy in Georgia's jail
Whose courage
You cowards can't break!
Angelo Herndon, do you hear us?
Do you hear our tread?
It shakes the lynchers
Like a reed in the wind.
Listen to our step—Negro,
White!
All in time—the same rhythm.
We are coming, Angelo.
Listen!

To be an honest writer down South is no easy matter. You may write all the mint-julep romances you want, and you may write about stars falling on Alabama, but you risk life and limb if you write about police clubs falling on Communists' heads in Georgia. As a result of the "notoriety" little Belle's poem achieved, the authorities went hot on her family's trail. They seized her older brother and indicted him for insurrection. As if that were not enough revenge, they forced the entire family to leave the state forever. . . .

3

My prolonged imprisonment began to wear down the nerves of my friends. A concerted drive to force the State Supreme Court of Georgia to render an early decision was initiated by the International Labor Defense, by various church organizations, by the American Civil Liberties Union, by the National Committee for the Defense of Political Prisoners, by the Communist Party and by others. Thousands of telegrams and resolutions poured down upon Governor Talmadge and the Georgia State Supreme Court demanding my freedom.

Mildly speaking, my situation was very precarious. A tangle of conflicting forces arose to make the prospect of an early acquittal appear very dim indeed. Just at that time a fierce political fight had to break out between Governor Talmadge and George Hamilton, his State Treasurer. It all had to do with a very delicate matter: the control of state highway funds, a source of enrichment for many an enterprising and grafting official. Governor Talmadge, being the more supple-minded of the two politicians fell upon an excellent stratagem. To win public approval for himself, he dragged a good old red herring into the brawl. With a melodramatic flourish for which the South's leading contender for the Hitler role is famous, "Our Gene" called the newspapermen together and informed them that he had received letters from "Communist" organizations threatening that unless he pardoned me he would be assassinated. To make the show more hair-raising, he threw a small army of National Guardsmen around the capitol to watch over his precious life. He kept it there in full military regalia for several weeks. Atlanta citizenry blinked in astonishment and was properly awed. *The Atlanta Georgian*, a Hearst paper, in its fidelity to the clutching-hand tradition of yellow journalism, ran a scare headline in its issue of June 13, 1934, reading:

CAPITOL GUARDED ON RED THREAT

The news article which followed it went on to say that the military guard had been drawn around the capitol by the Governor because "he has been bombarded by letters from all sections of the country threatening damage to his person and to state property unless he pardons Angelo Herndon, Negro Communist."

Mr. Hamilton, that noble defender of truth and liberty, suddenly sprang to the defense of the Reds. He pooh-poohed the Governor's circus tricks. Applesauce! said he in effect, "the Governor has attached no great significance to the threats, but felt that guards should be established." However, he was no match for Governor Talmadge when demagoguery and publicity stunts were concerned.

4

On May 24, 1934, the Georgia State Supreme Court handed down a decision upholding my conviction. It read in part:

"The defendant was indicted for the offense of attempting to incite insurrection, in violation of the Penal Code 56. The evidence authorized the verdict of guilty against him; and no substantial error of law having been committed, the court did not err in refusing a new trial.

"If the state were compelled to wait until the apprehended danger became certain, then its right to protect itself would come into being simultaneously with the overthrow of the government, when there would be neither prosecuting officers nor courts for the enforcement of the law. The evidence authorized the verdict, and the court did not err in refusing a new trial. Judgment affirmed. All the Justices concur, except C. J. Russell, absent on account of illness." *

We expected that such would be the outcome of our appeal. The Reverend Hudson became almost Biblical in his jubilations. He regarded my reverse as a personal triumph and he beat the timbrels and shouted "Hosannah" over it. He was determined to have me put on the chain gang while we appealed the case to the United States Supreme Court. But to our surprise, the State Supreme Court of Georgia actually issued a stay of the sentence pending appeal.

* For complete text see Appendix Six, p. 355.

5

Taking their cue, my prison guards now taunted and teased me at every step:

"You blasted coon, you will soon be sent to the chain gang! That's where you should have been all along. But they will 'take care' of you, once they get you out there."

To make matters worse they reversed their previous practice and kept from me all my letters, newspapers and books. This they did not do straightforwardly, but brought them to me and, displaying them in provoking fashion, went off with them, laughing. I know what beasts some men can be. I fully understand how as a result of circumstances they become degraded and conscienceless. But I have never been quite able to reconcile myself to the unnecessary cruelty they inflict so joyfully upon helpless human beings.

A new occurrence suddenly precipitated me into a state of great excitement. My application for bail, which had been denied for twenty-six months, was unexpectedly granted. However, there was a fly in the ointment. Did the officials have a little joke of their own up their sleeves? Possibly they thought that if they set a high bail I would find it impossible to raise it. I would thus have no alibi that I was being denied my constitutional rights, and so I would be obliged to stay in jail as long as it pleased them. When my lawyers informed me that my bail had been set at $15,000, I was ready to laugh.

Where, for goodness' sake, was I going to raise such a sum?

The lawyers of the International Labor Defense protested vigorously against such high bail. It was unheard of, they argued, that a man of my class and position be expected to raise such an enormous sum of money.

There were only twenty-three days left in which to raise the $15,000. If by that time the money was not deposited with the court, I would be sent to the chain gang. It was a race against time, a race in which I was not running, although it concerned me most vitally. But the International Labor Defense launched a spirited nationwide campaign for the bail money. It was an action which involved hundreds of thousands of workers. At first it looked disheartening, for to most workers who had heard of me I was a mere name, and to those who knew me I was an insignificant Negro worker with no particular standing in the working-class movement.

My jailers gloated over their certainty that the bail campaign would fail. At every opportunity they came to my cell to tease me.

"You'll never get out!" one of them jeered. "The Communist leaders certainly have gotten you into a lot of trouble, by gum, and now they are having a good time at your expense."

"Fifteen thousand dollars!" laughed another. "You're crazy if you think you can raise it!"

Because of the constant repetition of their jibes I actually began to doubt myself whether the money would be raised in time, if at all. Times were hard. Millions of workers were tramping the streets hungry-eyed, looking for jobs which were not to be gotten. It therefore seemed to me sheer madness to expect that the bail collection would be successful.

However, I am hardly the person to remain in a state of mental discouragement for long. It certainly was not because I was romantic. But from direct personal experience I knew that the workers would not rest until they had raised the money with which to snatch me from the chain gang.

Not receiving any newspapers, I could not find out how fast the bail was being raised, but as each day passed, and as the jibes of my jailers increased, my certainty that my freedom was rapidly approaching became stronger.

I then did a curious thing. I began to pack my few wretched belongings: my battered few books, my comb with half of its teeth missing, and a few patched and mended shirts. I tied these in a bundle with a piece of string. And as I packed I hummed to myself.

My conduct created a sensation. Word spread rapidly that Angelo Herndon was packing in preparation of leaving the jail. It was not for a long time that so much laughter had been heard in Fulton Tower as on that day. All those who were able, whether prison guards or prisoners, came to my cell to view the strange spectacle. It was clear that they all thought I had gone out of my wits.

"What you doin' there, son?" one of the older Negro prisoners asked, doubling up with mirth.

"Packing—don't you see?"

"When do you expect to leave, Your Honor?"

"Oh, I'll be leaving here any day now."

The prisoners and the guards nearly split their sides laughing.

"Bail set, ain't bail raised, son," another prisoner chided gently.

I did not answer but continued humming.

One guard sneered at me through the bars:

"Fifteen thousand *in dollars*, boy, is about the highest bail ever set in these parts. You ought to feel proud, you've made a world record. No cheap nigger's life was ever valued so high before."

I ignored him and continued my packing. I dusted and put away with loving care my two volumes of Marx' *Capital*, *The Gotha Program* and John Strachey's *The Coming Struggle for Power*. Unknown friends had sent them to me. With what interest I had pored over them, reading *and* re-reading them over and over again!

To me these were no mere books, but living, throbbing things, friends who had come to aid me in my days of dire need. They had been to me like a sword by day and a pillar of fire by night. They had helped me preserve my sanity through the nightmare of my twenty-six months of imprisonment. So that now, on the eve of re-emerging into the world, I was still standing upright, still unbroken, still full of the battle spirit, still unembittered.

6

The days that followed were endlessly long. The suspense was excruciating.

The response to the appeal was lukewarm at first. It was first printed in the *Daily Worker*, then reprinted in the Communist foreign-language press, such as the Jewish *Morgen Freiheit*, the Hungarian *Uj Elore*, the Finnish *Eteenpain*, the German *Der Arbeiter*, and the Italian *Il Lavoratori.* But after a few days some remarkable letters and contributions began to arrive. Because of the sentiments they expressed and because the small contributions represented sacrifice offerings, the International Labor Defense correctly came to the conclusion that within a short time a perfect torrent of such contributions would come pouring in for my bail fund. For, more than anything else, these letters and contributions represented the mass will and solidarity of the working class. A few examples will suffice in illustration.

Edwin Johnson wrote from Chicago, Illinois:

"I enclose $2.00 for Angelo Herndon bail. I am unemployed so I can't do very much, but I hope it will help some. Keep up the good work."

Helen Willis, living in New York, sent a little note with her contribution. It read:

"Good people—30c stamps. Best I can do. For Herndon bail."

One of the most inspiring communications came from a girl worker in Allentown, Pa. She wrote:

"I am nineteen years old. Have been out of work six months.

This ten dollars is my first pay. May it help free Angelo Herndon."

One worker in West Grove, Pa., sent a shy, guilty-sounding communication:

"This one dollar looks too trival to send."

There was nothing to apologize for. The spirit which moved him to send the dollar touched me very deeply.

One Southern worker who seemed fully to grasp my true condition wrote in a poetic vein:

"I enclose two dollars for the resurrection of Angelo Herndon."

Not all those who sent money for my bail fund agreed with my political views. One Socialist worker from New Jersey tried to explain this very frankly:

"Thank you for giving me the opportunity to assist in the Herndon fund. I am not a Communist like Herndon, but a Socialist. I shall strive to a united front of these cases."

To say that only workers and workers' organizations rallied to my defense would be to understate the matter. Liberals, intellectuals, business men, professionals and church bodies showed extraordinary interest and generosity in my behalf, for my case represented to them what the Dreyfus case had been in France and the Sacco-Vanzetti case in Boston—a conflict between reaction and free ideas.

The universal interest in my plight can best be illustrated by the following communication which came from a small town in Kentucky:

"Dear Sirs:—This $2.00 is donated by the Missionary Baptist Society. We are sending this small token with our prayers and best wishes. May the Lord replenish it."

Concern over my fate even reached out to me from beyond the ocean. I received heartening messages, and contributions were sent to the I.L.D. from almost every country in the world. From Vienna came the following greetings:

"To Comrade Angelo Herndon! Red Front! May our small contribution do all it can in order to achieve your immediate freedom. Viennese Sympathizers."

The future historian of the labor movement in America, on examining the records of my case, will surely remark on the extraordinary spirit of self-sacrifice manifested by both Negro and white workers in collecting the $15,000 redemption money for me. Some workers denied themselves clothing and even went without meals in order to be able to contribute their pathetic little mite to the bail fund. One poorly dressed white worker walked into the I.L.D. office in Newark, and blushing furiously, laid $200 in bills on the secretary's desk. Then, as he beat a hasty retreat, he muttered apologetically:

"This is for Angelo Herndon's bail. Thank you for accepting it."

It was most amusing to watch the jailers as the days went by. They were waiting impatiently for August 5th to arrive. That was the deadline that the court had fixed for the presentation of bail. The wretches even took bets on me as if I were a race horse!

"Ten dollars to your one that the $15,000 won't be raised by August 5th," was the challenge heard around me among the guards.

One of them, pointing brazenly at me, exclaimed:

"Hell, no! They'll never raise $15,000 in twenty-three days to get a nigger out of jail."

And to make my torment the keener, he went on to describe in the most vivid way possible how much the balls and chains with which I would be shackled weighed, and what kind of death by degrees would await me when I got on the chain gang.

Then he burst into a foul-mouthed frenzy, describing what they were going to do to me there.

I shuddered, and looking at him, saw through him and beyond him. I tried to shut out all the hideousness before me with reflections on ideal and worth-while things.

The Southern newspapers followed the collection of the bail fund as if it were the score in a baseball game. On July 23rd, they croaked with delight because only $538.60 had been raised. But only four days later the fund already totalled $5,000. Letters now began cascading into the I.L.D. office by the thousands. An entire staff of volunteer workers was on duty day and night, sorting postal-telegraph money orders and the contributions which arrived in special-delivery letters. On August 1st, only $4,614.60 stood between me and my freedom. Only three more days remained for the entire sum to be collected.

Chief Jailer Holland looked me up and down and laughed unbelievingly when he saw that I had made ready for my departure.

"Unpack that bag!" he ordered sternly.

Reluctantly I untied my bundle and, taking the second volume of *Capital*, sat down on my cot and before long lost myself in its knotty problems. Neither Chief Jailer Holland nor all the jailers in the world could reach me then. We spoke in different tongues. We moved in different worlds. Strangers!

7

My lawyer, Mr. Davis, came to see me one day. To his surprise and mine, the guards treated him with courtesy. At other times they snarled and snapped at him and put up all sorts of obstacles when he wished to see me. Our mystification increased further when they allowed us to meet in a private cell.

When Mr. Davis prepared to leave upon the conclusion of our conference I asked him to mail for me some twenty-five letters that I had written to various newspapers and to labor, fraternal and religious organizations. At our next meeting he told me that as he was walking out of the jail he was halted by one of the turnkeys, who forcibly took my letters from him and brought them to the Warden.

When Mr. Holland opened the letters he accused Mr. Davis of trying to smuggle insurrectionary material out of the jail. He warned him that if he wished to share the same fate with me, he'd better continue the way he was doing. What enraged him so was the following passage in one of my letters:

"The Fascist dogs are trying to kill me even before I get out. I have reliable information that they plan to lynch me if I am released on bail. They have increased the pressure against me since the Supreme Court's decision."

My discovery of the plot to lynch me came in an unexpected way. There was a certain white prisoner who, because of good conduct, was made a trusty in the Warden's office. He was an intelligent man, and occasionally he would stop and talk to me. In time, he and I became good friends. He would retail to me all the current gossip in the jail. Naturally enough, I had tried to convert him to my Communist views. I believe I succeeded completely in this. Now it happened that one day, as he was standing in my cell doorway arguing heatedly about something or other, Mr. Holland passed by and, spotting him in animated conversation with me, told him "to get the hell out of there." Furthermore, he upbraided him:

"You ought to be ashamed of yourself to talk to a nigger!"

Fortunately, my white friend was not ashamed to talk to niggers. I am afraid I had helped undermine his feeling of white superiority when I made him a gift of the pamphlet, *Why Communism?* by M. J. Olgin. He now stood his ground manfully and to my delight replied with an air of indignation to the Chief Jailer:

"He's as good as you are, and better!"

The Warden grew purple with anger. He walked off threatening to lock him up in solitary.

My friend became white as chalk at the threat. He already

knew the horrors of that kind of punishment. But it made him look only more grim and determined.

It was this incident which created a deep bond between us. I therefore took it quite naturally when late one night he stole up to my cell bars and called my name in a whisper. Frightened, I sprang out of my cot and, bending my face close to his on the other side of the door, listened to his warning message:

"Angelo, I just heard them talking about you down in the front office. I saw them read those letters they took from your lawyer. You better be careful now, because I heard them plot something dreadful. They are planning to lynch you, should you succeed in leaving on bail."

I silently gripped the hand of my white friend and, asking him to wait a moment, dashed off a note to the I.L.D. He promised to try and smuggle it out of the jail.

When the I.L.D. received my letter it immediately got on the job. It publicized the plot fully in the press and formally notified the police officials in all the cities that I would pass through by train to New York that they would be held responsible for my safety, because there was a lynch plot organized against me. Also the railroad company was informed of the matter and police protection was demanded from them.

When Theodore Dreiser, the novelist, heard of my predicament he telephoned Governor Talmadge from New York, demanding that he furnish full police protection for me out of the city of Atlanta. The conversation between the two men was a very strange one and I report it here as it was stenographically recorded:

Dreiser: This is Theodore Dreiser of New York speaking. We are sending a man down to take Angelo Herndon out of jail in a few days. We are informed that he has been threatened with lynching in case he is released.

Talmadge: I haven't heard about it.

Dreiser: We demand safe protection for him.

Talmadge: People down here don't get excited about things like that. We never molest a nigger unless he rapes a white woman. My nigger servants who are standing right here now can testify to that and tell you that that is the truth.

Dreiser: We are only asking you that Angelo Herndon leave the State of Georgia unharmed.

Talmadge: Oh, that fellow Herndon can live down here as long as he wants to, and so long as he behaves himself, nothing will ever happen to him.

Dreiser: Thank you very much. I just wanted to be sure.

8

By August 3rd, the bail fund had reached $16,324, and by midnight of August 4th it had skyrocketed to $18,723.85.

When the jailers heard of it, they looked stunned. One of them scolded me:

"Wait till you step outside of Fulton Tower, you'll wish you had stayed inside here, you God-damn coon —!"

The I.L.D. sent Mr. Joseph Brodsky, the chief of its legal staff, by airplane to Atlanta, in order to escort me to New York. And so on the morning of August 4th he breezed in with his usual jovial and reassuring manner. He said to me as he crushed my hand in his:

"We are leaving today, Angelo, say good-bye to your cell-mates."

No words can describe the joy and the excitement that came over me. My heart leaped up; it pounded in my chest like a kettle drum. I was afraid my nerves would not be able to hold together much longer, for they were strained to the breaking point. A big lump rose in my throat until it almost choked me. I could hardly restrain my tears.

I must admit that the prospect of going out again into the

world from which I had been away so long frightened me. I was filled with unreasonable misgivings. Would it be possible to adjust myself to life again? During the twenty-six months of my imprisonment I had lost practically all touch with it, had fallen out of step. How would it look to me now? Would my mother and my brothers and sister forgive me for all the sorrow I must have caused them unintentionally all this time? Would my comrades have become estranged from me? While time was holding its hands back for me in the vacuum of monotony and wretchedness in Fulton Tower, the world had marched on. I was afraid, so afraid, that it had already passed me by and that it was too late for me to catch up with it. The thought of meeting people again filled me with terror instead of making me happy. I was gripped by an unreasonable desire to hide myself somewhere in a cell far more secret than the one in which I had spent almost two and a half years of my life.

Mr. Brodsky left me for a while to go to the court house, there to have my release papers signed by the Reverend Hudson. The latter now felt inclined to assume his military role.

"You damn yellow cowards!" roared Colonel Hudson, addressing himself to Mr. Brodsky as the spokesman for all the Communists. "Why don't you come on down here and let's fight it out? You sit up there in New York and send telegrams. We ain't afraid to fight you! Just come on down here!"

Now Mr. Brodsky is a man of great urbanity and good humor. He knows when and how to laugh at absurdities whenever he strikes up against them. To all the rantings of Col. Hudson he exhibited a poker face. "I let him rave!" he later told me, laughing, describing his reaction. He saw that the Prosecutor was trying hard to provoke him into an argument by insult, so that he would have the pretext he was looking for not to sign my release papers. Certainly he was not going to give him that satisfaction!

9

At five o'clock that afternoon a guard came to my cell and sarcastically called out:

"Angelo Herndon, get your hat and coat and let's go home."

The news of my release spread through the jail. Both white and Negro prisoners crawled to the windows opening on the front gate side to bid me farewell. I followed the turnkey half dreaming. I could not grasp the full reality of what was happening to me. As I walked from the third floor to the first, all the big steel-plated doors were opened for me. Never before, it seemed to me, must they have opened so wide to let anyone pass. At each door stood an armed guard who eyed me with hostility. One of them sent a spiteful threat after me.

"We'll hang you next time, you black bastard!"

As I walked through the steel-lined corridor from compartment to compartment the words of the guard seemed to pursue me like specters in a nightmare.

Yes, they *would* hang me next time!

Touching was the farewell I received from my Negro and white fellow-prisoners. Most of them showed great pleasure over my release. They seemed to enjoy their own dreams of freedom in my realized dream. Some of the prisoners, however, were afraid to show their sympathy openly for me. As I followed the turnkey to the front office, these timid ones bowed their heads shamefacedly. But I knew just the same that in their hearts they wished me well.

10

A crowd of men milled round the front office of the jail as I entered it. I peered closely into their faces. I did not recognize any of them. Something about them filled me with deep alarm. Maybe it was the recent threat of lynching which suggested to me something sinister in their appearance. At any

BEN DAVIS, JR., ATTORNEY FOR ANGELO HERNDON

rate, they were not a sympathetic-looking lot. They were armed to the teeth with pistols and sawed-off shotguns. Not one friendly face among them—only expressions of contempt and hatred!

Was it possible that this was the lynch mob I so dreaded? I grew cold and clammy. It took all my will power to hold myself erect and outwardly calm.

When the time came for me to sign my discharge papers, I suddenly found Mr. Brodsky standing by my side. His cheerful, clever face reassured me. Seeing how upset I was he whispered in my ear:

"Don't worry, Angelo! Everything is all right! These men are here to protect you from the mob. They are from the railroad company."

It was as if a mountain had rolled off my chest. I smiled half-heartedly as I answered:

"I thought they were thugs who had come to lynch me. In any case they are thugs—only just lined up differently. This time they are on my side. Tomorrow they will be on their side—a lynch mob."

The sun was shining as I passed through the outer gates of the jail—a free man. I stopped on the sidewalk to wave good-bye to my fellow-prisoners who crowded the windows. A guard came running toward me yelling that I had better keep moving if I knew what was good for me. I ignored his orders and waved to the prisoners, calling out:

"Good-bye, fellows! Be brave! Heads up! Your turn will come next! Good luck!"

The prisoners, some of them deeply moved, cried back to me their good wishes and told me to carry on and not give up the fight.

A turnkey interrupted with a yell:

"Good-bye, hope to see you back for good."

I did not answer. My mind was preoccupied.

One great truth I discovered at the moment of my freedom: That as long as there will be men rotting unjustly in foul prisons, neither I, nor anyone else, can ever be free.

Freedom! That is a strange word. It may mean many things. But to me it means only one thing: a world which will not reduce men to the level of vile beasts, which will not drive them by need and a corrupt environment to rob and kill and deceive and commit every other sort of infamy.

I looked intently at the faces of the prisoners as they stood crowded at the windows, watching me go. First now, at the moment of my departure, I began to notice how really wretched they were. Their faces were so pinched, with jaundiced complexions, hollow-eyed and with a look of suffering in them that was so intense that it resembled madness most of all!

A chill went down my spine, overwhelmed by sheer horror.

"Well, how does it feel to be free again, Angelo?" Mr. Brodsky asked me suddenly, nudging me cheerfully in the ribs.

I tried to smile, but I could not. There was too much sadness in me.

"Free?" I answered questioningly. "I am going back now where I belong–in the front-line trenches of labor in the class war. I am afraid I won't be free for very long. The enemy will see to that."

"But you are sick! You deserve a rest," pleaded Mr. Brodsky.

I answered: "A man who loves his fellow-man must not grow tired–cannot afford to rest. There is too much work to be done–too little time to do it–too few to do it. All that has happened to me thus far has been for me a sort of apprenticeship in the revolutionary struggle–a kind of prelude to life, as I must live it."

I looked at the magnolia trees that hardly stirred in the quiet

August breeze. When I had entered Fulton Tower it was to them that I had directed my last farewell to freedom and beauty. I had feared that I would never see them again alive. How yearningly I had thought of them in the rotten prison stench when I was overcome by disgust and hatred for life. And there they were standing now, the same as I first saw them, but even fresher and greener. A great joy welled up in me. I too had struggled hard and had succeeded in keeping my spirit fresh and green and full of undying hope.

EPILOGUE

THE LIFE OF A MAN is like a river which winds in its course to the sea. It flows on in eternal continuity. Yet the sea is never full. Therefore, if I have chosen arbitrarily to bring my narrative to an end at this point it is entirely because my experience, and the effect it had on my attitude toward the world, reached its climax at the gates of Fulton Tower as they swung close behind me. What has followed after has only been a commentary upon what preceded. But because the commentary also has the vital breath of life in it, my story would be incomplete if I did not sketch briefly all that has happened to me after my temporary release from prison.

Before leaving Atlanta on that memorable day, August 5, 1934, I wired the following message to the International Labor Defense in New York:

> "We American workers must now tighten up our ranks in militant struggles that must free the Scottsboro boys, Thaelmann, Mooney and all class war victims, and eventually lead to the defeat of the pirate ruling class. This partial victory in connection with my case should be all the more convincing to those who have been doubtful or misled about the strength of mass pressure. I re-enter the struggle determined to carry on, come what may."

My journey from Atlanta to New York was full of stirring incidents. Not least among them was the sight of the sun as it rose at the rim of the horizon the following morning. It had been such a long, long time since I had seen daybreak! I could not look my fill of it. The fields were green and golden with ripening crops and glistened with dew in the soft morning light. I felt tired, very tired in spirit. But the purity and the peace in nature flowed into me like healing balm.

2

Everywhere the train stopped on the way I was met by enthusiastic crowds of workers and sympathizers. The news of my passage had preceded me. Everywhere it was the same thing, yet new each time because the demonstrations were without exception spontaneous and moving. In every city, whether in Washington, Baltimore, Philadelphia, Trenton or Newark, affectionate hands pulled me out of my car. I was hoisted up on the shoulders of sympathizers. The crowd gave vent to its feeling of joy because by its collective will I had been snatched, even if only temporarily, from the clutches of the chain-gang keepers. These mass receptions gave me a sense of emotional release. My tension, so great that it hurt, was eased.

People speak too lightly of the brotherhood of man. That day I experienced it completely. It filled me with a light so dazzling that I felt blinded.

When my train was about to pull out from Newark for New York I suddenly noticed a shabbily dressed Negro woman. She drew my attention because she was trying frantically to work her way through the crowd to me. When she finally reached me, she stood before me trembling with excitement. She clasped my hand tightly in hers. I waited expectantly, for it appeared as if she had something important to say to me. But she was so overcome with emotion that she could find no words. I looked into her eyes, from which tears were falling, and I too lost all power of speech. So both of us stood mutely looking at each other, hand clasping hand, until the whistle blew.

So great was my excitement that as I jumped on the train my fist was still clenched. But when the train began to move and I opened it I found a crumpled one-dollar bill.

3

When the train pulled into the Pennsylvania Terminal in New York I was met by a delegation representing the various organizations which had worked for my freedom. As they led me up the stairs into the station I heard the building rock with mighty cheers. The receptions I received in other cities were only preliminaries to what was to meet me here. The vast hall was thronged to suffocation with a cheering crowd of ten thousand, while thousands more overflowed into the streets. As they saw me their clenched fists swung forward in comradely salute. I swallowed hard. I felt my knees giving way. I hardly knew what was happening to me. Suddenly I found myself hoisted on the shoulders of Robert Minor and Ben Davis. The cheering became deafening. Men, women and children pelted me with flowers. I was almost smothered by them. Then someone started chanting. Others picked up the rhythmic cadence of the words. Soon they became cohesive, grew in volume and in power until they sounded like a clap of thunder. At first I could not make out what it was that they were chanting. Then it became unmistakable. It sounded like a war-cry:

Angelo Herndon must be freed! Angelo Herndon must be freed!

I knew they were not cheering me personally, but the unconquerable will of the working class. It was not merely my personal freedom they were demanding, but through me the freedom of all who are oppressed and exploited.

4

Only one discordant note rose up to mar the serene harmony of the first few days of my freedom. My release was the signal for our own Negro Uncle Toms and lickspittles to begin their yelping.

One of the most vicious attacks on me appeared in George Schuyler's column in the Pittsburgh *Courier* on August 25, 1934. Although a member of the National Board of the N.A.A.C.P., he nevertheless saw fit to revile me and also those who worked for my freedom. He wrote:

"Herndon is out on bail and will probably skip it like all the rest of his Communist friends."

Now there is nobody I find more offensive or coarse than a cold-blooded liar. I admit Mr. Schuyler's unprincipled attack stung me to the quick. So I immediately sent him the following telegram:

> "In your Pittsburgh *Courier* column of August 25, you say: 'Herndon is out on bail and will probably skip it like all the rest.' Just as you repeatedly knifed the Scottsboro boys by sneering at the mass fight for their freedom, so you attempt to knife me also. After thousands of workers and sympathizers have worked, sacrificed actually, to get together the $15,000 demanded by the Georgia lynchers for my bail, you announce that I will skip this bail. At this crucial point in my fight, you stab me in the back in an attempt to destroy the confidence the workers have in me. While I was in jail, you did not move a finger to help me. You never wrote a line to speed the collection of bail. Your statement about me has the effect of an invitation to the Georgia lynchers to revoke the bail. This is a police agent's action. No doubt your attack on me will win you the approbation of the lynch press of Georgia, just as your attack on the Scottsboro defense has already won

the approbation of the Alabama press.* I shall not skip the bail, which the workers have collected for me. If and when the time comes I shall return to Georgia, ready to continue the fight."

To this telegram, Mr. Schuyler replied in a fashion characteristic of him:

"My dear Mr. Herndon:

"Your telegram at hand. The capitalists have been so derelict in their duty that I have not sufficient funds to reply by wire as I would like to do. Knowing something of the technique of propaganda, I presume your wire was sent in order to serve as a basis for a 'news' release.

"My good friend, I admire your courage though I deplore your judgment anent returning to Georgia. If you should skip your bail, as have the other Communist brothers fallen afoul of the law, I would be among the first to laud your good sense. Such courage as yours is so rare among your comrades that it is well worth $15,000 to have you at liberty. I trust that you will ultimately win your case so that you may satisfy your ambition to return to Georgia and win over the black and white proletariat for Communism.

"Come up, to quote Mae West, and see me some time. I am always 'at home' to distinguished visitors. Bring my good friend Ben Davis with you.

"Sincerely yours,
(Signed) "George Schuyler"

Feeling it my duty to publicize my correspondence with Mr. Schuyler, I sent copies of it to all Negro newspapers in

* Mr. Schuyler wrote an article in the *American Spectator* attacking the I.L.D. defense of the Scottsboro case. Significantly enough, this article was reprinted with an editorial note of approval by the *Jackson County Sentinel* of Scottsboro, Ala., a reactionary newspaper which tried to whip up a lynch spirit against the Scottsboro boys during their trial in March, 1931.

the country. It goes without saying that everywhere it evoked a storm of protest and indignation. A group of Harlem intellectuals even threw a picket line around his house in Harlem. If they could not shame him privately they were determined to do it publicly.

5

The International Labor Defense arranged a speaking tour for me from coast to coast. Thousands of workers, Negro and white, intellectuals and liberals, churchgoers, trade unionists, Socialists, Republicans, Masons, Communists, college professors, university students, clergymen and school children—in fact, every segment of the population turned up at the meetings which I addressed. Wherever I went I was made to realize most dramatically that the decent people of America were aroused over my case. They did not only come to greet me and to listen to me; they also came to contribute their last pennies to my defense fund. They tried to make me feel personally that the destinies of all workers, regardless of race, nationality or color, are inextricably woven together. They were my brothers.

No one dwelt upon this theme more eloquently than the Reverend J. C. Austin, the pastor of the Pilgrim Baptist Church in Chicago. In addressing in my behalf a meeting of three thousand Negroes in his church he said:

> "Any man who does not want freedom is either a fool or an idiot, and if to want freedom is to be a Communist, then I am a Communist and will be until I die. From all I have learned of Communism, it means simply the brotherhood of man, and as far as I can see Jesus Christ was the greatest Communist of them all. A few weeks ago I stood in Red Square, Moscow, and raised my voice to the tune of the National Anthem of Russia. Just a week ago I stood in this church and talked to my congregation

on the subject 'Russia, the hope of the Negro.' I have been ordered not to let the I.L.D. use my church for a meeting to welcome Mr. Herndon because he is a Communist. I told them my church would always be open for those who stand for the universal brotherhood of man. Come here any time you want to hold a meeting, Mr. Herndon. Not only that, but you will find me always ready and willing to stand shoulder to shoulder with you, preach with you, pray with you, march with you and, if necessary, die with you for the common good of us all."

6

I had looked forward to my San Francisco visit with the greatest enthusiasm. The precise reason for this was that while there I would have an opportunity to visit the great working-class hero, Tom Mooney, in San Quentin prison.

I found Tom a mild, sad-eyed man. The confinement to which he had been subjected since 1916 had left its indelible marks on his face. It was lined and sallow and suggested high tension and great weariness. He was eager to discuss outside affairs, about which he spoke with greater penetration and knowledge than most men I have ever met. Despite all that has happened to him, he made upon me the impression of a strong, unyielding spirit.

I asked him:

"What do you think the United States Supreme Court will do about your case, Tom? Do you think they will let you go?"

His answer was much the same answer, allowing for different circumstances, I would have given had anyone asked me, "What do you think the United States Supreme Court will do about your case, Angelo?"

"I have no illusions about what they will do," answered Tom. "For eighteen years they have refused to have anything to do with my case. In fact, they have kicked and tossed me around so much that I cannot expect anything from them unless the protests of the working class will force them to free me."

"I suppose you know that Professor Moley has asked Governor Merriam to pardon you, so the workers will stop making such a noise about your frame-up?" I inquired.

"Yes, I know about that," answered Tom. "But you see there is Scottsboro, your case and mine, all coming up before the Supreme Court. Moley thinks that if Merriam pardons me the case will not go up there, and so they will be saved further exposure."

It seemed that he had been following very closely the developments in the cases of the Scottsboro boys and myself. Impulsively he extended his hand to me and clasped mine warmly, saying:

"I am glad to see you out, and for you to pay me a visit is indeed a pleasure. I know Georgia. I remember way back before the ruling class of California framed me how they used to treat Negroes. There was the 'Williams Farm' down there, where they used to work Negroes until they were almost dead. Then Williams, the plantation owner, would make them dig their own graves and kill them with an axe. I think he was put in prison later. As savage as they are, it is surprising that they let you go around the country speaking about your case."

When I extended to him my condolences over the death of his wonderful old mother, Tom's face turned gray and somber. He sounded tired and bitter:

"When my dear old mother died, and her dead body was brought to the gates of the prison so that I might see the last remains of the dear old soul who had fought and suffered for her son and her class, they would not let me go as far as the first door leading to the outside."

There were tears in Tom's eyes.

"She was a real fighter," he said, "who spent her last days on the battlefield, always agitating and organizing her class brothers and sisters for the final upheaval that will not only set her innocent son free, but break the chains that are bound around the necks of all workers."

I told Tom about what I had seen and read of the workers fighting for his freedom all over the world, and how there was never a meeting at which I spoke where the question of his freedom was not raised, and how warmly the workers received it.

Tom seemed very much pleased at what I told him. He was about to say something, but the guard rudely terminated the conversation.

Tom walked off crestfallen, his head bowed a little, and with a stoop in his shoulders.

7

On April 12, 1935, the United States Supreme Court sat listening to argument advanced by Whitney North Seymour, the noted constitutional lawyer retained by the International Labor Defense to represent me on the appeal. Mr. Seymour with great clarity and erudition tried to prove that the insurrection law under which I was jailed was unconstitutional.

For the State of Georgia appeared J. Walter LeCraw, who had been associated with the Reverend Hudson in the prosecution at my trial in Atlanta. Most extraordinary was his behavior. I could hardly believe my own eyes and ears. For the moment I forgot where I was. By the lynch plea he was making I thought I was in Judge Wyatt's court and not before the highest tribunal of the land. If Mr. Seymour and I were astonished, the nine justices were even more so. They even looked annoyed. He stood before them, wildly waving photostatic copies of the *Daily Worker*. It was about the worst rabble-rousing act I have ever seen. Was Mr. LeCraw trying to incite the justices of the United States Supreme Court to riot, I wondered with great amusement.

At one point the venerable Mr. Van Devanter asked the State's Attorney:

"Just what did the defendant do to be guilty of insurrection?"

Mr. LeCraw was slightly taken aback. Stammeringly he replied:

"Well, yer—yer Honors—the defendant had in his possession the *Daily Worker*, official organ of the Communist Party, U.S.A., Section of the Comm-u-nist Internationale-ee with headquarters in Moscoo, Rooshia."

A suppressed titter was heard among the spectators in the court room. Some of the justices almost ruined their dignity by smiling.

"No, I don't mean that. Just what actual crime did he commit?" persisted Mr. Van Devanter helpfully.

"He tried to set up a Nigger Republic in the Black Belt," replied Mr. LeCraw with exasperation.

This time the spectators in the court room did not try to repress their laughter—they choked with it, and the judges smiled broadly.

Fearing that the Supreme Court was going to decide unfavorably to the State of Georgia, Mr. LeCraw struck the attitude of Jefferson Davis and threatened the old gentlemen that should they decide against his state, Georgia was going to secede from the Union!

The nine justices looked at him with imperturbable solemnity. Whether they resented his threat or not, I could not tell because of their mask-like expression. However, Chief Justice Hughes announced that the court would take the appeal under advisement.

8

At last the Supreme Court came to a decision and on May 20, 1935, it issued the following opinion delivered by Justice Sutherland. It read in part as follows:

"An appeal from a decision of the Supreme Court of Georgia affirming a lower state court's judgment of conviction of attempting to incite insurrection, in violation of a Georgia statute, is not within the jurisdiction of the Supreme Court of the United States, although the statute is assailed as in violation of the Federal Constitution, since the Federal question was not seasonably raised or passed on, in the court below.

"The Federal question was raised in the lower state court in a preliminary attack upon the indictment, but the state supreme court declined to review the ruling of the trial court on the ground that the right to a review thereof was not preserved by exceptions, or assigned as error in due time in the bill of exceptions, as required by the established rules of the state. Such determination by state supreme court is conclusive on the Supreme Court of the United States. The presentation of the Federal question to the state supreme court on motion for rehearing is insufficient for its consideration by the Supreme Court of the United States. The rule that a Federal question may be raised in the Supreme Court of the United States for the first time where the state supreme court's ruling could not have been anticipated is not applicable." *

However, this decision was accompanied by a dissenting minority opinion, concurred in by the three liberals of the Court: Justices Cardozo, Brandeis and Stone. In sharp and challenging language they took to task the six justices who made the majority ruling.

* For full text of the majority opinion, see Appendix Seven, p. 391.

"It is novel doctrine that a defendant who has had the benefit of all he asks, and indeed of a good deal more, must place a statement on the record that if some other court at some other time shall read the statute differently, there will be a denial of liberties that at the moment of the protest are unchallenged and intact. Defendants charged with crime are as slow as are men generally to borrow trouble of the future. . . .

"For all that the record tells us, the prosecuting officer acquiesced in the charge, and did not ask the appellate court to apply a different test. In such a situation the appellant might plant himself as he did on the position that on the case given to the jury his guilt had not been proved. He was not under a duty to put before his judges the possibility of a definition less favorable to himself, and make an argument against it, when there had been no threat of any change, still less any forecast of its form or measure. He might wait until the law of the case had been rejected by the reviewing court before insisting that the effect would be an invasion of his constitutional immunities. . . .

"New strength is given to considerations such as these when one passes to a closer view of just what the Georgia court did in its definition of the statute. . . .

". . . The court disclaimed a willingness to pass upon the question as one of constitutional law, assigning as a reason that no appeal to the constitution had been made upon the trial or then considered by the judge. . . . Such a rule of state practice may have the effect of attaching a corresponding limitation to the jurisdiction of this court where fault can fairly be imputed to an appellant for the omission to present the question sooner. No such consequence can follow where the ruling of the trial judge has put the Constitution out of the case and made an appeal to its provisions impertinent and futile.

"In such circumstances, the power does not reside in a state by any rule of local practice to restrict the jurisdic-

TOM MOONEY AND ANGELO HERNDON

tion of this court in the determination of a constitutional question brought into the case thereafter. . . . If the rejection of the test of clear and present danger was a denial of fundamental liberties, the path is clear for us to say so. . . .

"The argument thus shut out is submitted to us now. Will men 'judging in calmness' . . . say of the defendant's conduct as shown forth in the pages of this record that it was an attempt to stir up revolution through the power of his persuasion and within the time when that persuasion might be expected to endure?

"If men so judging will say yes, will the Constitution of the United States uphold a reading of the statute that will lead to that response? Those are the questions that the defendant lays before us after conviction of a crime punishable by death in the discretion of the jury. I think he should receive an answer."

The majority decision had one concrete result: Instead of discouraging us, as our enemies expected, it only intensified our efforts. My lawyers petitioned United States Supreme Court Justice Roberts for a stay of execution of the sentence pending action on the motion for a rehearing. A two months' stay was granted.

So for that brief period I could still bask in the sun and walk as a free man among other men. After that—who could tell?

9

The Supreme Court's decision aroused a great deal of public indignation in liberal circles. Many newspapers carried editorials in which they condemned it as reactionary in the most scathing terms. The editorial in the New York *Post's* issue of May 22, 1935, expressed this widespread feeling of abhorrence and dismay.

"Herndon was arrested in July of 1932, a few days after he led an unemployed demonstration of white and Negro workers to demand relief. No disorder marked the demonstration. His 'crime' was the possession of Communist literature. He was convicted under a slave insurrection law of pre-Civil War era, providing the death penalty for 'bringing, introducing or circulating within the state any printed or written paper, pamphlet, or circular for the purpose of exciting insurrection, revolt, conspiracy or resistance on the part of slaves, Negroes or free persons of color.'

"Georgia officials frankly admit that if Herndon's conviction is upheld by the Supreme Court, they will use the statute against all who can be regarded as advocating Negro equality or the right of Negroes and whites to organize in the same union.

"Eighteen other persons, six of them women, are under indictment under the same law. They are union organizers, and there is no pretense that any of them have taken any direct part in any violent, unlawful or subversive acts.

"The race question is crucial in the struggle to organize the Southern worker and sharecropper. Maintenance of the color line is the core of anti-labor policy. The conviction of Herndon opens the way to crush the new labor and sharecropper organizations by the use of old slave laws, not only in Georgia, but in Arkansas and in other former slave-holding states.

"It opens the way to impose slavery not only on the black, but on the white. It threatens the whole standard of living of the South, and the lowering of this standard is a menace to Northern labor and to Northern manufacture. It constricts the national market, and it pulls down the standard of living everywhere.

"All honor is due Justices Cardozo, Brandeis and Stone, who dissented and upheld Herndon's right to a hearing. But more honor goes to the young Georgia Negro, Herndon, who had the courage, in the face of death and the chain gang, to help organize the most miserable, the most divided, the most exploited workers in this country.

"The fight to free Herndon is a fight to free Southern labor in factory and on farm. The fight to free Southern Labor is a fight to free Northern Labor as well from the menace of low wages and of terrorist tactics to maintain low wages."

10

The International Labor Defense believed that if it could only arouse strong enough public opinion for my case it would not only succeed in saving me from the chain gang, but it would save many other workers from a similar fate. To this end it began the stupendous task of collecting two million signatures to a petition addressed to "Our Gene," Governor Talmadge of Georgia, demanding my freedom.

The business of the petition in itself was highly dramatic. Such sincere devotion and sacrifice on a mass scale had rarely been equalled before, not only in this country, but in any other country in the world. People of all shades of opinion and in every worldly circumstance worked without rest to speed the collection of the signatures. Signed petitions came pouring in from as distant points as London, Johannesburg, the West Indies, Mexico and France. They came in by the thousands and startled even us, who with our own eyes had already seen so many wonderful manifestations of solidarity among the workers of the world.

It could hardly be said that my case symbolized Communism vs. Capitalism, as the lynch dervishes would have it—rather, a vast number of Americans looked upon it as a symbol of the clash between Democracy and Fascism, between the ideals of Thomas Jefferson's America and the doctrines of Hitler's Germany. This was why, although generally I was known as a Communist, many prominent legislators of both major parties not only signed my petition, but even wrote personal letters to Governor Talmadge, demanding my freedom and the repeal of the savage insurrection law. Many members of state legislatures and other public officials throughout the country did likewise. The City Council of Cleveland unanimously passed a resolution memorializing the Governor of Georgia in my behalf.

One of the dramatic devices with which the International Labor Defense planned to stimulate wider public interest in my case was a cage, an exact replica of the cages of torture in which the prisoners on the Georgia chain gang are forced to live. This cage, which was mounted on a truck, had cardboard pictures of prisoners in life-size who appeared chained inside. Volunteer workers also dressed in prison stripes exhibited themselves in the cage, just to give people an idea of how human beings look when they are degraded and brutalized. All over America this cage of the country's shame was driven. In every town that it stopped, workers, farmers, business men, professionals and young children crowded round it in great amazement to see with their own eyes the fruits of "Christian civilization." Open cries of disgust and shame were heard everywhere. Therefore, it was with more than polite interest that men and women, representing the real America and belonging to all classes and interests, affixed their signatures to the long petitions which hung poster-wise on the sides of the truck.

11

In order to achieve greater co-ordination and effectiveness, *The Joint Committee to Aid the Herndon Defense* was organized at the end of September, 1935.

A slight indication of the far-flung interest in my case may be seen in the names of the individuals and organizations who filed a brief, *amicus curiae*. These were Charles Houston of the National Association for the Advancement of Colored

People; George W. Lawrence, Thurgood Marshall, and James Marshall of Counsel; Arthur Garfield Hays and Morris L. Ernst for the American Civil Liberties Union; Bethuel M. Webster, Jr. of the Council of the Church League for Industrial Democracy; Miss Winifred Chappell of the Methodist Federation of Social Service; the Justice Commission of the Central Conference of American Rabbis; the Reverends W. Russell Bowie, Allen Knight Chalmers, Harry Emerson Fosdick, Hubert C. Herring and Rabbi Stephen S. Wise. Together with the Federal Council of Churches, the Socialist and Communist Parties and numerous other civic, religious and labor combincs, these aforementioned organizations were very active in collecting signatures and funds in my behalf.

12

At the height of this campaign, a delegation of prominent liberals and writers proceeded to Alabama and Georgia to protest both the Scottsboro and the Herndon decisions. In Alabama lynchers took pot-shots at the members of the delegation and when the latter demanded police protection from the Governor, he informed them very wittily that he could hardly be held responsible for people who wanted to have a little fun by shooting at themselves, implying thereby that the members of the delegation had tried to murder one another in the State of Alabama!

A little later at the railroad station in Atlanta the delegation was met belligerently by that old friend of the Negro people—American Legion Commander Kenneth Murrel—who delivered himself of the following defy:

> "When the group sent by the National Committee for the Defense of Political Prisoners appears before the Governor to ask a pardon for the nigger Communist Angelo Herndon, we will be right there with them. I have re-

ceived word that the National Office of the Legion will wage a definite fight against Herndon's pardon."

The Committee thanked him for his kind intentions and next called on Governor Talmadge, the man who boasted that he would like to be the Hitler of America. This distinguished gentleman, punctuating his illiterate remarks with pungent cussing, hemmed and hawed and tied himself up in knots trying to explain to the Committee that there was nothing he could do about my case.

On October 13, 1935, the Supreme Court turned down my petition for a re-hearing. It made no comment upon its decision. I was ordered to surrender myself to the Georgia authorities within twenty days to begin serving my sentence on the chain gang.

13

The reverse my appeal suffered at the hands of the United States Supreme Court galvanized all progressive forces in America into more intensified activity in my behalf. An emergency defense conference was hastily called in Harlem. New plans had to be worked out to meet new dangers. More than one hundred fraternal, political, social, church and labor organizations took part in the deliberations. Prominent among those who participated were Congressman Vito Marcantonio, Ashley B. Totten of the Brotherhood of Sleeping Car Porters, Anna Damon, the Reverend William Lloyd Imes, David Lasser of the Workers Unemployed Union, and Lester B. Granger of the National Urban League.

Mr. Marcantonio seemed deeply concerned about my case. In addressing the delegates, he said:

"During the closing weeks of Congress, Miss Damon, Secretary of the International Labor Defense, came down to Washington on the Angelo Herndon case. And we started at that time to obtain a number of signatures from the members of the House and from the members of the Senate. I don't recall just how many signatures we received, but you can rest assured of one thing—that the campaign for signatures down there will be kept on as part of the fight to free Angelo Herndon. I realize that in this fight for the freedom of Angelo Herndon we are fighting the combined forces of the last vestiges of feudalism and the most atrocious forms of capitalism in America. We are fighting here race prejudice plus the Bourbons and the reactionaries of America who are determined that labor, especially below the Mason and Dixon line, shall have no voice and show no protest, so that to me Angelo Herndon symbolizes a cause. If it were just a fight of an individual I would not be interested, but freedom for Angelo Herndon represents the cause of the right of the American working class, irrespective of race or creed to protest, to demand, and to agitate for a better deal in these United States."

I spoke after Mr. Marcantonio. Never before had I spoken with greater awareness of the secondary part my own personality was playing in the great drama of my case. Now was the time to speak up, for only a few days separated me from the chain gang, and perhaps eternal silence.*

When I finished speaking the Reverend Imes rose and with great earnestness made the following pledge to me:

"Fellow-worker and brother, Angelo Herndon, upon you has fallen the agony and the glory of symbolizing those heroic workers of America who, in their struggle for freedom and light, must bear the onslaught of all the dark and evil forces in this country. Just as you have

* For text of my speech see Appendix Eight, p. 404.

stood unswervingly with the working class and for the working class, so we pledge ourselves never to forget that as long as you are in chains, no worker of America can call himself free."

14

When the time for my surrender to the Atlanta authorities drew near, many people began to clamor their advice into my ears that I should skip bail; that I should run away to some foreign country where no one would know me.

That sort of freedom would be bought at too great a price, I protested.

Hundreds of thousands of people had believed in me and in my cause, had contributed money for my defense, had put me forward as a symbol of their struggle for human rights. Was I now going to let these people down?

I laughed. The advice was too absurd!

My friends looked very much disappointed.

Several Negro newspapers wrote articles and editorials urging me to save myself while there was still time. After all, fifteen thousand dollars was not the greatest amount of money in the world! The people who contributed would not mind. To go back would merely be to turn the other cheek to a ruthless enemy of the Negro people. According to their opinion, I had the moral right to run away and save myself from certain death.

My answer to all these urgings was that at half-past one on the afternoon of October 25, 1935, I boarded the train for Atlanta.

How different by contrast was my departure from my arrival. I had come to New York as a victim of capitalist injustice—broken in body and tired in spirit. But now my role was reversed. I was leaving as an emissary of the working class, bearing with me, and symbolizing by my voluntary surrender to the prison authorities, the revolutionary challenge of the working class. Far from being filled with gloom, I felt almost joyous. The strength of my comrades who saw me off at the station flowed into me and my spirits rose high. As the train with a great clangor pulled out, I had the overpowering certainty that I had no cause to grieve or to be afraid. I was being protected by the undespairing concern of the working class and by my own knowledge that what I was doing was the only right thing for a human being, for a class-conscious worker and an honest Bolshevik.

With mounting speed the train sped down the Atlantic coast. I looked hungrily out of the window at the passing landscape. All of nature seemed so radiant, pure and breathing peace and harmony. But who could tell—maybe this was going to be the last time I would ever look upon nature and its musings? The leaves on the trees looked golden and brown, and I fell into a revery as I watched them falling in the autumnal wind.

But I was soon shaken out of it by the sight of the cruel reality—a reality that for a brief space of time I had conveniently pushed back into the dim memory of my past. As our train thundered through South Carolina and Georgia I saw lynch mobs following bloodhounds on a manhunt. At the first station we stopped, I bought a newspaper and read about the alleged rape of a white girl by a Negro. My heart sank. Was that nightmare of persecution never to end?

All along the way, in plantation after plantation, and in every state I saw bales of cotton stacked one upon the other, rotting in the sun. The economic servitude of America's millions of tenant and sharecropper peons beggars description. Everywhere, as far as the eye could see, clustered the tumble-down shacks in which they lived. I raged within myself: A dog in a kennel, a horse in a manger, or a pig in a pig-sty was better housed than the people in these dwellings.

It was at this time that the rape of Ethiopia by the Italian Fascists was being justified at great length by the white capitalistic newspapers in this country because, they said, it would result in making the Abyssinian savages "civilized." And as I looked at the wretched, half-starved white and Negro sharecroppers toiling in the fields, I was amused at the thought of capitalist America's civilizing ardor for other peoples.

15

Before I went into the Sheriff's office in Atlanta to surrender myself, I sent the following message to all my friends and defenders:

> "If what I have done and what I do, if all I have suffered, and will still suffer, helps build the united front, then I have been successful. My fight has not been in vain. I will have been as successful as any human being, any worker could be in such a short span of life. I am now twenty-two years old. If life is spared me, and I am sure the people of America will see to that, if I am snatched from this slow death of a Georgia chain gang, then I will devote the rest of my life to the same work that caused my arrest. I searched for a unity of all the working men in America, white and black, in mine and office, to end the slavery I find my beautiful country in. I want to see shining workers' homes of marble where today these grimy shacks stand."

When I announced myself to the Sheriff, he looked unbelievingly at me. When his deputies heard of it, they came pouring into the room to see with their own eyes the lunatic who returned to jail of his own free will to serve a twenty-year sentence on the chain gang.

The Sheriff looked at me peculiarly. I was certain he too believed me crazy. I even thought I heard a rebuke in his voice when he said to me:

"Why didn't you skip the bail? Was $15,000 too much?"

I smiled to myself. What was the use of explaining? He would never have understood anyway. We spoke in different languages and our world was not the same.

16

Chief Jailer Holland grinned broadly when he saw me entering with the Sheriff.

"Well, well, there he is himself! What did I tell you when you left here—that I was going to see you soon, didn't I? Well, now you're back here and it's going to be a nice little family reunion. All the boys here will sure be glad to have you back."

"Thanks, Chief, for your kind welcome," I said, trying to keep a straight face.

A turnkey was assigned to lock me up in my cell in the Death House. As he led me through the corridors he lowered his voice and said to me confidentially:

"Now, listen here, Angelo, don't start raising any hell while you are here. I don't know how long you are goin' to be here, but I understand you ain't gonna be here long. I just want to put you wise. You know what they would like to do to you and if you cause any trouble that will only make things worse. That's for your good, my good and the good of the cause."

I marveled greatly over his concern for me. What did he mean by "good of the cause"? What cause? Of course I did not dare ask any questions. Time itself would answer them. I knew one thing though: that not everything that begins well, ends well. There surely was a hitch somewhere. But what was the use of speculating? I was prepared in spirit for whatever would befall me.

What an extraordinary transformation! Was I dreaming? Could I believe my own senses? All the jailers without exception seemed to have become humane all of a sudden. Were they the same bullying jailers that I had known for twenty-six months? I knew that something very drastic must have brought about such an astonishing change in them. I soon learned the cause for it. Almost overnight the protests of millions of people on my behalf had been the cause for this change. The spotlight of public opinion was on Fulton Tower, and the authorities, frightened out of their wits, scurried about like frightened rabbits, repairing the jail from roof to cellar. They installed practically every convenience known to modern prisons. We no longer slept on the cold cement floors, but on cotton mattresses! We even got clean linen and bathed twice a week! The food was delicious. Sunday dinner consisted of roast beef, fresh vegetables, ice-cream and cake!

I even did not experience any difficulty in getting reading material into the jail. No matter what I asked for was promptly delivered to me upon its arrival, and by Mr. Holland *himself*. The unexpected fame which I had suddenly achieved in the world made the prison officials almost respectful to me. They treated me with silk gloves and were constantly afraid that I might suddenly get a fit of balkiness and make a complaint! A complaint from me, they knew, would mean endless publicity of a very unpleasant nature and might even cause a public investigation of the prison. I spent most of my time reading and answering letters that I received from workers and sympathizers all over the world. My prison cell, for all its bars and guards, became a sort of sounding board to the whole country of the struggle of the Negro worker to achieve social and economic equality.

17

There were about thirty-five condemned prisoners in the Death House with me. I found them this time not much less depraved and quarrelsome than those I had met during my first stay. They fought with one another like tigers, and the prison constantly resounded with their ugly quarreling.

During my first night, sleep was impossible. Caged once more like an animal I paced up and down my cell counting every step mechanically, as if it were some sort of game I was playing with myself. The fighting among the prisoners shocked me all over again, as if I had never seen it before. And when I lay down I could not keep my thoughts quiet. All the misery in the world rose up like a mountain. I wished that I had the necessary strength to climb over this mountain and find on the other side my resignation to the reality of which I stood so badly in need. Evidently I was not strong enough to accomplish this. Maybe it was because I was only twenty-two years old. And maybe it was because the wells of my heart had not dried up yet. . . .

Suddenly, in the stillness of the sleeping prison, I heard an insinuating voice raised in song. I started up on my bunk. I thought my heart would stop beating from the excitement which the song awakened in me. There was something remarkable in that singing. It sounded more like a lamentation over the dead and a rebuke to the living than just a song. It must have been some poor unhappy wretch who like myself could not fall asleep and who out of the depths of his despair sang aloud. It was a chain-gang song.

Look a-yonder, yonder
Hard boiling sun
Is turning over,
It won't come down, O Lawd,
It won't come down.
Give me, give me a cold a'water
Before I die,
O Lawd, before I die.
I don't want no corn bread

Peas and molasses at supper time
No—at supper time.
Every mail day—mail day
I get a letter,
Son, come home,
O son, son, come home.
How can I go?
Shotguns and pistols
All around me
To blow me down
O Lawd, to blow me down.

A guard came running up and threatened the singing prisoner with solitary:

"Shut your God-damn trap, will ya! Haven't you got enough time to sing durin' the day?"

18

One night, to my surprise, a Negro prisoner came up to me and said:

"Mr. Herndon, I have read all about you speaking all over the country, but I never had a chance to hear you. Won't you speak for us tonight?"

I explained to him as best as I could that I could not possibly accept his invitation because the prison authorities were only looking for me to start some trouble in order to defame me before the world. However, when the prisoner assured me that he could arrange for my speaking without the jailers ever getting wind of it, I agreed to it. How this was effected, I am not at liberty to tell, because it would involve others. Suffice it that the technique this man boasted worked to perfection.

A curious thing happened upon the completion of my speech. One of the prisoners, a champion scrapper and cusser if ever there was one, jumped to his feet and put a motion to the others with solemn-faced formality: that, thereafter, anyone proved guilty of fighting or using profane language should be given two hundred fifty lashes on his bare buttocks by the kangaroo judge! The motion was carried by acclamation. I was so astonished, I could only laugh.

As the days went by, the Death House took on a Sunday-school atmosphere. The prisoners competed with one another in soft-spoken politeness and consideration. Let the cynical sneer and the incredulous lift an eyebrow, but the transformation I saw take place among my fellow-prisoners in that short space of time by means of education and example has shown me how imbecilic and stupid the American prison system is.

In the forty days of my stay in prison I succeeded in organizing and conducting classes in Negro history, trade unionism, Fascism and war. I could not stop marveling at the eagerness of these men, already standing in the shadow of death, to learn about their fellow-men and the world. I regarded it now as my principal duty to impress upon them the true meaning of life. I tried to console them in their darkest hours by distracting their minds from their own tragic plight and centering them upon universal problems. Perhaps, by describing to them in dark and realistic colors a world gone mad, I made the prospect of their early exit from this life no cause for great regret.

19

On November 12, 1935, my attorney, Mr. Seymour, argued for a writ of habeas corpus before Judge Hugh M. Dorsey of the Georgia Court of Appeals. He ripped to shreds the flimsy case of lies and stupidities that the state had woven together. He argued that the insurrection law was unconstitutional, and therefore my conviction was illegal.

In the meantime, the Joint Herndon Committee and the

International Labor Defense were not idle. They kept the case alive in every way possible. They made their persistent appeals to the conscience of America, employing the incident of my voluntary return to prison as proof of moral force and innocence of the crime for which I was framed.

The Southern reactionaries, on the other hand, also did their best to turn public sentiment against me. They succeeded well enough in certain quarters. Characteristic of these attacks was the editorial printed in the issue of November 24, 1935 in the *Atlanta Constitution.**

On December 7, 1935, Judge Dorsey delivered his ruling:

> "HELD AND ADJUDICATED: That the applicant's contention that this law in question as construed and applied in this case is in conflict with the Fourteenth Amendment to the Constitution of the United States, in that it is too vague and indefinite to provide a sufficiently ascertainable standard of guilt; and that it is also in conflict with Article 1, Section 1, Paragraph 3 of the Constitution of the State of Georgia for the same reason, and that his conviction and sentence are unconstitutional, illegal, void and of no effect, be and the same is hereby sustained."

He ordered me remanded to the custody of Sheriff Lowry of Fulton County for twenty days in default of $8,000 bail, in order to give the state sufficient time for exceptions and an appeal to the higher courts. However, that was not necessary, for just one hour after the decision was announced, the International Labor Defense had me out of prison on bail.

It appeared that the Supreme Court of Georgia to whom the state had appealed was much more "reliable and Southern" than Judge Dorsey, for on June 13, 1936, it reversed his opinion. Immediately, Mr. Seymour filed an appeal to the

* For editorial see Appendix Nine, p. 408.

United States Supreme Court and obtained a stay of execution until final adjudication by that court in February, 1937.

20

The question bothering all my friends and sympathizers now is: What will the Supreme Court decision be?

It can either be one of two things—freedom or the chain gang. Having lived so many lives in the poverty of my years I have acquired that little bit of elementary wisdom which compels me to expect the worst and yet hope for the best.

Again the question is being raised: If you are prepared for the worst, then why don't you run away? Why take chances? Haven't you had enough of lynch justice?

Run away? This is easier said than done, for I am not the kind that runs away.

It is even argued that just as good revolutionists as I have run away.

Maybe so, I answer, but each man must follow his own sense of duty toward his fellow-men and the cause he is serving.

I had an interesting discussion on this subject early in October, 1936, with a coal miner whom I visited in a small town in Pennsylvania. He put the matter very boldly to me:

"Run away, Angelo!" he said. "Run away before it is too late!"

"I can't run away," I answered. "There's too much at stake."

"But they will kill you if they get you on the chain gang!"

"Perhaps they will, but my place is here on the battlefield. Good soldiers must not run away. If they run away, they break the morale of their fellow-soldiers."

I saw that, in spite of his politeness, my good friend thought me a little mad. I therefore felt obliged to make it clear to him. So I said:

"No, brother, there is no running away for me. If I run away and you run away and everybody else who loves freedom and truth runs away, who will be left to fight the good battle? I am too healthy-minded to think of myself as a martyr. I know who I am and where I am going. I have my eyes open. Therefore I am not afraid. For I would rather die like a man than live like a dog. The great wonder of it all is that I am not alone in this. Throughout the world, in every land, millions upon millions of men and women are ready to lay down their lives for those things I hold most dear. Think of the thousands of Spanish men and women who have gone to their deaths recently in defense of liberty and human rights! It is no heroism on their part to have done so. And it is no heroism on my part to be prepared to carry on the fight the way I am doing. Death itself is not the greatest tragedy that can possibly happen to a man, rather, the greatest tragedy is to live placidly and safely and to keep silent in the face of injustice and oppression."

The stern and worried look on my friend's face vanished. A great softness and understanding crept into it. He clasped my hand firmly and murmured:

"I think I know what you mean now."

APPENDICES

APPENDIX ONE *

THE LEAFLET

WORKERS OF ATLANTA!
EMPLOYED and UNEMPLOYED—Negro and White—ATTENTION!
MEN and WOMEN OF ATLANTA:

Thousands of us, together with our families, are at this time facing starvation and misery and are about to be thrown out of our houses because the miserable charity hand-out that some of us were getting has been stopped! Hundreds of thousands of dollars have been collected from workers in this city for relief for the unemployed, and most of it has been squandered in high salaries for the heads of these relief agencies.

Mr. T. K. Glenn, president of the Community Chest, is reported to be getting a salary of $10,000 a year. Mr. Frank Neely, executive director of the Community Chest, told the County Commission Saturday that he gets $6,500 a year, while at the same time no worker, no matter how big his family, gets more than two dollars and a half to live on. If we count the salaries paid the secretaries and the investigators working in the thirty-eight relief stations in this city, it should not surprise us that the money for relief was used up and there is no more left to keep us from starvation. If we allow ourselves to starve while these fakers grow fat off our misery, it will be our own fault.

The bosses want us to starve peacefully and by this method save the money they have accumulated off our sweat and blood. We must force them to continue our relief and give more help. We must not allow them to stall us any longer with fake promises. The city and county authorities from the money they have already collected from us in taxes, and by taking the incomes of the bankers and other rich capitalists, can take care of every unemployed family in Atlanta. We must make them do it.

* See page 190.

At a meeting of the County Commissioners last Saturday, it was proposed by Walter S. McNeal, Jr., to have the police round up all unemployed workers and their families and ship them back to the farms and make them work for just board and no wages, while just a few months ago these hypocrites were talking about forced labor in Soviet Russia, a country where there is no starvation and where the workers rule! Are we going to let them force us into slavery?

At this meeting Mr. Hendrix said that there were no starving families in Atlanta, that if there is he has not seen any. Let's all of us, white and Negroes, together, with our women folk and children, go to his office in the county court house on Pryor and Hunter Streets Thursday morning at 10 o'clock and show this faker that there is plenty of suffering in the city of Atlanta and demand that he give us immediate relief! Organize and fight for unemployment insurance at the expense of the government and the bosses! Demand immediate payment of the bonus to the ex-servicemen. Don't forget Thursday morning at the county court house.

Issued by the
UNEMPLOYED COMMITTEE OF ATLANTA,
P. O. Box 339.

APPENDIX TWO

STATE OF GEORGIA, COUNTY OF FULTON.

IN THE SUPERIOR COURT
OF SAID COUNTY.

THE GRAND JURORS selected, chosen and sworn for the County of Fulton, to-wit:

1. Fred McSwain, Foreman

2. Frank C. Owens	12. R. S. Paden
3. Homer C. Hall	13. J. E. Bennett
4. P. A. Clark	14. C. L. Corlee
5. O. D. Witherspoon	15. R. S. Rust, Jr.
6. J. C. Slade, Jr.	16. J. W. Wray
7. F. R. Coleman	17. C. H. Turnipseed
8. M. T. McCullough	18. H. M. Peack
9. J. E. Varela	19. A. Levy
10. L. J. Smith	20. A. J. Collier
11. L. F. Green	21. C. B. Anderson

in the name and behalf of the citizens of Georgia, charge and accuse

ANGELO HERNDON

with the offence of:—

ATTEMPTING TO INCITE INSURRECTION

for that said accused, in the County of Fulton and State of Georgia, on the 16th of July, 1932, with force and arms did make an attempt to incite insurrection and did make an attempt to induce others to join in combined resistance to the lawful authority of the State of Georgia, with intent to the denial of the lawful authority of the State of Georgia and with intent to defeat and overthrow the lawful authority of the State of Georgia by open force and by violent means and by unlawful acts, said attempt to incite insurrection intended to be manifested by accused by unlawful acts and intended by accused to be accomplished by acts of violence, said attempt to incite insurrection being made by accused in the following manner to wit:

(1) Accused did call and did attend public assemblies and mass meetings in the homes of various persons whose names and addresses are to the Grand Jurors unknown and did make speeches to various persons to the Grand Jurors unknown, the purpose of said meetings and the purpose of said speeches being to organize, to establish and to set up a group and combination of persons white and colored, under the name and style of the Communist Party of America for the purpose of uniting, combining and conspiring to incite riots, to embarrass and impede the orderly processes of the courts and for the purpose of offering and making combined opposition and resistance to the lawful authority of the State of Georgia and for the purpose of overthrowing and defeating by force and violence the lawfully constituted authority of the State of Georgia, all of which said meetings were held in various places and on various occasions which are to the Grand Jurors unknown.

(2) Accused did by speech and persuasion, solicit and did attempt to persuade and solicit persons whose names are to the Grand Jurors unknown to combine with, to join and to confederate with and to become members of the Communist Party and the Young Communist League and to become members, agents and parties to and of the Communist Party of America, to the intent and purpose of creating, offering, establishing and waging war against the lawfully constituted authority of the State of Georgia for the purpose of overthrowing the lawfully constituted authority of the State of Georgia by acts of violence and by revolution and establishing in the place of said lawfully constituted authority of the State of Georgia a new government known as United Soviets Soviet Russia, sometimes called and known as the "Dictatorship of the Propertyless People."

(3) Accused did introduce and did circulate and did cause to be introduced and circulated and did aid and assist in introducing and circulating certain booklets, papers and other writings with the intent and purpose of inciting insurrections, riot, conspiracy, uprisings against the constituted authority of the State and for the purpose of establishing combined resistance to and against the lawful authority of the State of Georgia, the names and contents of said books, papers and writings in

part are as follows hereinafter, their full contents being of such a nature as that they cannot be copied in full in this indictment:

Book A. "*The Life and Struggles of Negro Toilers*" by Geo. Padmore. *Pg. 46.* Therefore unlike their black brother in Africa, the Negroes in the new world have had centuries of contact with the white capitalist civilization. But like the Negroes in Africa they are subjected to the same barbarous methods of imperialist plunder and exploitation. . . . In no other so-called civilized country in the world are human beings treated as badly as these 15 million Negroes. They live under a perpetual regime of white terror, which expresses itself in lynchings, peonage, racial segregation and other pronounced forms of white chauvinism. . . . They are absolutely at the mercy of every fiendish mob incited by the white landlords and capitalists. Bands of business and professional men make periodical raids upon the black countryside, where they lynch Negroes, burn homes and destroy the crops and other property belonging to the blacks. In most cases of lynching the Negroes are burned to death after their bodies have been soaked in gasoline, while others are hanged from trees. On these occasions the entire white community turned out to witness the bloody spectacles, which were made "Roman Holidays."

And many other passages of similar import as on page 48 of said book, White people are accused of burning the homes, destroying crops, killing live stock, poisoning drinking water wells, murdering and lynching unarmed men, women and children.

Book B. "*Party Organizer*"—Special Plenum Issue—Vol May-June 1332 No. 5 and 6. Issued by Central Committee Communist Party USA. Same being a book of instructions to the organizers of Communist Party and containing the details of methods of approaching factories, cotton mills, industrial plants and shops and containing instructions, doctrines, and teachings as to the methods of preparing and organizing strikes in the various shops, industrial plants, cotton mills and other places where people work, containing information as to methods of training and developing and organizing workers and leaders in the Communist Party and in building up and bringing on strikes, riots, and revolutions.

Book C. "*Communism and Christianism*" by Wm. Montgomery Brown, "Banish the Gods from the Skies and Capitalists from the Earth and make the World safe for Industrial Communism," in part as follows: Page 6. As the machinery of capitalist government, including the armed forces of the nations, conserves the monopoly by the capitalist class of the wealth taken from the workers, the working class must organize consciously and politically for acquiring the powers of government, national and local, in order that this machinery, including these forces, may be converted from an instrument of oppression into the agent of emancipation and the overthrow of privilege, aristocratic and plutocratic."

On pages 98 and 99 of said book: "The trouble with every reformatory socialism of modern times is, that it undertakes the impossibility of changing the fruit of the capitalistic state into that of the communistic one, without changing the political organization; but to do that is as impossible as to gather grapes from thorns or figs from thistles. Hence an uprooting and replanting are necessary (a revolution not a reformation) which will give the world a new tree of state.

Capitalism no longer grows the fruits (foods, clothes and houses) which are necessary to the sustenance of all the world. Hence it must be dug up by the roots in order that a tree which is so organized that it will bear these necessities for the whole world may be planted in its place.

Certain newspapers called *The Daily Worker* and *The Southern Worker* being the official organ of the Communist Party and containing various articles, criticising the courts of the United States and various states and designed and intended to scatter and carry and implant in the minds of the people and citizens of Georgia hatred and contempt against all constituted authority of the state with intent to the overthrow, denial and defeat of the lawfully constituted authorities of the State.

And all of the acts of the accused being done by accused with intent to formulate and to establish and to set on foot and to make effective combined resistance by force and violence to the lawful authority of the State of Georgia and to cause, produce and bring to pass the defeat, denial and overthrow by acts of violence, by unlawful means and by revolution, the lawfully constituted authority of the State of Georgia as above set forth and all of the acts of the accused were and are *contrary* to the laws of said State, the good order, peace and dignity thereof.

John A. Boykin,

Solicitor General, Special Presentment Prosecutor.

AR—JAIL

SPCL.

APPENDIX THREE *

ANGELO HERNDON'S SPEECH TO THE JURY

"GENTLEMEN OF THE JURY: I would like to explain in detail the nature of my case and the reason why I was locked up. I recall back about the middle of June 1932, when the Relief Agencies of the City of Atlanta, the County Commission and the city government as a whole, were cutting both Negro and white workers off relief. We all know that there were citizens who suffered from unemployment. There were hundreds and thousands of Negroes and whites who were each day looking for work, but in those days there was no work to be found.

"The Unemployment Council, which has connection with the Unemployed Committees of the United States, after 23,000 families had been dropped from the relief rolls, started to organize the Negro and white workers of Atlanta on the same basis, because we know that their interests are the same. The Unemployment Council understood that in order to get relief, both races would have to organize together and forget about the question whether those born with a white skin are 'superior' and those born with a black skin are 'inferior.' They both were starving and the capitalist class would continue to use this weapon to keep them further divided. The policy of the Unemployment Council is to organize Negroes and whites together on the basis of fighting for unemployment relief and unemployment insurance at the expense of the state. The Unemployment Council of Atlanta issued those leaflets after the relief had been cut off, which meant starvation for thousands of people here in Atlanta. The leaflets called upon the Negro and white workers to attend a meeting at the court house building on a Thursday morning. I forget the exact date. This action was initiated as the result of statements handed out to the local press by County Commissioners who said that there was nobody in the City of Atlanta starving, and if there were, those in need should come to the offices of the Commissioners

* See page 236.

and the matter would be looked into. That statement was made by Commissioner Hendrix.

"The Unemployment Council pointed out in its circulars that there were thousands of unemployed workers in the City of Atlanta who faced hunger and starvation. Therefore, they were called upon to demonstrate in this court house building, about the middle part of June. When the Committee came down to the court house, it so happened that Commissioner Hendrix was not present that morning. There were unemployed white women with their babies almost naked and without shoes to go on their feet, and there were also Negro women with their little babies actually starving for the need of proper nourishment, which had been denied them by the county of Fulton and State of Georgia and City of Atlanta as well.

"Well, the Negro and white workers came down to the Commissioners' office to show that there was starvation in the City of Atlanta and that they were in actual need of food and proper nourishment for their kids, which they never did receive. I think Commissioner Stewart was in the office at that time. The white workers were taken into his room and the Negroes had the door shut in their faces. This was done with the hope of creating racial animosity in order that they would be able to block the fight that the Negro and white workers were carrying on—a determined fight to get relief. The white workers were told: 'Well, the county hasn't any money, and of course, you realize the depression and all that but we haven't got the money.' We knew that the county did have money, but were using it for their own interest, and not for the interest of the Negro workers or white workers, either way. They talked to the white workers some considerable time, but when the white workers came out, they had just about as much results as the Negroes did—only a lot of hot air blown over them by the Commissioners, which didn't put any shoes on their little babies' feet and no milk in their stomachs to give them proper nourishment. No one disputed the fact they did keep the Negroes on the outside, but the white workers were in the same condition that their Negro brothers were in. In spite of the fact that the County Commissioners had published statements to the effect that there was no money in the county treasury to provide unemployment relief for the Negro and white workers, still the next day after the demonstration the County Commissioners voted $6,000 for relief, mainly because it was shown that for the first time in the history of Atlanta and the State of Georgia, Negro and white workers did join together and did go to the Commissioners and demand unemployment insurance. Have not they worked in the City of Atlanta, in different industries, different shops and other industrial concerns located in Atlanta for all their years, doing this work, building up the city where it is at the present time? And now, when they were in actual need of food to hold their bodies together, and when they came before the state and county officials to demand something to hold their bodies together, they were denied it. The policy of the Unemployment Council is to organize these workers and demand those things that are denied them. They have worked as slaves, and are entitled to a decent living standard. And, of course, the workers will get it if you ever organize them.

"After the successful demonstration, the solicitor's office had two detectives stationed at the post office to arrest anyone who came to take mail out of box 339. On Monday, July 11, 1932, I went to the post office to get mail from this box and was arrested by detectives, Mr. Watson and Mr. Chester. I had organized unemployed workers, Negro and white, of Atlanta, and forced the County Commissioners to kick in $6,000 for unemployment relief. For this I was locked up in the station house and held eleven days without even any kind of charges booked against me. I was told at the station house that I was being held on 'suspicion.' Of course, they knew what the charges were going to be, but in order to hold me in jail and give me the dirtiest kind of inhuman treatment that one could describe, they held me there eleven days without any charge whatsoever until my attorney filed a writ of habeas corpus demanding that they place charges against me or turn me loose. It was about the 22nd of July, and I still hadn't been indicted; there had been three sessions of the grand jury, and my case had been up before them each time, but still there was no indictment. This was a deliberate plot to hold me in jail. At the habeas corpus hearing, the judge ordered that if I wasn't indicted the next day by 2:30, I should be released. Solicitor Hudson assured the judge that there would be an indictment, which, of course, there was. Ever since then I have been cooped up in Fulton County Tower, where I have spent close to six months—I think the exact time was five months and three weeks. But I want to describe some of the horrible experiences that I had in Fulton Tower. I was placed in a little cell there with a dead body and forced to live there with the dead body because I couldn't get out of the place. The man's name was William Wilson, who fought in the Spanish-American war for the American principles, as we usually call it. He was there on a charge of alimony. His death came as a result of the rotten food given to all prisoners, and for the want of medical attention. The county physician simply refused to give this man any kind of attention whatsoever. After three days of illness, he died, and I was forced to live there with him until the undertaker came and got him. These are just some of the things that I experienced in jail. I was also sick myself. I could not eat the food they gave me as well as hundreds of other prisoners. For instance, they give you peas and beans for one dinner, and at times you probably get the same thing three times a week. You will find rocks in it, and when you crack down on it with your teeth, you don't know what it is, and you spit it out and there it is. They have turnip greens, and just as they are pulled up out of the ground and put in the pot, with sand rocks and everything else. But that's what you have to eat, otherwise you don't live. For breakfast they feed grits that look as if they were baked instead of boiled, a little streak of grease running through them, about two strips of greasy fatback. That is the main prison fare, and you eat it or else die from starvation. I was forced to go through all of this for five months without a trial. My lawyers demanded a trial time after time, but somehow the state would always find a reason to postpone it.

"They knew that the workers of Atlanta were starving, and by arresting Angelo Herndon on a charge of attempting to incite insurrection the unity of Negro and white workers that was displayed in the demonstration that forced the County Commissioners to kick in with $6,000, would be crushed forever. They locked Angelo Herndon up on such charges. But I can say this quite clearly, if the State of Georgia and the

City of Atlanta think that by locking up Angelo Herndon, the question of unemployment will be solved, I say you are deadly wrong. If you really want to do anything about the case, you must go out and indict the social system. I am sure that if you would do this, Angelo Herndon would not be on trial here today, but those who are really guilty of insurrection would be here in my stead. But this you will not do, for your role is to defend the system under which the toiling masses are robbed and oppressed. There are thousands of Negro and white workers who, because of unemployment and hunger, are organizing. If the state wants to break up this organization, it cannot do it by arresting people and placing them on trial for insurrection, insurrection laws will not fill empty stomachs. Give the people bread. The officials knew then that the workers were in need of relief, and they know now that the workers are going to organize and get relief.

"After being confined in jail for the long period of time that I have already mentioned, I was sick for several weeks. I asked for aid from the county physician and was refused that; the physician came and looked through the bars at me and said: 'What's the matter with you?' I told him, 'I'm sick, can't swallow water, my chest up here is tight and my stomach absolutely out of order, seems as if I am suffering with ulcers or something.' He would answer: 'Oh, there's nothing the matter with you, you're all right.' I explained: 'I know my condition. I know how I'm feeling.' He said: 'You will be all right.' Through friends I was able to get some medicine; otherwise I would have died.

"On Christmas Eve I was released. My bail was once $3,000 but they raised it to $5,000 and from that up to $25,000, just in order to hold me in jail, but you can hold this Angelo Herndon and hundreds of others, but it will never stop these demonstrations on the part of Negro and white workers, who demand a decent place to live in and proper food for their kids to eat.

"I want to say also that the policy of the Unemployment Council is to carry on a constant fight for the rights of the Negro people. We realize that unless Negro and white workers are united together, they cannot get relief. The capitalist class teaches race hatred to Negro and white workers and keep it going all the time, tit for tat, the white worker running after the Negro worker and the Negro worker running after the white worker, and the capitalist becomes the exploiter and the robber of them both. We of the Unemployment Council are out to expose such things. If there were not any Negroes in the United States, somebody would have to be used as the scapegoat. There would still be a racial question, probably the Jews, or the Greeks, or somebody. It is in the interest of the capitalist to play one race against the other, so greater profits can be realized from the working people of all races. It so happens that the Negro's skin is black, therefore making it much easier for him to be singled out and used as the scapegoat.

"I don't have to go so far into my case, no doubt some of you jurymen sitting over there in that box right now are unemployed and realize what it means to be without a job, when you tramp the streets day in and day out looking for work and can't find it. You know it is a very serious problem and the future looks so dim that you sometimes don't know what to do, you go nuts and want to commit suicide or something. But the Unemployment Council points out to the Negro and white workers that the solution is not in committing suicide, that the solution can only be found in the unity and organization of black and white workers. In organization the workers have strength. Now, why do I say this? I say it because it is to the interest of the capitalist class that the workers be kept down all of the time so they can make as much profit as they possibly can. So, on the other hand, it is to the interest of Negro and white workers to get as much for their work as they can—that is, if they happen to have any work. Unfortunately, at the present time there are millions of workers in the United States without work, and the capitalist class, the state government, city government and all other governments, have taken no steps to provide relief for those unemployed. And it seems that this question is left up to the Negro and white workers to solve, and they will solve it by organizing and demanding the right to live, a right that they are entitled to. They have built up this country, and are therefore entitled to some of the things that they have produced. Not only are they entitled to such things, but it is their right to demand them. When the State of Georgia and the City of Atlanta raised the question of inciting to insurrection and attempting to incite to insurrection, or attempting to overthrow the government, all I can say is, that no matter what you do with Angelo Herndon, no matter what you do with the Angelo Herndons in the future, this question of unemployment, the question of unity between Negro and white workers cannot be solved with hands that are stained with the blood of an innocent individual. You may send me to my death, as far as I know. I expect you to do that anyway, so that's beside the point. But no one can deny these facts. The present system under which we are living today is on the verge of collapse; it has developed to its highest point and now it is beginning to shake. For instance, you can take a balloon and blow so much air in it, and when you blow too much it bursts; so with the system we are living under—of course, I don't know if that is insurrection or not!"

CHIEF JAILER HOLLAND'S SPEECH TO THE JURY

"I absolutely did not make any threats of any sort about Herndon. I don't think I ever spoke to the man more than two or three times while he was there. With regard to approximate size of the cells, there's two sleeping bunks in the cell, the exact size I don't know, but there's plenty of room there; there is a commode in there, some of them, and wash basin; the commode is inside of the cell, all of the cells—well, I won't say every cell, either, there might be some cells where they haven't. The food there is not rotten, as I say; I ate breakfast there Sunday morning, the same food the prisoners were served. They all receive the same treatment. We don't make any distinction except in the case of murder, a fellow sentenced—the electric chair, we put them in some of the smaller cages. As to whether we have a white hospital ward, we have a ward where a lot of them sleep, but where a man is sick, sometimes we put him there. We do not have a colored ward, we have a ward where a lot of trusties sleep. We do not have a colored ward; we used to have, but we don't now. I would say it was somewhere back in 1925 or 1926 that we had one; we don't have a hospital ward there because we don't have occasion to have them. After a prisoner dies, his body is gotten out very quickly by the undertaker. As soon as we call there is one there in less than thirty minutes; I couldn't tell you how much time transpires between the death and the time we call the undertaker, because when the man makes his rounds with the flashlight he goes to every cell block, at least every hour; it is possible for him to walk by a cell and see a man on the cot and think he is sleeping when he is dead. A man died in jail last week, and a man sleeping right-side of him found him dead—the men wanted to give him his coffee and called for him, and the man lying in bed went and shook him and he said: 'Why, this man's dead,' but the man was up at four o'clock when they called the prisoners to come out, and that was six o'clock, and he was in Howard's undertaker's place before seven o'clock. It could not be possible for a man to die there and a day or so elapse without some deputy sheriff or somebody knowing he was dead, no such thing as that is possible; it is possible for a prisoner to send word that—cellmate is dead, but I have got men that don't do anything else but go around them cell blocks, not looking for dead bodies especially, but looking around to see what is going on. If I have any objections as to the unsanitary conditions of the jail, I investigate it. I always investigate, if I got any complaint whatever. I got a complaint from this man you are speaking about, from some foreign organization, that he wanted ham and eggs for his breakfast. I got that and I went and told him he would be served his breakfast just like anybody else, just whatever the jail feeds. As to whether the jail food is at all times free from such matter that would make the prisoners ill, I know it is good food, there is no fancy food, there is no fashionable stuff cooked for anybody; they buy good flour. As I stated, I had breakfast there Sunday morning. I eat there very often. I eat my dinner time and time again, day in and day out; dinner is set down there in the kitchen, the same food; I do not go out and buy food and bring it back to be cooked. If I go out and get food at all, I go out and get cooked food. I don't go out and get cooked food often. I do whenever I want to, and I can tell you another thing, if a prisoner in there has got something he wants cooked, we'll cook it for him. This fellow Wilson died there. If he had been bad off we would have moved him out and put him somewhere else and taken care of him, we do that, and put men to stay with them night and day, we put them sometimes in the hospital room—there's a room up there—a man bad off, and a doctor looks at him and says he is bad off, I move him; this man, Wilson, wasn't bad off. He died very suddenly; the doctor is here, he will tell you what he died with; my recollection is it was heart failure."

APPENDIX FIVE

SUMMARY FOR ANGELO HERNDON, DEFENDANT,
before FULTON COUNTY PETIT JURY
by Ben Davis, Jr., Chief Defense Trial Attorney

Gentlemen of the Jury: Don't try to organize for better conditions, and—especially you who are unemployed—don't try to fight for bread for yourselves and starving families; for if you do, Mr. Hudson will try to send you to the electric chair!

According to Mr. Hudson, it is a crime to ask for bread. It is a crime for poor Negro and white workers to exercise their constitutional rights to lawfully assemble and petition the government against their grievances. And, gentlemen of the jury, Herndon, a heroic young Negro boy must be sent to the electric chair because he organized black and white together—because Mr. Hudson must have his pound of flesh from the workers and the Negro people.

Mr. Hudson—I should say, Reverend Hudson—parades before you as a man of pure and holy principles. But let us examine his activities. On Sundays, Reverend Hudson preaches in a Methodist pulpit about a fair and just "God" who punishes injustice and iniquity with hell and damnation. But on Mondays, Tuesdays, Wednesdays—in short, on every other day of the week—he is busy sending innocent Negroes and poor whites to the infernal Georgia chain gang and the electric chair. Such a man cannot be rightfully called a "fair and impartial" prosecutor.

And how Mr. Hudson has tried to deceive you! He read amidst snorts and holy shrieks, from numerous pamphlets found in Herndon's possession, distorting their meaning, twisting their context to make it appear to you as if Communism is the doctrine of hatred between Negro and white workers.

In the first place, Reverend Hudson doesn't know any more about Communism than a pig knows about a full-dress suit. In the next place, he brazenly and dishonestly omitted all those passages which told of the lynchings of countless innocent

Negro workers—all those passages which told of the ruthless manner in which you, many of whom are white workers, are played against the Negro workers. Gentlemen of the Jury, the history of the South should be written in the blood of thousands of Negro lynch victims and in the sweat and suffering of the exploited poor whites.

Angelo Herndon is charged with attempting to incite insurrection. According to Reverend Hudson, it's insurrection to fight for bread—and when you fight, the Reverend Mr. Hudson, lord and master of the Methodist pulpit, wants to send you to the electric chair.

Gentlemen of the Jury, it is not Herndon who is the insurrectionist. It is the lynch mobs, the Ku Kluxers who are allowed to roam the land of this state burning innocent black people at the stake in defiance of every law of justice, humanity and right. If Reverend Hudson wants to send the insurrectionists to the electric chair, let him send the Ku Klux Klan to the electric chair; let him search out these terrorist bands who defy the laws of this state and of mankind right under his nose.

Gentlemen of the Jury, this is not a case of prosecution; it is one of persecution. Which one of you can say that he also will not be sitting in the scornful seat, listening at the righteous bellowing of Reverend Hudson, merely because you demanded food for your loved ones? Which one of you does not wish to clasp the hand of a young Negro boy who in the midst of every obstacle, every discrimination, dares to fight for the principles upon which this country was founded?

The Reverend Hudson says Herndon is stirring up racial hatred by advocating the doctrines of workers organizations. But I ask since when did it become racial strife for Negro and white workers to organize together for the betterment of their conditions? Is it not because young Herndon sat before you today and told you in the words of a man and not those of a cringing coward that he would never give up his principle of fighting for the workers and Negroes, that he sits framed before you today?

Gentlemen, this very case is a blot upon American civilization which boasts of liberty, democracy, freedom of speech and press.

And it is in the name of this very liberty and democracy that the Reverend Hudson is asking you to send this Negro youth to a horrible and unjustifiable death—merely because he fought for the rights of the poor and needy without regard to their race or color.

Gentlemen of the Jury, just as starvation, want and suffering knows no color or race line, neither does injustice and exploitation. What happens to Herndon today as you ponder his fate in the jury room is going to determine what is going to happen to you when the sharp pains of hunger tug at the helpless emaciated forms of your loved ones tomorrow.

By every principle of justice and fair play Herndon must be acquitted.

It is difficult to dignify the testimony of the state's witnesses with the name of evidence. Every one of the witnesses called by the Reverend Hudson is on the payroll of the state, men who dare not testify against their higher-up officials—detectives, jailers, assistant solicitor generals. Herndon is charged with attempting to incite insurrection, but the evidence shows that Herndon organized a demonstration of Negro and white unemployed for adequate relief. The rest of the testimony appears to have been fabricated in the "pure and spotless" mind of the Reverend Hudson.

The issue is simply this: Consider in your minds when you retire to that jury room whether you want to see a man burn in the electric chair because he had the courage to fight for the Negroes and whites who are hungry and without bread or jobs. Consider in your minds whether you want to see a Negro boy executed in the electric chair at a trial where Negro citizens have been denied their constitutional rights to sit on juries, a right which is guaranteed to every defendant and citizen by the Constitution of the United States, the document upon which this country was founded.

Gentlemen of the Jury, you have but one course before you, if you would uphold your oath, to bring back a verdict in accordance with the facts and consonant with justice—and that is a verdict of acquittal. Any other verdict will be a mockery of justice; any other verdict will be catering to the basest passion of race prejudice which the Reverend Hudson has sought to conjure up in you all; any other verdict will be making a scrap of paper out of the Bill of Rights, the Constitution of the United States and the State of Georgia, out of the democratic rights which are the property of every citizen whether his skin is black or white.

APPENDIX SIX

OPINION OF SUPREME COURT OF THE STATE OF GEORGIA

HERNDON v. STATE

178 Ga. 832

No. 9871.

May 24, 1934

Attempt to incite insurrection. Before Judge Wyatt. Fulton superior court. July 5, 1933.

John H. Geer, *Benjamin H. Davis Jr.*, and *Ewing C. Baskette*, for plaintiff in error.

John A. Boykin, solicitor-general, J. W. LeCraw, John H. Hudson, M. J. Yeomans, attorney-general, B. D. Murphy, and *J. T. Goree*, contra.

BELL, J.

Angelo Herndon was indicted in Fulton county for the offense of attempting to incite an insurrection. The offense is defined in Penal Code, § 56, as "any attempt, by persuasion or otherwise, to induce others to join in any combined resistance to the lawful authority of the State." Section 57 declares that any person convicted of this offense shall be punished by death unless the jury recommend mercy, in which event the punishment shall be confinement in the penitentiary for not less than five nor more than twenty years. In this case the jury found the defendant guilty, but recommended mercy and fixed his punishment at from eighteen to twenty years.

Before pleading to the merits, the defendant filed a motion to quash the indictment, and also a plea in abatement, alleging in each that he was a negro, and that members of his race were unlawfully, systematically, and intentionally excluded from the grand jury which indicted him, in direct violation of the Fourteenth Amendment to the Constitution of the United States and of paragraph 3, article 1, of the Constitution of the state of Georgia. The solicitor general did not demur, but filed a traverse to each of these proceedings, and the issues made thereby were by consent of counsel submitted for trial to the judge without a jury. After hearing evidence at length from jury commissioners and others, the judge overruled and denied both the motion and the plea. Upon the call of the panel of 48 jurors from which to select a trial jury, the defendant filed a challenge to the array based upon the same ground; namely, that negroes were unlawfully, systematically, and intentionally excluded from the panel for the January term, 1933, during which the defendant was about to be tried. As in case of the other preliminary proceedings, the solicitor general did not demur, but filed a traverse, and the issue thus made was likewise submitted to the judge for trial upon the evidence without a jury. After evidence was submitted, the motion was overruled.

The defendant was then tried upon the charge contained in the indictment with the result indicated. He made a motion for a new trial which contained the usual general grounds and a number of special grounds added by amendment. The motion was overruled upon all grounds, and the defendant brought the case to this court.

1. The rulings by the trial judge upon the motion to quash, the plea in abatement, and the challenge to the array were all made on January 16, 1933. No exceptions pendente lite were filed to any of these rulings, but they were assigned as error in the motion for a new trial and also in the bill of exceptions. The judgment refusing a new trial was rendered on July 5, 1933. The bill of exceptions was certified on July 12, 1933.

Under the settled rules of practice applicable in this state, the rulings and findings of the trial judge upon the preliminary issues could not properly be asserted as grounds of the motion for a new trial relating to the main and final issue as made by the indictment and the plea of not guilty; but the conclusions reached by the court on such preliminary or collateral issues should have been excepted to pendente lite, or assigned as error in due time in the bill of exceptions. Accordingly, the motion for a new trial, so far as it pertains to these matters, does not present any question of error for decision by this court.

The assignments of error upon the same rulings as contained

in the bill of exceptions are also fatally defective, though for the different reason that they were not made in time. In all criminal cases the bill of exceptions shall be tendered and signed within twenty days from the rendition of the decision complained of. This applies, of course, to the final bill of exceptions by which the case is brought to the appellate court. As to exceptions pendente lite, it is declared: "Exceptions tendered before the final judgment, for the mere purpose of being made a part of the record, shall be certified to be true by the judge, and ordered to be placed on the record. Such exceptions must be tendered during the term. But, if the court shall adjourn within less than thirty days from the date of the ruling complained of, such bills of exceptions pendente lite must be tendered within sixty days from the date of the order, decision, or ruling complained of." This provision of the law applies to both civil and criminal cases. "Where several rulings are complained of in a bill of exceptions in a criminal case, this court can consider only such as were made within 20 days before the tendering of the bill of exceptions, unless there be exceptions pendente lite." It follows that since the rulings of the court upon the preliminary issues were not excepted to pendente lite, nor assigned as error in the bill of exceptions within the time prescribed by law, the plaintiff in error is not entitled to a review of these rulings.

But even if we should go further and consider these rulings upon their merits, the result could hardly be different to the plaintiff in error. The burden was upon him to show by evidence that negroes were excluded from the jury lists on account of their race or color. Martin v. Texas, 200 U. S. 316. Nothing to the contrary was held in Neal v. Delaware, or in Carter v. Texas. In each of these cases the claim was disposed of as being insufficient in law, without affording the defendant the right to sustain it by proof. In the present case evidence was heard and findings were made thereon by the trial judge. Jury commissioners testified that negroes were never excluded by reason of their race or color, and that in fact members of this race were occasionally placed upon the lists for service on trial juries. The commissioners further testified: They recognized that there were taxpayers of Fulton county of the negro race who were qualified for jury service, but for the most part those who were thus qualified were professional men or holders of governmental positions and were excused by law from jury service. The population of Fulton county is large, and the commissioners could not well place every man on the lists who might be legally qualified. It seems that under this evidence the trial judge was not bound, as a matter of law, to find that negroes were excluded merely on account of their race or color. He could not have done so without imputing perjury to the jury commissioners who testified. This court, under its constitutional jurisdiction, would not be authorized to reverse the findings of the trial judge if they were supported by any evidence. In Martin v. Texas, supra, it was said that discrimination cannot be established by merely proving that no one of the defendant's race was on the jury, and that an accused person cannot, of right, demand a mixed jury, some of which shall be of his race, nor is a jury of that kind guaranteed by the Fourteenth Amendment to any race. It was further said in that case that "what an accused is entitled to demand, under the Constitution of the United States, is that, in organizing the grand jury as well as in the impaneling of the petit jury, there shall be no exclusion of his race, and no discrimination against them, because of their race or color." In Thomas v. Texas, it was said that the question of unlawful exclusion is one of fact. In Murray v. Louisiana, the evidence was similar to that produced in the present case, and it was said by the highest court that a careful inspection of the record failed to disclose any particular in which the accused was deprived of any right or immunity granted him under the laws or Constitution of the United States. The evidence in each of the following cases was materially stronger for the defendant (citing cases). In Rawlins v. State, it was said: "The law passed by the General Assembly for the purpose of carrying into effect the constitutional provision does not require that all persons possessing the constitutional qualifications shall be selected. It reposes in the jury commissioners, not only the authority to determine what men have these qualifications, but how many of such men shall be selected for jury duty in the county. The jury commissioners may select all belonging to this class, or they may select a lesser number. The jury list of the county is not to be made up of any given number, but this is a matter left to the discretion of the jury commissioners. The number of persons selected for jury service is to be determined by the jury commissioners in the exercise of a wise discretion, taking into consideration the whole number of persons liable to jury service, the volume of business to be transacted in the various courts which requires the presence of jurors, as well as the facilitation of business in such courts. They should keep in mind on the one hand the right of those entitled to a jury trial, whether in civil or criminal cases, and on the other hand the right of those who are subject to jury duty, making the list embrace such a number as will enable the courts to be carried on according to the spirit of the Constitution and the law, and at the same time not making the number so small that jury service would become burdensome upon those selected for that duty. One placed upon the jury lists by the commissioners is, so far as jury service is concerned, declared to be intelligent and upright. But the fact that a person's name is not upon the jury list of the county is no evidence that he is not intelligent and upright, nor that the commissioners did not consider him as such."

The grounds of the motion for a new trial referred to above were those numbered 9, 10, 11, and 12. Ground 13 complained of the rejection of evidence that negroes of Fulton county had served as jurors in the federal court. If exception had been duly preserved, this contention would not have contained merit, since the evidence was irrelevant.

2. In ground 25 it is complained that the court erred in refusing to allow the defendant's counsel to ask the jurors individually and severally, on the voir dire, the question, "Have you any prejudice against the defendant because he is colored, which would prevent you from arriving at a verdict on the trial of this case?" In this ground of the motion is the following statement: "Movant stated in his place that if prospective jurors on their voir dire had been permitted to answer the said question, defendant would have been better able to avail himself of his constitutional rights to select a fair and impartial jury for the trial of said case. The court refused to permit said question to be asked of said prospective jurors on their voir dire on the ground that the laws of the State of Georgia prohibited or

made no provision for such question to be asked severally and individually, but the court allowed on movant's motion said question to be propounded to the prospective jurors in groups of twelve as they were impaneled in the jury box. Movant insists that the refusal of the court to permit such question to be asked was prejudicial to movant, for the reason that movant did not have due opportunity to avail himself of his constitutional right to select a fair and impartial jury and because said refusal was and is a denial unto the defendant of equal protection of the laws and a denial unto him of the due process of law as guaranteed unto him by the fourteenth amendment to the constitution of the United States, section 1" (quoting it).

This ground of the motion fails to show cause for a new trial. The method of examining jurors on the voir dire is regulated by statute in this state. The provisions of this act are now contained in Penal Code 1910, §§ 999-1004. The questions to be propounded are stated in section 1001, and include inquiry (1) as to whether the juror has formed or expressed any opinion in regard to the guilt or innocence of the prisoner at the bar; (2) as to whether he has any prejudice or bias on his mind either for or against the prisoner at the bar; and (3) whether the mind of the juror is perfectly impartial between the State and the accused. Since the passage of the act of 1856, this court has consistently held that neither counsel for the state nor for the defendant may, as a matter of right, ask a juror upon the voir dire any other questions than those prescribed by statute. In Woolfolk v. State, it was said: "Questions could not be made more searching than these in order to determine the state of the juror's mind." But so careful was the law to provide for a fair and impartial jury that it did not stop with merely prescribing certain questions. It outlined a procedure whereby additional questions might be propounded. In § 1004, it is provided in effect that, when any juror has been found competent "as aforesaid," he may yet be put upon the judge as a trior and shown to be incompetent at any time before the submission of evidence on the main issue. The judge, acting as a trior, is not confined to the statutory questions, but, in order to test the juror's qualification, may ask him any question except such as would tend to inculpate or disgrace him. It is true the additional examination may not be had as a matter of right, unless the juror is challenged and put upon the court as a trior. But the machinery provided for testing the juror's competency would seem to meet all constitutional requirements. In the Woolfolk case, supra, it was held that the statutory procedure was not in violation of the Constitution of Georgia or the United States. The defendant here did not pursue this procedure, but sought, without challenging any juror, to propound additional questions to each of them. "Under the practice in this state of trying the competency of jurors, only the statutory questions can be asked in the first instance. If the juror answers the statutory questions satisfactorily, and is pronounced prima facie competent, and the parties put him before the court as trior, aliunde evidence of the untruthfulness of his answers must be offered, and it is not competent to propound questions to the juror himself to show his incompetency. It is within the province of the court to permit a further examination of the juror himself in rebuttal of the testimony offered to show his incompetency. While the defendant may not, as a matter of right, extend the examination beyond the statutory questions without first putting the juror on the court as a trior, it is yet true that the court may in its discretion allow additional questions. As a matter of fact, the court did allow the additional question in the instant case. The question was actually propounded to each and every juror. The question was put to them, however, in panels of 12, and the whole substance of the complaint is that each juror was not interrogated individually and severally. Since the judge had a discretion as to whether he would allow the question, and did allow it, he might, within the same discretion, have permitted the requested individual examination, and thus was not strictly correct so far as he may have held, as stated in the motion, that the law prohibited such examination. The legal misconception, however, did not deprive the defendant of more than the mere right to have the judge exercise a discretion as to whether the question should be put to the jurors singly or in panels, involving a mere matter of procedure, with respect to which the statute is silent, and not relating to any substantive right. In Williams v. State, followed in Wilkerson v. State, it was held that the examination on the voir dire should be made separately as to each juror, but this was based upon a construction of the statute and related merely to the statutory questions and not to such additional questions as might be asked only in the discretion of the court. The statute provides that on trials for felonies "any juror" may be put upon "his" voir dire, and the following questions shall be propounded to "him." Then follows the prescribed questions, all of which were presumably propounded singly in this case. It was obviously the quoted singular words which constrained the decision in the Williams case. In the present case, the judge, having exercised his discretion so as to allow an additional question, did not violate any substantial right of the defendant in refusing, for any reason, to permit the question to be propounded to each juror separately as requested. It should be noted further in this case that the defendant in his motion for a new trial does not complain that the action of the judge was erroneous upon the ground that he failed to exercise a discretion with which he was vested by law; but the assignment is that an absolute constitutional right was denied to movant. The judge pursued the course prescribed by statute, except that he went further in the defendant's favor than the statute required him to do. The statute was not attacked as being unconstitutional, and it is merely claimed that the action of the court, not the statute, deprived the defendant of a constitutional right. Did the court, merely in requiring the one question to be propounded collectively, as indicated, instead of singly, deny to the defendant any right guaranteed to him by the Fourteenth Amendment of the Federal Constitution? We do not think the Constitution was ever intended to be reduced to so thin a tissue. In West v. Louisiana, it was said: "The limit of the full control which the state has in the proceedings of its courts, both in civil and criminal cases, is subject only to the qualification that such procedure must not work a denial of fundamental rights, or conflict with specific and applicable provisions of the Federal Constitution." In Jordan v. Massachusetts, the United States Supreme Court, quoting L. & N. R. Co. v. Schmidt, said: "It is no longer open to contention that the due process clause of the 14th Amendment to the Constitution of the United States does not control mere forms of procedure in state courts or regulate practice therein. All its requirements are complied with, provided in the proceedings which are claimed not to have been due process of law the person condemned has had sufficient notice, and adequate opportunity has been afforded him to defend." It was further said in the Jordan case that "When the essential elements of a court having jurisdiction in which an opportunity for a hearing is afforded are present, the power of a state over its methods of procedure is substantially unrestricted by the due process clause of the Constitution."

It cannot be said that the defendant was denied due process of law or the equal protection of the laws merely because the question was propounded to the jurors in panels of 12 and not separately. Certainly nothing to the contrary was held in Aldridge v. U. S. In that case the court refused to permit any sort of inquiry as to whether the jurors had any racial prejudice such as would prevent a fair and impartial verdict. Furthermore, the Aldridge case was appealed from the District of Columbia, and an examination fails to show the existence of any statute in the District similar to the Georgia law. The same is true of the statutes of the several states from which decisions are cited in the Aldridge case. The question here is also different from that presented in Bailey v. United States. Under the rule in the federal District Court (in Georgia) from which the case was appealed, the names of the jurors were not published or communicated to any one prior to the convening of court. It was pointed out in the decision that "the only information as to the persons whose names were on that list possessed by appellants and their counsel before the right of challenging was to be exercised was that derived from looking at the prospective jurors and hearing their names read from the list and their answers to the three questions propounded by the court." It was held that the right of challenge was one of the most important of the rights secured to the accused, and that "it should not be required to be exercised before an opportunity is given for such inspection and examination of prospective jurors as is reasonably necessary to enable the accused to have some information upon which to base an exercise of that right." It is not contended here that the defendant was surprised or circumscribed by any such rule as was of force in the federal District Court.

The present case is further distinguished from the Bailey case upon the broad ground that in that case, as well as in the Aldridge case, supra, the court summarily "disposed of the requests, wholly and absolutely refusing to permit the additional questions urged." This is not to say that the decision in the Bailey case was in conformity with the statute law of this state.

3. The defendant was arrested without a warrant by police officers of the city of Atlanta. At the time of his arrest certain documents were found in his personal possession, in a "box under his arm," and this box and its contents were taken into custodv by the arresting officers. Following the arrest, the defendant stated that he was rooming at a certain place to which the officers then carried him. The room identified by the defendant as his place of abode was searched and other documents were found. Ground 1 of the motion for a new trial complains of the ruling of the court admitting in evidence the "documents found in the personal possession of movant * * * in a box under his arm," the evidence having been objected to upon the ground that the solicitor general had "not exhibited any search warrant which authorized any officer to search defendant's person, nor has the solicitor exhibited any search warrant which authorizes any officer to enter the defendant's room and seize the box and contents contained therein." This ground of the motion contains several additional statements as reasons why the court should not have admitted the evidence. These additional statements cannot be considered. It is the province of this court to consider only such questions as were presented to the trial court. Accordingly, an assignment of error on the admission of evidence is limited by the objections made at the time the evidence was offered. The objections cannot be enlarged by the addition of new matter as argument or grounds of error in the motion for new trial. It may be said now that other grounds of the motion for a new trial contained the same defects, and attention is here called to that fact in a general way, in order to avoid needless repetition as we come to consider the other grounds. In the main we shall notice only such objections to the evidence as were made at the time the evidence was of-

fered, and statements regarding the record will be limited accordingly.

The evidence obtained by the alleged illegal search and seizure was not inadmissible upon that ground. In the argument here the defendant relies upon the provisions of the Constitution which are contained in Civil Code 1910, § 6362, relating to illegal searches, and it is further urged with great earnestness that the evidence should have been excluded in view of the similar provisions contained in the Fourth Amendment of the Federal Constitution. So far as the objections relate to an application of the State Constitution, the case is controlled by the decision in Calhoun v. State. It was held in that case that evidence discovered by the search of a person while he was under an illegal arrest, if relevant, is not inadmissible as contravening the constitutional provision against compelling a person to give testimony against himself. It was further held that articles taken from the premises of the accused may be admitted in evidence against him, notwithstanding that they were discovered by an unlawful search and seizure. In such cases the criterion is, Who furnished or produced the evidence? If the person suspected is made to produce the incriminating evidence, it is inadmissible, but if his person or belongings are searched by another, and the accused is not compelled to do any act or to produce any evidence tending to incriminate himself, the evidence thus discovered may be used against him, although it was obtained "without a vestige of authority." In the present case, it does not appear that the defendant was compelled to do any act or to produce any evidence. The decision in the Calhoun case, supra, was rendered by a full bench, and requests to overrule it have been denied in Kennemer v. State.

With reference to the like provisions of the Federal Constitution as contained in the Fourth Amendment, it has been repeatedly held by the Supreme Court of the United States that these provisions refer to powers to be exercised by the government of the United States and not to those of the individual states. See the discussion and citations in Johnson v. State. Moreover, the Supreme Court of the United States has also held that these provisions do not apply to evidence obtained by state or city officers so as to exclude it even in federal prosecution, where the officers were not acting with a view to such prosecution or in conjunction with federal officers in obtaining the evidence. It is also the federal rule that, where the defendant knows before the trial of the possession by the prosecution of physical evidence and the manner in which it was obtained, he cannot wait until the trial to make objection thereto, but should make his objection beforehand, and, failing to do so, he waives the right to object to the introduction of the evidence at the trial. So, in any possible view of the instant case, the court did not err in admitting the evidence referred to in the first special ground of the motion for a new trial.

There is no merit in ground 8, contending that the documentary evidence was inadmissible because the state did not introduce evidence to show that it was insurrectionary. The evidence was not objected to upon this ground, and besides this the literature referred to in this ground was in plain language and would speak for itself.

4. In ground 4 it is contended that the court erred in permitting a witness for the defendant to testify on cross-examination: "A negro doesn't happen to have the right to marry my daughter, under the laws of this State. I do not know how many states there are in the Union where they do have that right." This evidence was objected to on the sole ground, "There is nothing whatever in the Communist 1932 election platform about intermarriage." In ground 5, it is complained that the court erred in allowing the prosecuting attorney to propound the following question, "Do you understand the Communist position equal rights for negroes to mean the right of a colored boy to marry your daughter, if you have one?", over the objection that the question is "irrelevant and immaterial and calls for a conclusion of the witness." In ground 6, it is contended that the court erred in permitting the prosecuting attorney to ask the following question, "Did you know there are twenty states in the United States where the two races (white and negro) intermarry or mix?", over the same objection as quoted from ground 5.

Upon a consideration of ground 4 in connection with the brief of evidence and with grounds 5 and 6, it is clear that the evidence objected to as stated in ground 4 was given under the following circumstances: The evidence tended to show that the defendant was sent to Atlanta as an organizer for the Communist Party, and that certain literature found in his possession was forwarded to him from the headquarters of this party in New York. Witnesses testified to admissions by the defendant of these facts. Among the documents was what purported to be a platform of the Communist Party as promulgated during the presidential campaign of 1932. Plank 4 was as follows: "Equal rights for the negroes and self-determination for the Black Belt." The witness had testified that he was familiar with all of the principles contained in the platform, and that he was in sympathy with some of them. On cross-examination the assistant solicitor interrogated him as to the meaning of plank 4, and finally asked him if he understood it to mean the right of a colored boy to marry the witness's daughter, if he had one. To this question the witness gave the reply as to the law of Georgia. The solicitor then asked him about other states, and his reply is the second statement of the testimony objected to. Other documents found in the defendant's possession and introduced in evidence tended to show that the Communist Party did advocate racial and social equality for the negro. These documents were admitted in evidence without objection, except for invalid reasons as indicated in division 3 of this opinion. It is a general rule of practice based upon sound principle that the admission of evidence over a party's objection will in no event require the grant of a new trial when substantially the same evidence is admitted without objection. Thus, the question of racial and social equality, including, of course, the right of intermarriage, was already in the case in such a way that the jury were bound to know of it in any event, and, so, the testimony objected to did not introduce a new factor. The defendant, therefore, could not be harmed by this testimony. The witness was correct in his statement as to the law of Georgia. Penal Code, § 678. It is to be remembered also that the sole objection was that there was nothing in "party 1932 platform" about intermarriage. While the assistant solicitor had asked about the platform, the witness made a detour and spoke of an entirely different subject, namely, the law of Georgia. It is thus apparent that the admissibility of the testimony did not depend upon the contents of the party platform, and that the court did not err in admitting it over the sole objection urged.

Referring now to grounds 5 and 6, we notice that each of these grounds omits all reference to evidence, the assignments of error being aimed only at the questions themselves. "In order to raise a question for decision by this court as to whether the trial court erred or not in overruling objections of the defendant to questions propounded by the solicitor general to a witness, the answers to the questions should be shown, and a reference to the brief of the evidence is not sufficient." A ground of a motion for new trial must be complete in itself, without reference to other parts of the record. If a question standing alone is inherently improper and prejudicial, the remedy is a motion for a rebuke or for a mistrial.

But to look further still, the witness was on cross-examination. The defendant himself, on direct examination, had interrogated the witness, not only as to the party platform of 1932, but had asked some other questions in reference to communism. In response to the defendant's examination, the witness testified that, without being informed as to the definition of communism, he could not answer the question as to whether he was "sympathetic with Communism." He did testify, however, "I find elements within Communism with which I agree." The defendant himself had brought about an expression of the attitude of the witness introduced by him. As noted above, the evidence tended to show that the tenets of the Communist Party included racial and social equality for the negro (see documentary evidence quoted below, in division 11 of this opinion). This witness, like any other witness, was subject to cross-examination. The right of cross-examination, thorough and sifting, belongs to every party as to witnesses called against him. This is a right which may be claimed by the state as well as by any other party.

Finally, the jury could not reasonably have been drawn from the main issue by any of the happenings referred to in grounds 4, 5, and 6. They were presumed to be intelligent and upright. They were aware of the fact that the defendant was on trial for the offense of attempting to incite an insurrection. A definition of this offense was later given to them in the charge. They must have known that the defendant could not be convicted merely because he may have become aligned with a party which advocated racial equality, and also that neither the statement of the witness nor the questions of the state's attorney could throw any affirmative light on the issue of guilt or innocence of the accused. Regardless of every other consideration in relation to these grounds, we should be compelled to attribute to the jurors a lesser degree of intelligence and uprightness, than we are willing or authorized to do, before we could hold that the occurrences referred to in these grounds were such as to vitiate the verdict. The jurors had sworn that they had no such racial prejudice themselves as would prevent the rendition of a fair and impartial verdict, and we cannot assume that they were inflamed by anything alluded to in the grounds under consideration, as urged in the briefs, but not alleged in the motion for a new trial.

This case differs quite materially on its facts from Williams v. State, where the court did not effectually restrain highly inflammatory arguments by the prosecuting attorney, notwithstanding repeated objections thereto.

5. In ground 2, it is complained that the court erred in refusing to permit a witness who was a college instructor, and who was introduced by the defendant, to "qualify as an expert to testify to the non-insurrectionary character of the documentary evidence introduced by the State." The motion states that the witness gave certain testimony showing his proficiency in the subject of economics and his acquaintance with anarchistic, sociological, and Communistic literature, and also testified that he had written articles of an economic nature. This ground of the motion fails to set forth the "documentary evidence" as to which an opinion of the witness would have been sought, nor is it averred that the witness would have answered that it was "non-revolutionary" or "non-insurrectionary." To constitute a good assignment of error the exception should have stated at least the substance of the documentary evidence as to which the witness was expected to give an opinion, and it is also the rule that "A ground of a motion for new trial, which assigns error because the court excluded certain testimony of a witness, will not be considered, where the movant has failed to show that the court was advised as to what the answer of the witness would be." The motion does

not even indicate that the witness was expected to give an opinion as to the meaning of technical language, but, so far as appears, it was the purpose of the defendant to interrogate him as to the meaning of words as familiar to the jury as to any one else. "An expert may aid the jury, but he cannot perform the functions of a juror, and, under the guise of giving testimony, state a legal conclusion."

In ground 3, it is contended that the court erred in permitting the same witness, on cross-examination, to testify as follows: "I am acquainted with what is known as the Communists of Soviet Russia or the Soviet Union, of the present form of government in the nation of Russia, that it is a government which succeeded the Kerensky government, which succeeded the former Czarist government; that it was brought about by a revolution, putting out the Czar and the assassination of the Czar and his family some time later, not necessarily as the result of a revolution. As to the Russian revolution, history so regards, that there was a revolution, the Czarist government overthrown, the Kerensky government took charge, and after about six months another revolution of bloodless character in which the present regime succeeded the Kerensky government; I wouldn't attempt to dispute that as an historical fact." The defendant objected to this evidence at the time the same was offered on the following ground: "Those were all questions that necessitate an opinion and required [the witness] to answer with particular detailed knowledge of political science." This evidence was not inadmissible for the reason urged by the defendant. The facts stated by the witness were of an historical nature and were generally known. The jury presumably knew of them anyway, and the defendant was not harmed by the admission of the testimony.

6. In ground 7 of the motion for new trial it is alleged that during the progress of the trial the judge erred, "in that he did intimate that movant was guilty" by the following statement made in the presence of the jury while a witness for movant was testifying: "The Court: 'If Emory University is guilty of anything, we will try them; I think even if Emory University had actually attempted to incite riot, it wouldn't be material in this case, it is a question what this defendant has done!'" The record contains a note by the trial

judge to the effect that the remark was made in ruling on an objection to testimony. Whether or not the statement might have been subject to criticism, it was not made as a part of nor during the instructions to the jury. The proper mode of excepting to statement was by motion for mistrial, and the defendant failed to adopt this procedure. He could not abide the chance of a favorable verdict, and "after the return of an adverse verdict, have that verdict set aside" on a motion for a new trial.

7. In ground 14 error is assigned upon an instruction of the court which contained the definition of insurrection as in the Penal Code, § 55. The court further instructed the jury as to the legal statutory definition of an attempt to incite insurrection, and of course it was not improper, in connection therewith, to define the offense of insurrection, the purpose being to give the jury a better understanding of the elements of the offense for which the accused was being tried. The jury were specifically told that the defendant was being tried for an alleged attempt to incite insurrection. It was not error, as contended, to fail in the same connection to instruct the jury as to the method or means by which to determine the meaning of the offense "combined resistance to the lawful authority of the State," as contained in the definition of insurrection.

8. In ground 15 it is alleged that the court erred in charging the jury "that mere possession of literature insurrectionary in its nature on the part of the accused wouldn't warrant a conviction in this case, nor would engaging in academic or philosophic discussions of abstract principles of economics or politics or other subjects however radical or revolutionary in their nature." This charge was excepted to on the ground that it assumed that the literature introduced in evidence was insurrectionary and thus invaded the province of the jury. There is no merit in this contention. And this is specially true, in view of the additional instructions to the effect that all elements of the crime must appear from the evidence and the defendant's statement, to the satisfaction of the jury, that the court "can express no opinion and does express no opinion as to what has been proven."

In ground 16 it is contended that the court erred in charging: "That advocacy, however reprehensible morally, is not sufficient to convict the defendant where there is no evidence to indicate that the advocacy would be acted upon immediately. In order to convict the defendant, gentlemen, it must appear clearly by the evidence that immediate serious violence against the State was to be expected or advocated." It is contended that this charge was argumentative, and intimated that advocacy had been proved, also that the alleged advocacy of movant was reprehensible morally; and that the charge otherwise unduly emphasized the contentions of the state. These exceptions were not substantial.

In ground 17 error was assigned upon an instruction that "an attempt to commit an act which is, in fact, a crime is not complete unless the alleged crime is dangerously near completion; that the mere possession of radical literature, as I have before stated, alone is not sufficient to constitute the crime of attempting to incite insurrection." The exceptions to this charge were that it intimated that the literature was radical, that said charge failed to disclose to the jury the method by which they should determine whether the literature was radical or not, and unduly stressed the contentions of the state. There was no merit in these exceptions.

In ground 18 error is assigned upon an instruction relating to admissions or incriminatory statements. The exceptions were that the charge was argumentative in the constant reference to "incriminatory statements," and contained an expression of opinion that such statements had been proved, and was confusing and misleading; also that the charge was not applicable to any facts or evidence adduced upon the trial of the case. None of these exceptions were meritorious. As to the correctness of the charge, see Morris v. State.

Ground 19 assigns error upon a charge to the effect that the state contended that the defendant was guilty of an attempt to incite insurrection, and that the defendant, on the other hand, "claims that he is guilty of nothing—that he is not guilty of attempting to incite to insurrection"; that the state has set out its contentions in the indictment, to which the defendant pleaded not guilty, which "raises a clear-cut issue of fact for this jury to determine under the evidence in the case and under the rules of law," as given in the charge. The exceptions were that the charge failed to point out the issue of fact to be determined by the jury, intimated an opinion that, while the defendant may not be guilty of the crime charged, he must have been guilty of some crime, and that it was not applicable to any facts or evidence adduced upon the trial. Obviously these exceptions were groundless, if not frivolous. The same is true of the exceptions to the charge referred to in ground 20 of the motion, which exceptions are so insubstantial as not to require specific reference thereto.

With reference to the instruction excepted to respectively in grounds 16 and 17, it appears from the specifications in the bill of exceptions, and from the transcript made in compliance therewith, that the defendant requested the court to give each of these charges. Certainly he should not except to a charge which he requested.

9. In ground 21 error was assigned upon the refusal of the court to give a charge that all evidence of the Ford and Foster Clubs be excluded from consideration by the jury, since (as contended by the defendant) the Communist Party in this state is a legal party and therefore entitled to existence in this state.

Ground 22 complains of the refusal of a request to charge that there is a wide difference between demonstration and insurrection; that "demonstration" is the public exhibition of one's sympathy towards a social or political movement, and that "insurrection" is resistance with force against the lawful authority of the state of Georgia.

The fact that the Communist Party may have been allowed to enter the names of its candidates upon the official ballot did not legalize its doctrines if they were in fact insurrectionary. Accordingly, there is no merit in ground 21.

The requested definition of the word "demonstration" was too limited in its scope, and for this reason, if not for others, the court properly refused the request referred to in ground 22.

10. Grounds 23 and 24 complained that a witness for the state was allowed to use the term "darkey" in referring to the defendant, the contention being that the word was a term of opprobrium, and that its use was highly prejudicial to the defendant. To this objection, which was urged at the time, the court replied, "I don't know whether it is or not,"

but directed the witness to refer to the accused as the "defendant."

The term "darkey," as applied in this state to a person of color, is not opprobrious. Webster's New International Dictionary states one of the definitions as, "A Negro. Colloq."; and contains nothing to indicate that it is a term of opprobrium.

11. Having determined that no substantial error of law was committed, we now consider the question of whether the evidence was sufficient to support the verdict. Before proceeding to examine the evidence, however, it is proper to determine the exact nature of the offense alleged to have been committed. Sections 55, 56, and 57 of the Penal Code are as follows: "Insurrection shall consist in any combined resistance to the lawful authority of the State, with intent to the denial thereof, when the same is manifested, or intended to be manifested, by acts of violence." (§ 55) "Any attempt, by persuasion or otherwise, to induce others to join in any combined resistance to the lawful authority of the State shall constitute an attempt to incite insurrection." (§ 56) "Any person convicted of the offense of insurrection, or an attempt to incite insurrection, shall be punished with death; or, if the jury recommend to mercy, confinement in the penitentiary for not less than five nor more than twenty years." (§ 57).

The defendant was not on trial for the offense of insurrection, nor for an attempt to commit that offense. He was indicted simply for an attempt to incite an insurrection, which by section 56 is made a distinct and independent crime under the laws of this state. Accordingly, the principles which might be applied in passing upon an alleged attempt to commit insurrection, or upon an alleged attempt to commit any other crime, are without any sort of relevancy to the present case. In U. S. v. Ford, it was said: "The indefinite nature of the offense, at common law, of an attempt to commit a crime, has induced the enactment of many statutes in England and this country, setting forth, in express terms, what acts shall constitute an attempt to commit the crimes referred to in such statutes." In such a case, the statute, of course, will govern. As indicated above, however, the defendant here was not indicted for an attempt to commit any offense whatsoever, but was charged with the doing of that which constituted an independent crime under the law of Georgia, namely, an attempt to induce others to join in combined resistance to the lawful authority of the state. The word "join," as used in the statute, should be given its ordinary signification. It is defined in Webster's New International Dictionary as "to come together so as to be united and connected," "to unite," "to form a union," or "to enter into association or alliance." The statute means then that any attempt to induce others to come together in any combined resistance to the lawful authority of the state shall constitute an attempt to incite an insurrection and shall be punishable as stated. It is immaterial whether the authority of the state was in danger of being subverted or that an insurrection actually occurred or was impending. In State v. Tachin, it was held competent for the state to make it an offense to attempt by speech to incite hostility and opposition even to the government of the United States. See, also, in this connection, State v. Diamond, 27 N. M. 477.

In State v. Quinlan, where the defendant was convicted under a statute making it a crime to advocate, encourage, or incite the killing or injuring of any person, or class of persons, it was held to be immaterial whether any person or class of persons were in fact killed or injured, "the gravaman of the offense being in the incitement or encouragement, and not in the actual commission of the offense." So, in the present case, it is unimportant that the defendant may not have been successful, if he did in fact attempt to induce others to join in any combined resistance to the lawful authority of the state, as charged. Nor was it necessary that he attempted to induce any large number of persons to commit the offense of insurrection, since the offense could be committed by two or more persons. In re Charge to Grand Jury: Force must have been contemplated, but, as said above, the statute does not include either its occurrence or its imminence as an ingredient of the particular offense charged. State v. Tachin, supra. Nor would it be necessary to guilt that the alleged offender should have intended that an insurrection should follow instantly or at any given time, but it would be sufficient that he intended it to happen at any time, as a result of his influence, by those whom he sought to incite. It was the intention of this law to arrest at its incipiency any effort to overthrow the state government, where it takes the form of an actual attempt to incite others to insurrection. In Gibson v. State, supra, it was said of section 4250, now section 56: "This does not contemplate an attempt by the defendant at insurrection, or to commit insurrection by himself, but an attempt to incite others to join in insurrection. A person may commit the offence of an attempt to incite others to join in, or to commit insurrection who neither promises nor attempts to join in it, or commit it himself. He may stand aloof entirely when it is committed, and still he may, by his influence, have incited it, and may be responsible for it." It was further said in that case that the section as to penalty prescribed "a penalty for attempt at insurrection, but none for an attempt to incite insurrection." Hence, the defendant was discharged in that case because the statute failed to prescribe a penalty for the specific offense of which he was convicted. This defect, however, was cured by the act of December 12, 1871, so that the provisions as to penalty are now as stated in the Penal Code, § 57. From what has been said, the question here is simply this: Did the evidence show that the defendant made any attempt to induce others to come together in any combined forcible resistance to the lawful authority of the state? This is the only question to be determined under the evidence.

The evidence, which included certain admissions by the defendant, established the fact that he had come to Atlanta from another state as an organizer for the Communist Party, and that he had no other interest in view. The evidence did not show the exact time of his arrival, but it appeared that under an assumed or different name he rented a post office box for the reception of mail in the Atlanta post office in September, 1931, and it was a fair inference that he had not resided here for any considerable length of time and had not become identified with any local business enterprise. He was indicted in July, 1932, and it appeared that in the meantime he had actively espoused the cause of the unemployed, and had inspired a mass demand for an appropriation by the county authorities for their relief. The jury were authorized to find that his chief objective was to press the cause of the Communist Party, and that his agitations with reference to local conditions were not the result of any particular interest which he may have had in the local welfare, but were pursued merely as a method of fomenting a state of discontent and unrest as a goodly premise for his party program, or, in other words, as a means to an end. The jury, on seeing that his principal mission was to spread the doctrine of the Communistic Party, could weigh the other circumstances in the light of this fact. In view of it, the documents found in his possession assumed an added significance, and the use to which the defendant may have applied them became an easier question for solution by the jury. Were these not the tools to be used by the defendant in the execution of his mission? Did he remain in Atlanta for about a year without using them? He told the officers that he was sent to Atlanta as a paid organizer for the Communist Party, and that the literature was sent to him from the headquarters of this party in New York City. Did he take the means and instruments supplied to him and fail to use them? Was he active or inactive as an agent of his employer? How far did he go in the discharge of the responsible duties assigned to him? The defendant was apparently busy at the time of his arrest, since he had just approached his post office box and taken out his mail, and was carrying at the time a box containing communistic literature. The number of this box was 339.

The evidence showed that he had distributed circulars "Issued by the Unemployed Committee of Atlanta, P. O. 339," and that he was in fact the author of these circulars. While the circulars here referred to may not have been of any considerable importance within themselves, they showed the defendant's connection with the unemployment committee, and with the other evidence it was a fair conclusion that the name "Unemployment Committee" was a term common in the Communist Party applicable to its workers or propagandists. It was not shown directly that he ever distributed any literature except two classes of circulars of a more or less harmless character, but the case depended mainly upon circumstantial evidence and must not be measured by the limits of the direct evidence introduced. To say that the defendant did no more than was shown by the direct evidence would deny to the state all right to the benefit of circumstantial evidence, and this, of course, cannot be done.

With reference to admissions, the defendant stated to one of the arresting officers that "he was sent here by this communist party as an organizer for them, representing this communist party." He also stated that the material, or literature, found in his possession was "sent to him from headquarters of this Communist Party in New York." He directed the officers to his room in which a part of the literature was found.

Shortly after his arrest he was taken before Mr. E. A. Stephens, assistant solicitor general, who testified as follows: "He stated that he came here from Lexington, Kentucky, where he was an employee of some coal mine company, he stated that a man by the name of E. Doran came there and got him interested in the Communist Party, and that he joined the Nation Communist Party at Lexington, Kentucky, * * * he stated that he was sent to Atlanta to take the position of Organizer for the Communist Party; * * * he stated he was paid $10 a week, sometimes in cash and sometimes in money orders. At that time he stated to me that his duties were, as organizer for the Communist Party, to call meetings, educate or disseminate information regarding the party at these meetings, to distribute literature, to secure members for the organization and generally to work up an organization of the Communist Party in Atlanta. * * * He said he had held or attended two meetings, and then later when questioned about where they were held he designated the meeting places of three meetings that he had called and had been held. * * * He did give me the names of persons that he said were members of the organization, said he only have [had] five or six actual members at that time—actual members, as he put it—said the meetings were sometimes in vacant houses and sometimes in private houses * * * he made these statements to me freely and voluntary; I want to state, further, among the other things he said in talking to me about this quantity of literature here in the suitcase and in the grip, a part of which you will notice has never been taken out of the wrapper—there are several packages like this—in questioning him what this was sent to him for, he stated for distribution at his meetings, the same with reference to many of the books that he had in these two receptacles there * * * he said that he called the meetings and held them and conducted the meetings; as to whether he said he made any speeches at any of those meetings, I don't know that the word 'speech' was used." The localities of the meetings were given and were shown to be situated in Fulton county.

Other evidence was introduced which showed that the defendant had induced others to become members of the Communistic Party, about twelve in all. What purported to be minutes of three meetings were also found in the defendant's possession. Some of the minutes made reference to "section committees," and from the evidence as a whole the jury were authorized to find that the phrase "section committee," like the term "unemployed committee," was a designation applied to a subordinate division of the Communist Party. In his statement to the jury he denied none of the testimony to which reference has been made, and made no explanation or statement whatsoever with regard to the literature.

Among the documents were nine "Membership Books * * * of the Communist Party of the U. S. A." containing the names of persons "admitted" to the party in Atlanta. These books also contained what purported to be "extracts from the Statutes of the Communist Party of the U. S. A.," some of which were as follows: "A member of the Party can be every person from the age of eighteen up who accepts the program and statutes of the Communist International and the Communist Party of the U. S. A., who becomes a member of a basic organization of the Party, who is active in this organization, who subordinates himself to all decisions of the Comintern and of the Party, and regularly pays his membership dues. * * * The Communist Party, like all sections of the Comintern, is built upon the principle of democratic centralization. These principles are: * * * Regular reporting of the Party committees to their constituents. Acceptance and carrying out of the decisions of the higher Party committees by the lower, strict Party discipline, and immediate and exact applications of the decisions of the Executive Committee of the Communist International and of the Central Committee of the Party. * * * The basis of the Party organization is the nucleus (in factories, mines, shops, etc.) which all Party members working in these places must join. The nucleus consists of at least three members. Newly organized nuclei must be endorsed by the leading committee of the Section in which the shop nuclei are organized. * * * The strictest Party Discipline is the most solemn duty of all Party members and all Party Organizations. The decisions of the CI and the Party Convention of the CC and of all leading committees of the Party, must be promptly carried out. Discussion of questions over which there have been differences must not continue after the decision has been made. * * *" In the same membership books we find the following question and answer: "What is the Communist Party? The Party is the vanguard of the working class and consists of the best, most class conscious, most active, the most courageous members of that class. It incorporates the whole body of experience of the proletarian struggle, basing itself upon the revolutionary theory of Marxism and representing the general and lasting interests of the whole of the working class. The Party personifies the unity of proletarian principles, of proletarian will and of proletarian revolutionary action. (From the program of the Communist International.) We are the Party of the working class. Consequently, nearly the whole of that class (in time of war and civil war, the whole of that class) should work under the guidance of our Party, should create the closest contacts with out [our] Party. (Lenin.) He who weakens, no matter how little the iron discipline of the Party of the proletariat (especially during the period of dictatorship), effectually helps the bourgeoisie against the proletariat (Lenin)."

The authenticity of the literature was effectually admitted by the defendant, and thus no reasonable question can be raised in this case as to the reality of its apparent source, whether it purports to be an expression from the New York headquarters or from the main party organization, wherever located.

The defendant himself was admittedly a member of the party, and he showed that he was connected with a "party committee." Did he accept its discipline, program, and statutes, and endeavor to execute them as other members were required to do? These were questions to be considered by the jury, and we cannot say that they should have been answered favorably to the accused. When he solicited members and thus pledged them to the party program, what, indeed, was contemplated? Was it an "attempt to induce others to join in combined resistance to the lawful authority of the State?" This was a question to be answered by the jury in the light of that program, and here let us notice some of the additional literature bearing upon the motive and intent of the party organization, and which the jury had before them for their study and consideration.

One of the documents was a booklet entitled "The Communist Position on the Negro Question." On the outside cover was a map of the United States, under which was the following: "Self Determination for the Black Belt." The map had a dark belt across it, beginning with a portion of Arkansas and Louisiana, and extending generally eastward through the states of Mississippi, Alabama, Florida, and Georgia, and thence up the coast through several states. The belt included about two-thirds of the state of Georgia, mostly in the central section, from west to east. On page 28 of the pamphlet appeared the following: "In the South, the fight must be fearlessly developed against the thievery and robbery of the Southern capitalists and landlords; against their whole system of enslaving the Negroes based on Jim Crowism and lynch terror. We must fight there not merely against inequality, but against the whole system by which this inequality is enforced. In the first place, our demand is that the land of the Southern white landlords for years filled by the Negro tenant farmers, be confiscated and turned over to the Negroes. This is the only way to insure economic and social equality for the tenant farmers. Secondly, we propose to break up the present artificial State boundaries established for the convenience of the white master class, and to establish the State unity of the territory known as the 'Black Belt,' where the Negroes constitute the overwhelming majority of the population. Thirdly, in this territory, we demand that the Negroes be given the complete right of self-determination; the right to set up their own government in this territory and the right to separate, if they wish, from the United States. Around these demands for the Negroes, as I have outlined them here—with the revolutionary white workers in the very fore-front of the struggle—the unity of white workers, small farmers and the Negro masses must be established. Not promises: but action. But the Negroes have listened to many promises. Every political faker has promised equality and freedom. The white workers can win the confidence of the Negro masses, not by promises, but by action."

The matter last quoted appeared to be an extract from a speech nominating a candidate for vice president of the United States on the Communist ticket for 1932; but, even so, it appeared in a pamphlet entitled "The Communist Position on the Negro Question," and came to the defendant with the implied, if not express, approval of the party headquarters in New York. In any view, it illustrated the program in Georgia, and shed light upon the purpose and intent of the defendant in soliciting members, and in otherwise executing his mission as the party agent.

This pamphlet which carried the map of the "Black Belt," also contained the following: "Resolutions of the Communist International on the Negro Question in the United States." "Resolution of Communist International, October, 1930. 1. * * * The struggle of the Communists for the Equal Rights of the Negroes applies to all Negroes, in the North as well as in the South. The struggle for this slogan embraces all or almost all of the important special interests of the Negroes in the North, but not in the South, where the main Communist slogan must be: The right of self-determination of the Negroes in the Black Belt. These two slogans, however, are most closely connected. The Negroes in the North are very much interested in winning the right of self-determination of the Negro population of the Black Belt and can thereby hope for strong support for the establishment of true equality of the Negroes in the North. In the South the Negroes are suffering no less, but still more than in the North from the glaring lack of all equality; for the most part the struggle for their most urgent partial demands in the Black Belt is nothing more than the struggle for their equal rights, and only the fulfillment of their main slogan, the right of self-determination in the Black Belt, can assure them of true equality. * * * It is the special duty of the revolutionary Negro Workers to carry on tireless activity among the Negro working masses to free them of their distrust of the white proletariat and draw them into the common front of the revolutionary class struggle against the bourgeoisie. * * * The slogan of the right of self-determination occupies the central place in the liberation struggle of the Negro population in the Black Belt against the yoke of American imperialism. But this slogan, as we see it, must be carried out only in connection with two other basic demands. Thus, there are three basic demands to be kept in mind in the Black Belt, namely, the following: (a) Confiscation of the landed property of the white landowners and capitalists for the benefit of the Negro farmers. The landed property in the hands of the white American exploiters constitutes the most important material basis of the entire system of national oppression and serfdom of the Negroes in the Black Belt. More than three-quarters of all Negro farmers here are bound in actual serfdom to the farms and plantations of the white exploiters by the feudal system of 'share cropping.' Only on paper and not in practice are they freed from the yoke of their former slavery. The same holds completely true for the great mass of black contract laborers. Here the contract is only the capitalist expression of the chains of the old slavery, which even today are not infrequently applied in their natural iron form on the roads of the Black Belt (chain-gang work). These are the main forms of present Negro slavery in the Black Belt, and no breaking of the chains of this slavery is possible without confiscating all the landed property of the white masters. Without this revolutionary measure, without the agrarian revolution, the right of self-determination of the Negro population would be only a Utopia or, at best, would remain only on paper without changing in any way the actual enslavement. (b) Establishment of the state unity of the Black Belt. At the present time this Negro Zone—precisely for the purpose of facilitating national oppression—is artificially split up and divided into a number of various States which include distant localities having a majority of white population. If the right of self-determination of the Negroes is to be put into force, it is necessary wherever possible to bring together into one governmental unit all districts of the South where the majority of the settled population consists of Negroes. Within the limits of this State there will of course remain a fairly significant white minority which must submit to the right of self-determination of the Negro majority. There is no other possible way of carrying out in a democratic manner the right of self-determination of the Negroes. Every plan regarding the establishment of the Negro state with an exclusively Negro population in America (and of course still more exporting it to Africa) is nothing but an unreal and reactionary caricature of the fulfillment of the right of self-determination of the Negroes, and every attempt to isolate and transport the Negroes would have the most damaging effect upon their interests. Above all, it would violate the right of the Negro farmers in the Black Belt not only to their present residences and their land, but also to the land owned by the white landlords and cultivated by Negro labor. (c) Right of self-determination. This means complete and unlimited right of the Negro majority to exercise governmental authority in the entire territory of the Black Belt, as well as to decide upon the relations between their territory and other nations, particularly the United States. It would not be right of self-determination in our sense of the word if the Negroes in the Black Belt had the right of self-determination only in cases which concerned exclusively the Negroes and did not affect the whites, because the most important cases arising here are bound to affect the whites as well as Negroes. First of all, true right to self-determination means that the Negro majority and not the white minority in the entire territory of the administratively united Black Belt exercises the right of administering governmental, legislative, and judicial authority. At the present time all this power is concentrated in the hands of the white bourgeoisie and landlords. It is they who appoint all officials, it is they who dispose of public property, it is they who determine the taxes, it is they who govern and make the laws. Therefore, the overthrow of this class rule in the Black Belt is unconditionally necessary in the struggle for the Negroes' right to self-determination. This, however, means at the same time the overthrow of the yoke of American imperialism in the Black Belt on which the forces of the local white bourgeoisie depend. Only in this way, only if the Negro population of the Black Belt wins its freedom from American imperialism even to the point of deciding ITSELF the relations between its country and other governments, especially the United States, will it win real and complete self-determination. One should demand from the beginning that no armed forces of American imperialism should remain on the territory of the Black Belt. * * * As stated in the letter of the Political Secretariat of the E. C. C. I. of March 16, 1930, the Communists must unreservedly carry on the struggle for the self-determination of the Negro population in the Black Belt in accordance with what has been sct forth above. It is incorrect to say that the Communists are only to carry on propaganda or agitation for the right of self-determination, but not to develop any activity to bring this about. No, it is of the utmost importance for the Communist Party to reject any such limitation of its struggle for this slogan. Even if the situation does not yet warrant the raising of the question of uprising, one should not limit oneself at present to propaganda for the 'Right of Self-Determination' but should organize mass actions such as demonstrations, strikes, tax boycott movements, etc. * * * It would be a mistake to imagine that the right of self-determination slogan is a truly revolutionary slogan only in connection with the demand for complete separation. The question of power is decided not only through the demand of separation, but just as much through the demand of the right to decide the separation question and self-determination in general. A direct question of power is also the demand of confiscation of the land of the white exploiters in the South, as well as the demand of the Negroes that the entire Black Belt be amalgamated into a State unit. Hereby every single fundamental demand of the liberation struggle of the Negroes in the Black Belt is such that if once thoroughly understood by the Negro masses and adopted as their slogan it will lead them into the struggle for the overthrow of the power of the ruling bourgeoisie, which is impossible without such revolutionary struggle. One cannot deny that it is just possible for the Negro population of the Black Belt to win the right to self-determination during capitalism; but it is perfectly clear and indubitable that this is possible only through successful REVOLUTIONARY STRUGGLE for power against the American bourgeoisie, through WRESTING the Negroes' right of self-determination from American Imperialism. Thus, the slogan of right to self-determination is a real slogan of NATIONAL REBELLION which to be considered as such, need not be supplemented by proclaiming struggle for the complete separation of the Negro zone, at least not at present. * * * It is particularly incumbent on Negro Communists to criticize consistently the half-heartedness and hesitations of the petty-bourgeois national-revolutionary Negro leaders in the liberation struggle of the Black Belt, exposing them before the masses. * * * Simultaneously, Negro communists must carry on among the Negro masses an energetic struggle against nationalist moods directed indiscriminately against all whites, workers as well as capitalists, Communists as well as imperialists. Their constant call to the Negro masses must be: REVOLUTIONARY STRUGGLE AGAINST THE RULING WHITE BOURGEOISIE, THROUGH A FIGHTING ALLIANCE WITH THE REVOLUTIONARY WHITE PROLETARIAT."

The booklet from which the foregoing statements are quoted contained a foreword as follows: "The documents presented in this pamphlet are the result of the very best and most careful thought, study and experience of our Party. The correct line on our Party has been hammered out in years of bitter struggle—struggle with the enemies of Bolshevism. * * * But in the furious struggle against our enemies, and against the influence of these enemies upon our own ranks; with the indispensable guidance of the Communist International—our Party has hammered out its BOLSHEVIK line on the Negro question."

Another document found in the defendant's possession was a book entitled "Communism and Christianism," and containing the following statements: "As the machinery of capitalist government, including the armed forces of the nation, conserves the monopoly by the capitalist class of the wealth taken from the workers, the working class must organize consciously and politically for acquiring the powers of government, national and local, in order that this machinery, including these forces, may be converted from an instrument of oppression into the agent of emancipation and the overthrow of privilege, aristocratic and plutocratic. The trouble with every reformatory socialism of modern times is, that it undertakes the impossibility of changing the fruit of the capitalist state into that of the communistic one, without changing the political organism; but to do that is as impossible as to gather grapes from thorns or figs from thistles. Hence an uprooting and replanting are necessary (a revolution not a reformation) which will give the world a new tree of state. Capitalism no longer grows the fruits (foods, clothes and houses) which are necessary to the sustenance of all the world. Hence it must be dug up by the roots in order that a tree which is so organized that it will bear these necessities for the whole world may be planted in its place. The people in Russia have accomplished this uprooting and replanting (this revolution) in the case of their state, and those of every nation are destined to do the same in one way or another, each according to its historical and economical development, some with much violence, most, I hope with but little."

The evidence also included a document entitled "An Appeal to Southern Young Workers." Following are some of the statements contained in this document: "The Young Communist League is the champion not only of the young white workers but especially of the doubly oppressed Negro young workers. The Young Communist League fights against the whole system of race discrimination and stands for full racial, political, economic and social equality for all workers. * * * The Young Communist League is a section of the Young Communist International, the revolutionary leader of the young workers the world over and accepts the guidance of the Communist Party of America. The Young Communist League fights for: * * * FULL POLITICAL, SOCIAL AND RACIAL EQUALITY FOR THE NEGRO WORKERS. * * * SMASH THE NATIONAL GUARD, THE C. M. T. C. AND R. O. T. C."

Still another document was one entitled "Party Organizer," and containing a number of articles on the Communistic Party, on what it advocates, and the manner of organizing workers.

In his statement to the jury the defendant said in part: "We know the system we are living under is on the verge of collapse; no matter what system we are living under, it has developed to its highest point and comes back—for instance, you can take a balloon and get so much air in it, and when you get too much it bursts; so with the system we are living under

—of course, I don't know whether that is insurrection or not, but the question, it has developed to its highest point."

The defendant here apparently expressed the view that a crisis was impending. Did this statement not indicate a belief that the conditions were opportune for a revolution or insurrection and that now or soon would be a seasonable time to strike? We repeat that the case does not turn alone upon the direct evidence that circulars advocating unemployment relief were distributed. It must not be overlooked that the defendant was an organizer and induced a number of persons to become members of the Communist Party, the purpose and intent of which are thoroughly illustrated by the documentary evidence from which we have quoted. The establishment of the "Black Belt" by peaceful and through lawful processes could not have been reasonably anticipated. It called for "breaking up State lines" with even the right of secession from the present national government. The literature fairly teems with such expressions as "confiscation," "revolution," "rebellion," and "violence," even distinguishing a "reformation" and advocating an "uprooting" in its stead. The jury were amply authorized to infer that violence was intended, and that the defendant did attempt to induce others to combine in such resistance to the lawful authority of the state.

In Carr v. State, this court said that: "A combination of persons working together in a campaign with the intent and purpose to overthrow the present government of the United States or the states of the federal Union, by the establishment of a proletarian dictatorship through resistance to the federal government and by the smashing of the National Guard, cannot be considered as an inoffensive peaceful aggregation of citizens merely advising that course with the anticipation that the present government will quietly lay down its authority and embrace the principles and form of the proletarian dictatorship of Soviet Russia." This statement was in reference to the use of literature containing some of the expressions which are found in this record and quoted in the present opinion. In Gitlow v. People, the Supreme Court of the United States had for consideration a "Manifesto," which in tone and substance was similar to the documentary evidence in the instant case, and not stronger in its tendency to insurrection.

In Carr v. State, supra, Mr. Justice Gilbert, speaking for this court, quoted at length from the decision in the Gitlow case. We now refer to the quotations there made as illustrating the opinion of the highest court on the nature and purport of such literature. Some of the language is so pertinent that we also take the liberty of quoting again, in part, as follows: "The Manifesto, plainly, is neither the statement of abstract doctrine nor, as suggested by counsel, mere prediction that industrial disturbances and revolutionary mass strikes will result spontaneously in an inevitable process of evolution in the economic system. It advocates and urges in fervent language mass action which shall progressively foment industrial disturbances and through political mass strikes and revolutionary mass action overthrow and destroy organized parliamentary government. It concludes with a call to action in these words: 'The proletarian revolution and the Communist reconstruction of society—the struggle for these—is now indispensable. * * * The Communist International calls the proletariat of the world to the final struggle!' This is not the expression of philosophical abstraction, the mere prediction of future events; it is the language of direct incitement. The means advocated for bringing about the destruction of organized parliamentary government, namely, mass industrial revolts usurping the functions of municipal government, political mass strikes directed against the parliamentary State, and revolutionary mass action for its final destruction, necessarily imply the use of force and violence, and in their essential nature are inherently unlawful in a constitutional government of law and order. That the jury were warranted in finding that the Manifesto advocated not merely the abstract doctrine of overthrowing organized government by force, violence and unlawful means, but action to that end, is clear. * * * That utterances inciting to the overthrow of organized government by unlawful means present a sufficient danger of substantive evil to bring their punishment within the range of legislative discretion, is clear. Such utterances, by their very nature, involve danger to the public peace and to the security of the State. They threaten breaches of the peace and ultimate revolution. And the immediate danger is none the less real and substantial, because the effect of a given utterance cannot be accurately foreseen. The State cannot reasonably be required to measure the danger from every such utterance in the nice balance of a jeweler's scale. A single revolutionary spark may kindle a fire that, smouldering for a time, may burst into a sweeping and destructive conflagration. It cannot be said that the State is acting arbitrarily or unreasonably when in the exercise of its judgment as to the measures necessary to protect the public peace and safety, it seeks to extinguish the spark without waiting until it has enkindled the flame or blazed into the conflagration. It cannot reasonably be required to defer the adoption of measures for its own peace and safety until the revolutionary utterances lead to actual disturbances of the public peace or imminent and immediate danger of its own destruction; but it may, in the exercise of its judgment, suppress the threatened danger in its incipiency. In People v. Lloyd, it was aptly said: 'Manifestly, the legislature has authority to forbid the advocacy of a doctrine designed and intended to overthrow the government without waiting until there is a present and imminent danger of the success of the plan advocated. If the State were compelled to wait until the apprehended danger became certain, then its right to protect itself would come into being simultaneously with the overthrow of the government, when there would be neither prosecuting officers nor courts for the enforcement of the law.' "

The evidence authorized the verdict, and the court did not err in refusing a new trial.

Judgment affirmed. All the Justices concur, except RUSSELL C. J., absent on account of illness.

Index 889

ANGELO HERNDON
v.
STATE OF GEORGIA

SUPREME COURT OF THE UNITED STATES

NO. 665. DECIDED MAY 20, 1935.

On appeal from the Supreme Court of Georgia.

WHITNEY NORTH SEYMOUR (Walter Gellhorn, Herbert T. Wechsler and Carol King with him on the brief) for appellant; J. Walter LeCraw, Assistant Solicitor General of Georgia (M. J. Yeomans, Attorney General, John A. Boykin, Solicitor General, B. D. Murphy, Assistant Attorney General and John H. Hudson, Assistant Solicitor General, with him on the brief) for appellee.

SUPREME COURT OF UNITED STATES—Appeal from State Supreme Court affirming judgment of conviction in criminal case—Absence of Federal question—

An appeal from a decision of the Supreme Court of Georgia affirming a lower state court's judgment of conviction of attempting to incite insurrection, in violation of a Georgia statute, is not within the jurisdiction of the Supreme Court of the United States, although the statute is assailed as in violation of the Federal Constitution, since the Federal question was not seasonably raised or passed on, in the court below.

The Federal question was raised in the lower state court in a preliminary attack upon the indictment, but the state supreme court declined to review the ruling of the trial court on the ground that the right to a review thereof was not preserved by exceptions, or assigned as error in due time in the bill of exceptions, as required by the established rules of the state. Such determination by state supreme court is conclusive on the Supreme Court of the United States. The presentation of the Federal question to the state supreme court on motion for rehearing is insufficient for its consideration by the Supreme Court of the United States. The rule that a Federal question may be raised in the Supreme Court of the

United States for the first time where the state supreme court's ruling could not have been anticipated is not applicable.

Mr. Justice SUTHERLAND delivered the opinion of the Court:

Appellant was sentenced to a term of imprisonment upon conviction by a jury in a Georgia court of first instance of an attempt to incite insurrection by endeavoring to induce others to join in combined resistance to the authority of the State to be accomplished by acts of violence, in violation of Sec. 56 of the Penal Code of Georgia. (Note No. 1.) The supreme court of the state affirmed the judgment. 178 Ga. 832; rehearing denied, 179 Ga. 597. On this appeal, the statute is assailed as contravening the due process clause of the Fourteenth Amendment in certain designated particulars. We find it unnecessary to review the points made, since this court is without jurisdiction for the reason that no Federal question was seasonably raised in the court below or passed upon by that court.

It is true that there was a preliminary attack upon the indictment in the trial court on the ground, among others, that the statute was in violation "of the Constitution of the United States," and that this contention was overruled. But, in addition to the insufficiency of the specification (Note No. 2), the adverse action of the trial court was not preserved by exceptions *pendente lite* or assigned as error in due time in the bill of exceptions, as the settled rules of the state practice required.

In that situation, the state supreme court declined to review any of the rulings of the trial court in respect of that and other preliminary issues; and this determination of the state court is conclusive here. John v. Paullin, 231 U. S. 583, 585; Atlantic Coast Line R. R. Co. v. Mims, 242 U. S. 532, 535; Nevada-California-Oregon Ry. v. Burrus, 244 U. S. 103, 105; Brooks v. Missouri, 124 U. S. 394, 400; Central Union Co. v. Edwardsville, 269 U. S. 190, 194-195; Erie R. R. Co. v. Purdy, 185 U. S. 148, 154; Mutual Life Ins. Co. v. McGrew, 188 U. S. 291, 308.

The Federal question was never properly presented to the state supreme court unless upon motion for rehearing; and that court then refused to consider it. The long-established general rule is that the attempt to raise a federal question after judgment, upon a petition for rehearing, comes too late, unless the court actually entertains the question and decides it. Texas &c. Ry Co. v. Southern Pacific Co., 137 U. S. 48, 54; Loeber v. Schroeder, 149 U. S. 580, 585; Godchaux Co. v. Estopinal, 251 U. S. 179, 181; Rooker v. Fidelity Trust Co., 261 U. S. 114, 117; Tidal Oil Co. v. Flanagan, 263 U. S. 444, 454-455, and cases cited.

Petitioner, however, contends that the present case falls within an exception to the rule—namely, that the question respecting the validity of the statute as applied by the lower court first arose from its unanticipated act in giving to the statute a new construction which threatened rights under the Constitution.

There is no doubt that the Federal claim was timely if the ruling of the state court could not have been anticipated and a petition for rehearing presented the first opportunity for raising it. Saunders v. Shaw, 244 U. S. 317, 320; Ohio v. Akron Park District, 281 U. S. 74, 79; Missouri v. Gehner, 281 U. S. 313, 320; Brinkerhoff-Faris Co. v. Hill, 281 U. S. 673, 677-678; American Surety Co. v. Baldwin, 287 U. S. 156, 164; Gt. Northern Ry. Co. v. Sunburst Co., 287 U. S. 358, 367. The whole point, therefore, is whether the ruling here assailed should have been anticipated.

The trial court instructed the jury that the evidence would not be sufficient to convict the defendant if it did not indicate that his advocacy would be acted upon immediately; and that—"In order to convict the defendant . . . it must appear clearly by the evidence that immediate serious violence against the State of Georgia was to be expected or was advocated." Petitioner urges that the question presented to the state supreme court was whether the evidence made out a violation of the statute as thus construed by the trial court, while the supreme court construed the statute (178 Ga., p. 855) as not requiring that an insurrection should follow instantly or at any given time, but that "it would be sufficient that he (the defendant) intended it to happen at any time, as a result of his influence, by those whom he sought to incite," and upon that construction determined the sufficiency of the evidence against the defendant. If that were all, the petitioner's contention that the federal question was raised at the earliest opportunity well might be sustained; but it is not all.

The verdict of the jury was returned on January 18, 1933, and judgment immediately followed. On July 5, 1933, the trial court overruled a motion for new trial. The original opinion was handed down and the judgment of the state supreme court entered May 24, 1934, the case having been in that court since the preceding July.

On March 18, 1933, several months prior to the action of the trial court on the motion for new trial, the state supreme court had decided Carr v. State, 176 Ga. 747. In that case section 56 of the Penal Code, under which it arose, was challenged as contravening the Fourteenth Amendment. The court in substance construed the statute as it did the present case. In the course of the opinion it said (p. 750):

> "It (the state) can not reasonably be required to defer the adoption of measures for its own peace and safety until the revolutionary utterances lead to actual disturbances of the public peace or imminent and immediate danger of its own destruction; but it may, in the exercise of its judgment, suppress the threatened danger in its incipiency. * * * 'Manifestly, the legislature has authority to forbid the advocacy of a doctrine designed and intended to overthrow the government without waiting until there is a present and imminent danger of the success of the plan advocated. If the State were compelled to wait until the apprehended danger became certain, then its rights to protect itself would come into being simultaneously with the overthrow of the government, when there would be neither prosecuting officers nor courts for the enforcement of the law.'"

The language contained in the subquotation is taken from People v. Lloyd, 304, Ill. 23, 35 and is quoted with approval by this court in Gitlow v. New York, 268 U. S. 652, 669.

In the present case, following the language quoted at an earlier point in this opinion to the effect that it was sufficient if the defendant intended an insurrection to follow *at any time*, etc., the court below, in its original opinion, (178 Ga. 855), added—"It was the intention of this law to arrest at its incipiency any effort to overthrow the State government, where it takes the form of an actual attempt to incite others to insurrection."

The phrase "at any time" is not found in the foregoing excerpt from the Carr case, but it is there in effect, when the phrase is given the meaning disclosed by the context, as that meaning is pointed out by the court below in its opinion denying the motion for a rehearing (179 Ga. 600), when it said that the phrase was necessarily intended to mean within a reasonable time—"that is, within such time as one's persuasion or other adopted means might reasonably be expected to be directly operative in causing an insurrection."

Appellant, of course, cannot plead ignorance of the ruling in the Carr case, and was, therefore, bound to anticipate the probability of a similar ruling in his own case, and preserve his right to a review here by appropriate action upon the original hearing in the court below. It follows that his contention that he raised the federal question at the first opportunity is without substance, and the appeal must be dismissed for want of jurisdiction.

It is so ordered.

Mr. Justice CARDOZO:

The appellant has been convicted of an attempt to incite insurrection in violation of Section 56 of the Penal Code of Georgia. He has been convicted after a charge by the trial court that to incur a verdict of guilt he must have advocated violence with the intent that his advocacy should be acted on immediately and with reasonable grounds for the expectation that the intent should be fulfilled.

The appellant did not contend then, nor does he contend now, that a statute so restricted would involve an unconstitutional impairment of freedom of speech.

However, upon appeal from the judgment of conviction the Supreme Court of Georgia repudiated the construction adopted at the trial and substituted another. Promptly thereafter the appellant moved for a rehearing upon the ground that the substituted meaning made the statute unconstitutional, and in connection with that motion invoked the protection of the Fourteenth Amendment.

A rehearing was denied with an opinion which again construed the statute and again rejected the construction accepted in the court below. Now in this court the appellant renews his plaint that the substituted meaning makes the statute void.

By the judgment just announced the court declines to hear him. It finds that he was tardy in asserting his privileges and immunities under the Constitution of the United States, and disclaiming jurisdiction dismisses his appeal.

I hold the view that the protection of the Constitution was seasonably invoked and that the court should proceed to an adjudication of the merits. Where the merits lie I do not now consider, for in the view of the majority the merits are irrelevant. My protest is confined to the disclaimer of jurisdiction.

The settled doctrine is that when a constitutional privilege or immunity has been denied for the first time by a ruling made upon appeal, a litigant thus surprised may challenge the unexpected ruling by a motion for rehearing, and the challenge will be timely. Missouri v. Gehner, 281 U. S. 313, 320; Brinkerhoff-Faris Trust & Savings Co. v. Hill, 281 U. S. 673, 678; American Surety Co. v. Baldwin, 287 U. S. 156, 164; Great Northern R. Co. v. Sunburst Oil & Refining Co., 287 U. S. 358, 367; Saunders v. Shaw, 244 U. S. 317, 320. Within that settled doctrine the cause is rightly here.

Though the merits are now irrelevant, the controversy must be so far explained as to show how a federal question has come into the record. The appellant insists that words do not amount to an incitement to revolution, or to an attempt at such incitement, unless they are of such a nature and are used in such circumstances as to create "a clear and present danger" (Schenck v. United States, 249 U. S. 47, 52) of bringing the prohibited result to pass.

He insists that without this limitation a statute so lacking in precision as the one applied against him here is an unconstitutional restraint upon historic liberties of speech. For present purposes it is unimportant whether his argument be sound or shallow. At least it has color of support in words uttered from this bench, and uttered with intense conviction, Schenck v. United States, supra; cf. Whitney v. California, 274 U. S. 357, 374, 375; Fiske v. Kansas, 274 U. S. 380; Gitlow v. New York, 268 U. S. 652, 672, 273; Schaefer v. United States, 251 U. S. 466, 482.

The court might be unwilling, if it were to pass to a decision of the merits, to fit the words so uttered within the framework of this case. What the appellant is now asking of us is an opportunity to be heard. That privilege is his unless he has thrown it away by silence and acquiescence when there was need of speech and protest.

We are told by the state that the securities of the Constitution should have been invoked upon the trial. The presiding judge should have been warned that a refusal to accept the test of clear and present danger would be a rejection of the restraints of the Fourteenth Amendment.

But the trial judge had not refused to accept the test proposed; on the contrary, he had accepted it and even gone a step beyond. In substance, he had charged that even a present "danger" would not suffice, if there was not also an expectation, and one grounded in reason, that the insurrection would begin at once.

It is novel doctrine that a defendant who has had the benefit of all he asks, and indeed of a good deal more, must place a statement on the record that if some other court at some other time shall read the statute differently, there will be a denial of liberties that at the moment of the protest are unchallenged and intact. Defendants charged with crime are as slow as are men generally to borrow trouble of the future.

We are told, however, that protest, even if unnecessary at the trial, should have been made by an assignment of error or in some other appropriate way in connection with the appeal, and this for the reason that by that time, if not before, the defendant was chargeable with knowledge as a result of two decisions of the highest court of Georgia that the statute was destined to be given another meaning.

The decisions relied upon are Carr v. The State (No. 1), 176 Ga. 55, and Carr v. The State (No. 2), 176 Ga. 747. The first of these cases was decided in November, 1932, before the trial of the appellant, which occurred in January, 1933. The second was decided in March, 1933, after the appellant had been convicted, but before the denial or submission of his motion for a new trial. Neither is decisive of the question before us now.

Carr v. The State, No. 1, came up on demurrer to an indictment. The prosecution was under Sec. 58 of the Penal Code, which makes it a crime to circulate revolutionary documents. (Note No. 1.)

All that was held was that upon the face of the indictment there had been a wilful incitement to violence, sufficient, if proved, to constitute a crime.

The opinion contains an extract covering about four pages from the opinion of this court in Gitlow v. New York, supra. Imbedded in that long quotation are the words now pointed to by the state as decisive of the case at hand. They are the words of Sanford, J., writing for this court. 268 U. S. at p. 669. "The immediate danger is none the less real and substantial, because the effect of a given utterance cannot be accurately foreseen."

A state "cannot reasonably be required to defer the adoption of measures for its own peace and safety until the revolutionary utterances lead to actual disturbances of the public peace or imminent and immediate danger of its own destruction; but it may, in the exercise of its judgment, suppress the threatened danger in its incipiency."

To learn the meaning of these words in their application to the Georgia statute we must read them in their setting. Sanford, J., had pointed out that the statute then before him, the New York criminal anarchy act, forbade the teaching and propagation by spoken word or writing of a particular form of doctrine, carefully defined and after such definition denounced on reasonable grounds as fraught with peril to the state.

There had been a determination by the state through its legislative body that such utterances "are so inimical to the general welfare and involve such danger of substantive evil that they may be penalized in the exercise of its police power." 268 U. S. at p. 668.

In such circumstances "the question whether any specific utterance coming within the prohibited class is likely, in and of itself, to bring about the substantive evil, is not open to consideration. It is sufficient that the statute itself be constitutional and that the use of the language comes within its prohibition." 268 U. S. 670.

In effect the words had been placed upon an expurgatory

index. At the same time the distinction was sharply drawn between statutes condemning utterances identified by a description of their meaning and statutes condemning them by reference to the results that they are likely to induce. "It is clear that the question in such cases (i. e. where stated doctrines are denounced) is entirely different from that involved in those cases where the statute merely prohibits certain acts involving the danger of substantive evil, without any reference to language itself, and it is sought to apply its provisions to language used by the defendant for the purpose of bringing about the prohibited results." pp. 670, 671. Cf. Whitney v. California, supra; Fiske v. Kansas, supra.

The effect of all this was to leave the question open whether in cases of the second class, in cases, that is to say, where the unlawful quality of words is to be determined not upon their face but in relation to their consequences, the opinion in Schenck v. United States, supplies the operative rule. The conduct charged to this appellant—in substance an attempt to enlarge the membership of the Communist party in the city of Atlanta—falls, it will be assumed, within the second of these groupings, but plainly is outside the first.

There is no reason to believe that the Supreme Court of Georgia, when it quoted from the opinion in Gitlow's case, rejected the restraints which the author of that opinion had placed upon his words. For the decision of the case before it there was no need to go so far. Circulation of documents with intent to incite to revolution had been charged in an indictment. The state had the power to punish such an act as criminal, or so the court had held. How close the nexus would have to be between the attempt and its projected consequences was a matter for the trial.

Carr v. The State, No. 2, like the case under review, was a prosecution under Penal Code, Section 56 (not Section 58), and like Carr v. The State, No. 1, came up on demurrer. All that the court held was that when attacked by demurrer the indictment would stand. This appears from the headnote, drafted by the court itself. After referring to this headnote, the court states that it may be "useful and salutary" to repeat what it had written in Carr v. The State, No. 1. Thereupon it quotes copiously from its opinion in that case, including the bulk of the same extracts from Gitlow v. New York. The extracts show upon their face that they have in view a statute denouncing a particular doctrine and prohibiting attempts to teach it. They give no test of the bond of union between an idea and an event.

What has been said as to the significance of the opinions in the two cases against Carr has confirmation in what happened when appellant was brought to trial. The judge who presided at that trial had the first of those opinions before him when he charged the jury, or so we may assume. He did not read it as taking from the state the burden of establishing a clear and present danger that insurrection would ensue as a result of the defendant's conduct. This is obvious from the fact that in his charge he laid that very burden on the state with emphasis and clarity. True, he did not have before him the opinion in prosecution No. 2, for it had not yet been handed down, but if he had seen it, he could not have gathered from its quotation of the earlier case that it was announcing novel doctrine.

From all this it results that Herndon, this appellant, came into the highest court of Georgia without notice that the statute defining his offense was to be given a new meaning. There had been no rejection, certainly no unequivocal rejection, of the doctrine of Schenck v. United States, which had been made the law of the case by the judge presiding at his trial.

For all that the record tells us, the prosecuting officer acquiesced in the charge, and did not ask the appellate court to apply a different test. In such a situation the appellant might plant himself as he did on the position that on the case given to the jury his guilt had not been proved. He was not under a duty to put before his judges the possibility of a definition less favorable to himself, and make an argument against it, when there had been no threat of any change, still less any forecast of its form or measure. He might wait until the law of the case had been rejected by the reviewing court before insisting that the effect would be an invasion of his constitutional immunities.

If invasion should occur, a motion for rehearing diligently pressed thereafter would be seasonable notice. This is the doctrine of Missouri v. Gehner and Brinkerhoff-Faris v. Hill. It is the doctrine that must prevail if the general securities of the Constitution are not to be lost in a web of procedural entanglements.

New strength is given to consideration such as these when one passes to a closer view of just what the Georgia court did in its definition of the statute. We have heard that the meaning had been fixed by what had been held already in Carr v. The State, and that thereby the iminence of the danger had been shown to be unrelated to innocence or guilt.

But if that is the teaching of those cases, it was discarded by the very judgment now subjected to review. True, the Georgia court, by its first opinion in the case at hand, did prescribe a test that, if accepted, would bar the consideration of proximity in time. "It is immaterial whether the authority of the state was in danger of being subverted or that an insurrection actually occurred or was impending." "Force must have been contemplated, but * * * the statute does not include either its occurrence or its imminence as an ingredient of the particular offense charged."

It would not be "necessary to guilt that the alleged offender should have intended that an insurrection should follow instantly, or at any given time, but it would be sufficient that he intended it to happen at any time, as a result of his influence, by those whom he sought to incite."

On the motion for rehearing the Georgia court repelled with a little heat the argument of council that these words were to be taken literally, without "the usual reasonable implications." "The phrase 'at any time,' as criticized in the motion for rehearing, was not intended to mean at any time in the indefinite future, or at any possible later time, however remote." "On the contrary the phrase 'at any time' was necessarily intended, and should have been understood, to mean within a reasonable time; that is, within such time as one's persuasion or other adopted means might reasonably be expected to be directly operative in causing an insurrection." "Under the statute as thus interpreted, we say, as before, that the evidence was sufficient to authorize the conviction."

There is an unequivocal rejection of the test of clear and present danger, yet a denial also of responsibility without boundaries in time. True, in this rejection, the court disclaimed a willingness to pass upon the question as one of constitutional law, assigning as a reason that no appeal to the Constitution had been made upon the trial or then considered by the judge. Brown v. State, 114 Ga. 60; Loftin v. Southern Security Co., 162 Ga. 730; Dunaway v. Gore, 164, Ga. 219, 230.

Such a rule of state practice may have the effect of attaching a corresponding limitation to the jurisdiction of this court where fault can fairly be imputed to an appellant for the omission to present the question sooner, Erie R. Co. v. Purdy, 185 U. S. 148; Louisville & Nashville R. Co. v. Woodford, 234 U. S. 46, 51. No such consequence can follow where the ruling of the trial judge has put the Constitution out of the case and made an appeal to its provisions impertinent and futile. Cf. Missouri v. Gehner, supra; Rogers v. Alabama, 192 U. S. 226, 230.

In such circumstances, the power does not reside in a state by any rule of local practice to restrict the jurisdiction of this court in the determination of a constitutional question brought into the case thereafter. David v. Weschsler, 263 U. S. 22, 24. If the rejection of the test of clear and present danger was a denial of fundamental liberties, the path is clear for us to say so.

What was brought into the case upon the motion for rehearing was a standard wholly novel, the expectancy of life to be ascribed to the persuasive power of an idea. The defendant had no opportunity in the state court to prepare his argument accordingly. He had no opportunity to argue from the record that guilt was not a reasonable inference, or one permitted by the Constitution, on the basis of that test any more than on the basis of others discarded as unfitting. Cf. Fiske v. Kansas, supra.

The argument thus shut out is submitted to us now. Will men "judging in calmness" (Brandeis, J., in Schaefer v. United States, supra, at p. 483) say of the defendant's conduct as shown forth in the pages of this record that it was an attempt to stir up revolution through the power of his persuasion and within the time when that persuasion might be expected to endure?

If men so judging will say yes, will the Constitution of the United States uphold a reading of the statute that will lead to that response? Those are the questions that the defendant lays before us after conviction of a crime punishable by death in the discretion of the jury. I think he should receive an answer.

Mr. Justice Brandeis and Mr. Justice Stone join in this opinion.

NOTES

Judge Sutherland's opinion

Note No. 1—"Sec. 56. Any attempt, by persuasion or otherwise, to induce others to join in any combined resistance to the lawful authority of the state shall constitute an attempt to incite insurrection."

"Insurrection" is defined by the preceding section. "Sec. 55. Insurrection shall consist in any combined resistance to the lawful authority of the State, with intent to the denial thereof, when the same is manifested, or intended to be manifested, by acts of violence."

Note No. 2—Maxwell v. Newbold et al., 18 How. 511, 516; Messenger v. Mason, 10 Wall. 507, 509; Capital City Dairy Co. v. Ohio, 183 U. S. 238, 248; Harding v. Illinois, 196 U. S. 78, 85, 86-88.

Mr. Justice Cardozo

Note No. 1—Sec. 58. If any person shall bring, introduce, print, or circulate, or cause to be introduced, circulated, or printed, or aid or assist, or be in any manner instrumental in bringing, introducing, circulating, or printing within this State any paper, pamphlet, circular, or any writing, for the purpose of inciting insurrection, riot, conspiracy, or resistance against the lawful authority of the State, or against the lives of the inhabitants thereof, or any part of them, he shall be punished by confinement in the penitentiary for not less than five nor longer than twenty years.

APPENDIX EIGHT

TEXT OF HERNDON SPEECH AT EMERGENCY CONFERENCE

"You have already been told that this monstrous frame-up of myself is not something that has been directed against an individual, but is symbolic of a people as well as the oppression that all workers face. I wonder if those of you who have not been South, who have not had a chance to see what conditions are like, have an idea of what the workers have to go through. I have worked for a number of years organizing black and white workers in various states in the South. We know that Negroes constitute the overwhelming population of the people in the Black Belt. They are forced to work for any number of years, and no matter what they produce, no matter how hard they may work, they are always in debt and tied down to slavery. Should they try to escape there are means of stopping them. There is the chain gang; there are the organizations such as the Ku Klux Klan, the Red Shirts, the Men of Justice. But the South is becoming a different South from what it has been. Negro and white workers are organizing together, and it is because of this that I have been condemned to serve eighteen to twenty years on the barbarous Georgia chain gang. The ruling class oppressors know what this movement means for them; they know that once black and white organize together, it will mean the end of their tyrannical rule. That is why they have decided to do me to my death. That is why there are wholesale lynchings, burnings at the stake; that is why there are Scottsboro cases.

"The Civil War did not free the Negro nor did it free the white workers. We must put the question plainly: How can the Negro people be free when the white workers themselves are not free?

"The Supreme Court of another day handed down the infamous Dred Scott decision, making slave-catching the law of the land and declaring that a Negro has no rights that a white man is bound to respect. Now they have handed down another Dred Scott decision. We can no longer have illusions about the rights of Negroes written into the Constitution. Negroes have no rights—no right to vote, to sit on juries, to think and act as free men. These rights will become a reality only when we band together to put them into effect.

"The period in which we are living today is so crucial that the fate of the whole human race is at stake. And it seems that my fate has already been decided by the cruel lynchers and despots of the State of Georgia. Within a few days I must give myself up to be tortured for twenty years on a chain gang, because I was born with a black skin, and above all because I had the courage to challenge their rule.

"The Negro people, oppressed and enslaved as they are, will not remain silent and indifferent to such outrages. The Negro people have already shown that they are willing to die in defense of their rights. They will unite with white workers, will show the ruling class that they will fight not only until Angelo Herndon is free, but until the very jails and chain gangs and the whole system of oppression and robbery are done away with. This question is of such importance that it transcends any political differences we may have among us. In my case the ruling class has tried to trample underfoot those rights guaranteed to all civilized human beings. But I am convinced that we will be able to meet this challenge and to assure them that the American workers and the American people will not submit to this kind of Fascist rule.

"We love this country. Why not? We have built it, we have made it what it is. The blood and bones of our forefathers are mingled in its soil. We have produced everything, and we are entitled to what rightfully belongs to us. The fact that I am a Communist infuriated the rulers of Georgia. They would rather see their Negro servants come crawling on their knees asking for their hypocritical mercy. But let me say this: Before I would get down on my knees and beg them for their mercy, I would rather see myself put to death. If I were to do such a thing, then I would deserve nothing short of such a tragic fate. But I choose my own course. I would rather die standing up fighting for my principles, rather than sit idly by while my people are being trampled underfoot.

"Today, when the world is in danger of being pushed into another blood-bath, when Negroes are being shot down and lynched wholesale, when every sort of outrage is taking place against the masses of people—today is the time to act, if there ever was such a time in the history of the world.

"The tortures and horrors of the chain gangs of the South rival those of the Spanish Inquisition. Even to see them is to find it hard to believe. They have built little boxes like telephone booths, in which prisoners are locked. The door is shut, a rope is tied around the prisoner's neck, and he is strung up with his toes just touching the ground. Steam is then turned on. A few years ago Arthur Maillefert, a young white boy, traveling in search of a job was arrested for vagrancy in Florida and put on the chain gang. The overseers cut the bottom out of a barrel, placed the barrel around his neck and made it impossible for him to raise his arms. If a man were to sit down from weariness in such a contraption, his neck would be broken. That is what happened to young Maillefert.

"Do you think that they would have had any difficulty or any trouble in doing away with me? This is not the first case where a Negro worker was involved. Many cases happen where Negro workers are framed and murdered, arrested on flimsy excuses, tried and sentenced to die in the electric chair. And most of these farcical trials never take more than fifteen or twenty minutes. These things you hear nothing about. It would have been the same way with me. They would have called me to trial, sentenced me to death, and nothing would have been said or done about it. But thanks to the organized struggle led by the International Labor Defense, which rallied the masses of people irrespective of color, creed or political opinion in my defense, not only has my own life been saved thus far, but the struggle against the Georgia insurrection law has taken on tremendous proportions.

"It is to be understood that no man has ever lived more than ten years on the chain gang. And in the case of myself, I would not last one year. There are many ways they can get rid of me. They can shoot me in the back and then say I tried to escape. But I know that if the pressure of the masses is great enough, if we are on the job every day and every night, they will not dare to carry through their usual practice and do me to my death.

"The composition of the conference, the various people

who have spoken from this platform, assures me that you will continue the fight for the Negro people, for the freedom of all oppressed peoples, and then I am sure it will not be long before we can smash the chain gangs and the whole system of which they are a part.

"What is my interest in all this? My only desire is that the Negro people become equals in every walk of life; that all workers have the right to enjoy the things they have produced, to control their own destinies, instead of being robbed by a few worthless parasites. Therefore, I call upon you to extend and broaden the fighting alliance of all workers, black and white, native and foreign born.

"It was such tremendous pressure that forced the hangman of Hitler's Germany to free Dimitroff and his co-defendants. We can do the same thing in the United States. Too long have we allowed them to commit such outrages. They murdered Sacco and Vanzetti; they put Tom Mooney in jail for life; they are still trying to kill the Scottsboro boys. But today we are stronger than we were when Sacco and Vanzetti were executed. Today we have a mighty defense organization, the I.L.D., which through its work has kept the Scottsboro boys alive, and everywhere rallied the masses in defense of labor's rights, in defense of the trade-union movement.

"Only five more days remain before I must surrender myself to the chain gang. Now more than ever must we develop the united campaign of mass protest which will bring the voice of millions into the State of Georgia: 'The slave insurrection law must be wiped out!'

"You and other justice-loving people of America must be the ones to smash the insurrection law, to free the Scottsboro boys, to free me, to put an end, at last, to the barbarous regime of the South. Continue that fight; it is a fight for your own freedom as well as for mine."

APPENDIX NINE

EDITORIAL

ATLANTA CONSTITUTION—November 24, 1935

SEARCH THEM OUT

Handbills signed "The Young Communist League of Atlanta" have recently been circulated throughout the city, many of them having been posted in conspicuous places in the center of the city. This group of Reds, presumably financed from Russia, as are other branches of the "league" in the United States, hide behind a post-office box number in Birmingham, knowing that the giving of a local address would mean instant arrest.

The anonymous handbills are a challenge to the police authorities of Atlanta and every effort should be exercised to round out this group of radicals who would spread their poisonous doctrines among the ignorant classes of the city.

Such groups seize upon every development offering opportunity to flame racial and industrial passion and prejudice. In this effort to cause trouble in Atlanta they have hit upon the Herndon case, which for many months has been used by national Communist organizations in the effort to foment disorders. Money from communistic organizations carried this case to the United States Supreme Court which refused to review it.

Regarding Herndon's case. A. L. Henson, Georgia Americanism chairman of La Société des Quarante Hommes et Huit Chevaux (a subordinate organization of the American Legion), who has kept in close contact with the case from its inception, says:

"Angelo Herndon was not arrested for distributing communistic literature, but for inciting a group of Georgia's population to armed insurrection and seizure of a major portion of five Southern states for the establishment of a Soviet republic, independent of the United States.

"He possessed and presented a written contract of the communistic party, plans of attack on the native population and seizure of lands and property and maps defining territory to be conquered. It is not a violation of Georgia laws to distribute Communist literature, and freedom of speech is as safe here as in any other state."

Notwithstanding, the Young Communist League of Atlanta, in its false and scurrilous circular, claims that "the constitutional rights of the Georgia people to freedom of speech, a free press and freedom of assembly is on trial here." What happened in this particular case was that the Reds, obsessed with their plans to create unrest and dissatisfaction in the Southeast, overstepped the liberal bounds that exist in the United States and planned insurrection and overthrow of the Federal government.

This is what they are trying to do in all parts of the country. Alien agitators, financed by the Soviet internationale, have been ordered from Russia to insinuate themselves into the labor unions, for the purpose of causing strikes and harassing the employers. Communist schools exist in many cities, teachers of Communism have been spotted in many of our colleges and universities, and Communist periodicals are being openly published in some industrial cities.

Free speech is the inalienable right of an American citizen, but it was never intended that this constitutional guarantee should be used to permit aliens to preach and teach the overthrow of our government.

Other sections of the country may remain insensitive to activities of the Reds, but Atlanta can be expected to crush this type of over-radicalism whenever it shows its ugly head above the slime in which it breeds.

Those styling themselves the "Young Communist League of Atlanta" should be arrested and punishment given them such as will be a convincing warning that Atlanta will not condone efforts to stir up strife and discontent under the banner of "free speech."